The Craft of Church Planting

The Craft of Church Planting

Exploring the Lost Wisdom of Apprenticeship

Christian Selvaratnam

scm press

© Christian Selvaratnam 2022

Published in 2022 by SCM Press
Editorial office
3rd Floor, Invicta House,
108–114 Golden Lane,
London EC1Y 0TG, UK

www.scmpress.co.uk

SCM Press is an imprint of Hymns Ancient & Modern Ltd
(a registered charity)

Hymns Ancient & Modern® is a registered trademark of
Hymns Ancient & Modern Ltd
13A Hellesdon Park Road, Norwich,
Norfolk NR6 5DR, UK

British Library Cataloguing in Publication data
A catalogue record for this book is available
from the British Library

978-0-334-06181-6

Typeset by Regent Typesetting
Printed and bound by
CPI Group (UK) Ltd

Contents

Part 5 Conclusions

For Amanda, Kate,
Philip and Hannah

Abbreviations of Bible Translations

Unless noted otherwise, scripture translations are from The New Revised Standard Version with Apocrypha (Anglicised Edition).

ESV   English Standard Version (Anglicised Edition)
KJV   The King James Bible
NIV   New International Version (Anglicised Edition)
NLT   New Living Translation

Foreword

by the Most Revd Stephen Cottrell

There is nothing new about church planting – every church was planted once. There is therefore much to discover from current and historic practice.

Church planting is a craft to be learned, and Christian Selvaratnam is a wise and experienced teacher. He describes church planting as a ministry-adventure. This is an exciting way of thinking about the church creatively that allows for the Christian message to be adapted and applied to fit specific contexts. It is a form of art or, as the title suggests, a craft to be carefully learnt, honed, practised and lived out.

Christian writes passionately about the need for proclaiming the gospel message. This surely lies at the heart of what we believe, and what as Christians we should live out. As disciples of Christ, we learn the craft of being Christ-centred by studying Scripture with other Christians. Being a church planter hones creativity into a specific context – taking the wisdom of Scripture and shaping it into something that is life-giving today through good theology and learning from traditional and practical wisdom.

In emphasizing church planting as a craft, Christian shows us that it is something we can learn and pass on to others. He highlights the 'master-apprenticeship' relationship but pushes beyond this to community training. Building a church is more than one-dimensional, it relies on the wisdom, experience and tradition of a community and the support of communities.

Creator and craftsman, creation and creativity and art are all explored in this book, drawing the reader into a world that takes Scripture and imaginatively explores the beauty of the Creator and the place of the creation within this. There's an artistry to the craft of church planting, which draws its inspiration from the creator but also points beyond itself to something much bigger.

The questions peppered throughout the book imply that this is a book to be read slowly, engaging closely with the text; it will also make it a useful tool for a group of people. Church planting is not a solitary activity. Just as eating is more enjoyable in the company of others, so too praying together and studying Scripture together is enriched through shared wisdom, collective memory and learning.

Drawing on the rich history of mission, Christian shows how church planting is not something new, even though the term itself may be. He touches on the medieval church, for whom church planting was about the establishment of the first church in a new region. Apprenticeship is an underlying theme in the book, and reference to the *Didache* offers a fresh perspective on thinking about discipleship and the 'Way of Life' for Christians. He quotes Irenaeus, who said that 'the Church is planted like Paradise in this world'. The sentence that precedes this reads: 'Flee to the Church, and be brought up in her bosom, and be nourished by the Lord's Scriptures.' What a wonderful description of the life-giving nature of the Gospel of Christ that should be lived out by the Church throughout the world. The Church as the Body of Christ should be a place where all people find a safe haven and a place of nurture and refreshment.

Christian describes a church planter as someone called to lead in evangelistic mission, develop new leaders, and start new churches – or breathe life into existing ones. This book helpfully explores how this craft can be taught and practised. It is a well-researched book, which is written with wisdom and passion. Christian is not afraid to share his own personal stories, allowing others to learn not only from his mistakes but from his many successes. It is a rich contribution to the current dialogue about being church, and offers invaluable insight into the craft of church planting.

Stephen Cottrell
Archbishop of York

PART I

Introductions

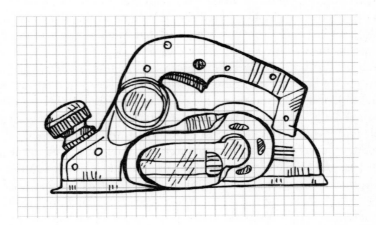

Out of a thousand people who study sacred scripture normally a hundred attain the readiness for the study of the Mishnah; out of these, ten attain the readiness for the Talmud, and out of these, only one will achieve mastery and becomes a master.

Kohelet Rabbah

Note: *Kohelet Rabbah* (or Ecclesiastes Rabbah) is a Jewish commentary on Ecclesiastes compiled between the sixth and eighth century. *Kohelet Rabbah* 7.41 is quoted in Reinhard Neudecker, 'Master-Disciple/Disciple-Master Relationship in Rabbinic Judaism and in the Gospels', *Pontificia Universitas Gregoriana*, Vol. 80, No. 2, 1999, 245–61, 248.

Personal Introduction

> I will build my church, and the gates of Hades will not prevail against
> it. I will give you the keys of the kingdom of heaven …
>
> *Jesus Christ (Matthew 16.18–19)*

Church planting: 'the most amazing thing I've ever heard'

It was just over 20 years ago – my wife and I were getting ready to become
church planters for the first time. Two years earlier some close friends
had planted a new church. We'd followed them closely, given money to
help with the costs, listened to their story, prayed for them, made visits
and shared their journey. Somewhere along the way we caught the bug
for church planting and less than a year after our friends planted their
church, we 'got the call'. We were a few weeks away from moving to the
North of England to start a new church.

A few days before we left, we spent an evening with some friends and
neighbours to say our final goodbyes. At the time we were living in a
small village where everyone liked to know everyone else's business.
While I don't imagine that we were the biggest news in the village, I do
remember there was some curiosity about why we were leaving. During
the evening, a local farmer asked me: 'What exactly is it that you are
going to do?' So, I told him our story.

We were part of a church that existed to invite people to follow Jesus
– one of the ways we did this was by starting new churches. My wife and
I felt called to this ministry-adventure and had been praying about where
and when we should go. As a result of much seeking God, working with
others, and some confirming events, we had concluded that God was calling us to the city of York in the North of England to start a new church.

We expected it to start small, like a seed being planted, but we hoped our new church would be a place where people with no church connection might discover Jesus Christ for themselves. When I finished telling my friend the story there was a short pause, then he said: 'That's the most amazing thing I've ever heard ... it sounds heavenly.' I suspect he didn't know he was agreeing with a great saint, Irenaeus of Lyons, who wrote in the second century that 'the Church is planted like Paradise in this world' (at the time, neither did I).[1] I have never forgotten his positive reaction and genuine intrigue with the idea of founding a new church. Moreover, I agree with him – I think that starting new churches is an amazing adventure. I still think that, more than two decades later.

In the 1990s church planting in England was still something of a novelty, but over the last few decades it has become more mainstream, particularly for younger leaders. Once upon a time, every cool kid in church aspired to be a preacher.[2] Years later, being a youth worker was the thing everyone wanted to do. A few years ago, it seemed every young leader dreamed of being a hipster worship leader. Now, everybody wants to be a church planter, or at least sometimes it feels that way. What is certainly true is that grass-roots interest in church planting is growing. For example, a few years ago, as part of a sermon, I asked my church, 'Who feels that at some point soon they will be involved in a church plant?' Almost every hand went up. My impromptu straw poll is an illustration of the growing grass-roots interest in church planting, especially in the younger generations of the church today. Although younger age-groups are increasingly absent from the Christian church, my church was demonstrating a more hopeful maxim: the 'missing generation' are the mission generation.

That isn't to say that church planting is easy, in fact it's harder than it looks. For a start, in addition to being the minister of a church, a church planter also needs to be an entrepreneur, an innovator, a dreamer and visionary, a strategist, an evangelist, a fundraiser, a team builder and more. Church planters need to be good at many key skills and this means they need great training and appropriate learning opportunities.

For 14 years, until 2021, I was the Ordained Leader of G2, a church plant based in York in the United Kingdom.[3] G2 was started as a missional experiment to discover whether a church hosted in a neutral location, outside the sometimes forbidding and austere buildings of the Church of England, might connect with a new group of people who did not attend church. G2 has been particularly effective in reaching the under 30s generation, who are commonly referred to as Millennials: more than 70 per cent of the adult members of G2 are part of this age-group. Over the last decade, G2 has been active in raising up leaders from this younger generation using simple apprenticeship models that focus on hands-on training, supervision, reflective learning, experience-based development and team learning. These basic practices have proved to be highly effective in developing a large cohort of young leaders, public speakers, evangelists, student workers, youth workers, worship leaders and church planters. Over 14 years, these have included more than 50 people who have gone to work for Christian organizations or who have been ordained in the Church of England.

During a personal retreat a few years ago, I spent some time considering the focus of my ministry over the next two decades, until I reach retirement age. I concluded that I felt called to play my part in the revitalization of the Church of England and the wider Christian church in three key ways: leading in evangelistic mission, developing new leaders and starting new churches. The seeds of this book are rooted in my personal experience of church planting and working with church planters in various contexts over the last 30 years. In that period, I have co-founded and led two church plants, trained and sent out numerous church planters, and advised others on how to develop church planting. I have also developed resources for church planters. These include a short book: *Alpha as a Church Planting Tool*,[4] undergraduate and postgraduate teaching material on church planting for Anglican and Baptist ministers in training,[5] a course called *Exploring Church Planting* for churches wanting to engage in church planting,[6] and training material for strategic directors of church planting. Through these engagements and others, I have had the opportunity to be personally involved with a large group of church planters encompassing a wide range of styles of church planting.

It has taken me more than 20 years of practitioner experience and some recent research to write this book. I've discovered a lot since that evening with my farmer friend and my first experience of founding a new church. Much of what I have learned has been gained through on-the-job experience, from the tutoring of more experienced practitioners, from reading about the history of the Church, and from mixing with other church planters. Some of the things I understand now I didn't learn until I was on my second church plant, and most of these learnings have been discovered through trial and error and trying again. Most recently, the clarity of some of what I know only came when I started training church planters – illustrating the saying 'you never really know something until you teach it to someone else'.[7]

Although the styles and models of church planting that I have experienced are diverse, I have observed in each context the significance of the role of a skilled pioneer leader in the successful founding and sustaining of new Christian communities. Moreover, I have noticed that many pioneer leaders and church planters have been frustrated with the experience of their formal ministerial preparation, typically because they have found the methods used in institutional training often do not help them develop as pioneers and practitioners. There is a crucial reason for this, which brings me to the point of this book. I've become convinced that church planting is not an optional interest or set of additional ministerial activities, the directions for which can be passed on through an academic process. Church planting is a craft. It is learned through active ministry with experienced practitioners who, in the right conditions, can pass these skills to apprentices so that they can then improvise the craft in new contexts. The aim of this book is to capture this process and help today's church rediscover the lost art of apprenticeship at its core.

I hope this book helps you discover this life-changing wisdom and inspires your own adventures in church planting: 'the most amazing thing I've ever heard'.

Notes

1 Irenaeus, *Against Heresies*, 5.20.2. Irenaeus of Lyons was one of the Fathers of the Church – influential theologians from the Patristic Era whose writings were formative in the early development of Christian doctrine. Irenaeus is probably referring to *plantatio Ecclesiae*, which is unpacked in Chapter 9.

2 The assumption that a calling to Christian ministry is principally a calling to preach is made, for example, by Martyn Lloyd-Jones when describing the period in England immediately after the end of the Second World War: *Preaching and Preachers* (Hodder & Stoughton, 1998).

3 Some of the story of G2 is written up in Christian Selvaratnam, 'Reclaiming the Missing Generation', in *Global Voices: Stories of Church Planting from Around the World*, edited by Winfield Bevins (Asbury Church Planting Initiative: 2019), 71–86.

4 Alpha is an evangelistic tool comprising a series of interactive sessions that explore the Christian faith. See Christian Selvaratnam, *Alpha as a Church Planting Tool* (London: Alpha International, 2017) for an overview of how Alpha can be used as a church planting tool.

5 The Common Awards modules I have designed are Church Planting in Perspective (TMM3861) and Advanced Church Planting in Perspective (TMM46120), at https://www.durham.ac.uk/departments/academic/common-awards/policies-pro cesses/curriculum/modules (accessed 28.1.2022).

6 *Exploring Church Planting*, a five-week introduction to church planting for anyone. Developed by St Hild College, published and distributed by CCX Media at the Gregory Centre for Church Multiplication.

7 A common saying with variations attributed to different people, this version is by John C. Maxwell, *The 360 Degree Leader with Workbook: Developing Your Influence from Anywhere in the Organization* (Thomas Nelson: 2011), 236.

2

Background:
The Best and Worst of Times

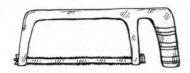

> It was the best of times, it was the worst of times,
> it was the age of wisdom, it was the age of foolishness,
> it was the epoch of belief, it was the epoch of incredulity,
> it was the season of light, it was the season of darkness,
> it was the spring of hope, it was the winter of despair,
> we had everything before us, we had nothing before us,
> we were all going direct to Heaven, we were all going
>   direct the other way
> – in short, the period was so far like the present period …
> *Charles Dickens*, A Tale of Two Cities[1]

The best and worst of times

Anyone involved in church planting today can identify with the paradox of the words above written by Charles Dickens in 1859: 'the period was so far like the present period'. In Dickens' fiction, London is thriving and peaceful whereas Paris is declining into a terrible drama that will become the Reign of Terror and the French Revolution: 'Along the Paris streets, the death-carts rumble, hollow and harsh.'[2] Ministry-life is often like this – a hybrid of 'London' and 'Paris' type experiences where good circumstances and bad co-exist in the same realm. Rarely is something all good or all bad, and often complex organizations have positive and less-positive narratives unfolding at the same time.

I suggest that today it is both 'the best of times' and 'the worst of times' for the historic Churches of the Western World.[3] This book will explore aspects of some 'springs of hope' from multiplying churches and the new initiatives that are termed 'church plants', but this is currently a minority report – the overall picture is still one of a 'winter of despair'.

The default context used in this book is England and the Church of England. (You may also notice my bias towards the North of England where I live.) While the story of each historic denomination and each Western nation is different, the overall picture of the Church is the same. In England, the average church attendance has been in decline for decades and is continuing to fall. If present trends continue, in just over ten years many of the historic Christian denominations may cease to be of national significance, and some may have closed altogether.[4]

The Doom statistics

There are many depressing reports on the decline of the church – a friend of mine calls them collectively the 'Doom statistics'.[5] All the Doom statistics tell a similar story: the attendance of most local churches and the total attendance in all the historic denominations is declining; this decline is most acute in younger age groups, who attend church less than their parents' and grandparents' generations.[6] The glory days of full – or supposedly full – churches have passed,[7] and we are, say some, 'one generation away from extinction'.[8] This depressing picture is illustrated by the internal statistics from the Church of England gathered just before the beginning of the effects of Covid-19, which show an overall picture of 'catastrophic decline' over the last ten years. Of the 15,496 churches surveyed, 41 per cent were in 'significant decline' and at the end of 2019 half of parishes in the Church of England had a usual Sunday service attendance of just 26 adults and two children, or fewer.[9] In addition, we have yet to see the lasting impact of Covid-19 on the church – many analysts believe the Coronavirus pandemic will accelerate and increase the existing decline of the church.[10] As one commentator on these data says, 'The church in its present form will have to die. It is dying.'[11] A few years ago one archdeacon offered an emotive description of the demise of the Church when he said,

> An empty church is like the empty palace of a long-forgotten king and people walk past and say, 'The king is dead.'[12]

Like many observers, the journalist Jeremy Paxman laments the Church's decline. He notes that the Church of England now has fewer members than The Royal Society for the Protection of Birds.[13] Quite possibly it is the worst of days for the Church in England. Is there hope?

The hope of church planting

This book is about church planting: an ancient ministry that offers hope for the present decline of the Church. Although the term 'church plant-ing' is modern,[14] the practice is ancient. Every local church was once started; thus, church planting is the history of the origins and growth of the church. Medieval Roman Catholics referred to this as *plantatio Ecclesiae*, a phrase which means 'church planting' in the sense of the first establishing of the church in a new region. The British Isles has a long and rich history of this pioneering form of ministry. Ancient tradition records that Christianity arrived in England when Roman artisans and merchants spread the message of Jesus, in the first or second century.[15] This was followed, several hundred years later, with two significant movements of mission and church planting. In the late sixth century, the Gregorian mission led by Augustine of Canterbury began in Kent and spread north and west bringing Roman Christianity through evangelism and church planting. Shortly after, in the early seventh century, Celtic missionaries from Ireland and Scotland travelled south to evangelize the North of England. These first missionaries included Aidan of Lindisfarne and Cuthbert, and later Hilda of Whitby and Bede.[16] The evangelistic efforts of these 'Northern Saints' resulted in the establishment of inno-vative expressions of Christianity – in the form of monastic church plants – across Northumbria in the North of England.[17] Since these early times, England has experienced various cycles of religious decline followed by mission and then church growth, the latter typically resulting in the establishing of new worshipping communities and revitalization of the church.[18]

Other seasons of church planting in England include church growth in early medieval times, the English Reformation, early Methodism,[19] 4,000 new churches following the Industrial Revolution (many of these new churches were 'Tin Tabernacles'[20]), Victorian church planting,[21] Queen Anne's 50 New Churches,[22] church planting in the inter-war period,[23] and most recently the Fresh Expressions of Church movement, Resource Churches,[24] and other late-twentieth and twenty-first-century church planting movements.[25]

The Church of England report cited above offers two threads of hope in the present situation: 10 per cent of existing churches are growing and all the church plants included in the data have grown and they have seen their membership collectively double since 2016.[26] It might be too early to say it is 'the best of times': at the moment, the bad news (of church decline) significantly outweighs the good news (of church planting, church revitalization and church growth). But there is a 'spring of hope' and perhaps the dawn of a 'season of light'.

The Church of England has been in decline since the beginning of the twentieth century and we have had decades to construct a plausible response.[27] Although several great initiatives have been proposed, to date none have fully taken stock of the challenge of our current situation.[28] This type of bad-news good-news paradox is hard to navigate. But decline is the elephant in the room that can no longer be ignored, the can that cannot be kicked any further down the road. How do we approach this challenge?

Clouds and sand

There are two common responses to the doom statistics: some bury their head in the sand, others keep their head in the clouds. Both groups are ignoring the challenges but in different ways. We've been burying our heads in the sand for a long time: finding ever-more positive-sounding ways to report the statistics, defending the small,[29] merging declining parishes,[30] changing vocabulary,[31] and focusing on faithfulness against fruitfulness.[32] Oftentimes these activities, and others, are simply procrastination born out of an unwillingness to address the challenges of a church that is declining in numbers. But equally bad is keeping our heads in the clouds, which also manifests in different forms: unqualified bold appeals to the faithfulness of God and expressions of denominational arrogance ('surely God wouldn't let ...'), appeals to the longevity of our history ('we've been here more than 400 years'), the comfort of buildings (because buildings convey a sense of permanence), and focusing efforts on reports, debates and theological discussion.[33]

So, some have their head in the sand, and some have their head in the clouds – we need a framework to move forward. I recently discovered some encouragement and wisdom from the Diocese of Bradford that might help resolve this dilemma. This is what they have to say:

> The times are difficult for all and the Church of England in every diocese has very real problems to face and decisions to make. But God has blessed the work abundantly in the past and He will continue to bless if faith and courage do not fail.[34]

Wise and encouraging words which we might imagine were written recently; however, the Diocese of Bradford was dissolved in 2014.[35] These words – that recognize the scale of a great challenge and are nevertheless hopeful in the faithfulness of God – are taken from the minutes of the Bradford Diocesan Board of Finance in 1946 as they, and the nation, began to move on from the effects of the Second World War. Despite being 75 years old, this statement echoes the sense of worry and concern that many of us feel about the decline of the church, especially as we emerge from the global pandemic. Bradford proposes that we do two things: recognize and engage with the full scope of the present challenges and commit to taking appropriate and bold action; and remember and celebrate God's past faithfulness, including his promises to us, and choose to believe that God is generous and faithful, so we can act with courage and humble confidence.[36] We can only do this by engaging boldly and humbly with God.

Fixing our eyes on Jesus

Two Bible passages come to mind which illustrate the fortitude of the Bradford response, the first is from the book of Hebrews:

> Therefore, since we are surrounded by such a great cloud of witnesses … let us run with perseverance the race marked out for us, fixing our eyes on Jesus, the pioneer and perfecter of faith. For the joy set before him he endured the cross, scorning its shame, and sat down at the right hand of the throne of God. Consider him who endured such opposition … so that you will not grow weary and lose heart. (Hebrews 12.1–3 NIV)

Jesus accepted his cross as he looked to his future vindication. He neither rejected his suffering nor saw it as the final word over his life. J. B. Phillips translates verse two like this: 'For he himself endured a cross and thought nothing of its shame because of the joy he knew would follow his suffering.'[37] No servant is above their master: if Jesus faced his challenges and held on to God's promises, so can and should we. And, since Christ has modelled this way forward, he has made it holy and even a means of grace.

The second passage is about Abram from the Old Testament.

> Without weakening in his faith, he faced the fact that his body was as good as dead – since he was about a hundred years old – and that

Sarah's womb was also dead. Yet he did not waver through unbelief regarding the promise of God, but was strengthened in his faith and gave glory to God, being fully persuaded that God had power to do what he had promised. (Romans 4.19–20 NIV)

Like Jesus, Abram faced the reality of his limitations and challenges; nevertheless, he believed God's promises and even grew stronger in his confidence by praising God and remembering that God could do what he had promised. These two great witnesses remind us how we can recognize the scale of the great challenge and be actively hopeful in God for a better future.

Proclaim the gospel afresh to every generation

Every Church of England deacon, priest and bishop knows these words from the preface to the Declaration of Assent:

> The Church of England is part of the One, Holy, Catholic and Apostolic Church, worshipping the one true God, Father, Son and Holy Spirit. It professes the faith uniquely revealed in the Holy Scriptures and set forth in the catholic creeds, *which faith the Church is called upon to proclaim afresh in each generation.*[38] (Emphasis added)

The mission and commission of the Church calls us to be perpetually proclaiming the gospel afresh to each generation. The 'faith' of the Church doesn't change – it is focused on the Trinitarian God, who is uniquely revealed in the Bible and affirmed through the historic catholic creeds. But our proclamation of this faith is to be applied dynamically and afresh to each generation and context.[39] Sometimes this means we need new expressions of church.

When introducing a position paper on church planting from the House of Bishops, the Bishop of Islington, who is the Church of England lead bishop for church planting, explained: 'In every generation, and with every tradition, the Church of England has planted new churches to reach new people in new places in new ways.'[40] As we have already noted, often this comes as a response to the worst of times.

Here is how the House of Bishops describe their commitment to church planting:

> Planting new churches is a long-established and effective means of establishing the presence of a Christian community to witness to the

gospel in new places, and of enabling that witness to be shared with more people in all places. It is integral to how the Church of England has shown its commitment to apostolicity and sought to express its catholicity.[41]

And also:

We welcome planting new churches as a way of sharing in the apostolic mission by bringing more people in England to faith in Christ and participation in the life of the Church.[42]

I believe we are at the beginning of another period when all congregations, across the Christian denominations, need to increase their commitment to the apostolic mission of the church – to bring more people to faith in Christ through a fresh proclamation of the gospel which will result in new churches.

Notes

1 Charles Dickens, *A Tale of Two Cities* (Glasgow: William Collins, 2017), 1.

2 Dickens, *Cities*, 412.

3 Throughout this book, I use 'Church' (with a capital letter) when I refer to a denomination, a network, or group of churches; and 'church' (lower case) when I refer to an individual local church. I have preserved the capitalization of 'church' in quoted material.

4 To be clear, I do not believe the Church in England will die for two key reasons. First, the English church has known pastimes of low numbers which has in turn provoked action that led to growth – we've been here before. Second, the parts of the Church of England that are growing (currently about 10 per cent) are vigorous and multiplying quickly. However, I believe we will continue to see net decline for more than a decade before we return to overall growth.

5 My friend Tim May refers to any of the data that describes the decline of the church as 'the Doom Statistics'.

6 Attendance is not the best measure of the health of the church; however, it is often used as a convenient proxy. Decreased church attendance in younger generations has recently been described as 'an 18 year-old is eight-times less likely to be in church on Sunday than an 81 year-old': *Everyone Counts: Growing the Church for All* (London: Archbishops' Council of the Church of England, 2014).

7 Although Robin Gill challenges the idea that many large church buildings constructed in the Victorian era were ever full. See his *The Myth of the Empty Church* (London: SPCK, 1993).

8 George Carey, a former Archbishop of Canterbury, quoted in 'Crisis of Faith', *The Spectator*, 13 June 2015, at https://www.spectator.co.uk/article/crisis-of-faith (accessed 28.1.2022).

9 These data are from *Statistics for Mission 2019*, at https://www.church

ofengland.org/sites/default/files/2020-10/2019StatisticsForMission.pdf (accessed 28.1.2022). The phrases 'catastrophic decline' and 'significant decline' are from David Keen's blog commentary on this report, at http://davidkeen.blogspot.com/2020/10/last-chance-to-see-church-of-england.html (accessed 28.1.2022).

10 For example, The Barna Group believe that one consequence of Covid-19 'could be a significant reduction in the number of churches in America'. David Kinnaman, the president of Barna Group, estimates that as many as one in five churches – and one in three mainline ones – could close for good within the next 18 months. An impact that Barna suggest 'would represent a rapid acceleration of a long-term decline in American religiosity', at https://www.economist.com/united-states/2020/05/23/the-virus-is-accelerating-dechurching-in-america (accessed 28.1.2022).

11 David Keen, 'Last Chance To See ... Church of England Membership and Attendance Stats 2019', *Opinionated Vicar*, at http://davidkeen.blogspot.com/2020/10/last-chance-to-see-church-of-england.html accessed (accessed 28.1.2022).

12 Quoted in Justin Brierley, 'Nicky Gumbel and the Evangelization of the Nation', Premier Christianity, July 2015, at https://www.premierchristianity.com/Past-Issues/2015/August-2015/Nicky-Gumbel-and-the-evangelization-of-the-nation, para. 18 (accessed 28.1.2022).

13 Jeremy Paxman. 'The Church of England's Fight to Survive as Congregations Dwindle, Is the Church on the Brink of Extinction?' *Financial Times*, 7 Sept. 2017, at https://www.ft.com/content/fced3f20-9294-11e7-a9e6-11d2foebb7fo para. 9 (accessed 28.1.2022).

14 Roland Allen, *Missionary Methods; St. Paul's or Ours: A Study of the Church in the Four Provinces* (Connecticut, NY: Martino Publishing, 2011).

15 John R. H. Moorman, *A History of the Church in England* (Harrisburg, PA: Morehouse Publishing, 1994), 3.

16 Bede, *The Ecclesiastical History of the English People* 3.3–5, 4.23, 4.27–28, see Venerable Bede, *The Ecclesiastical History of the English People*, edited by Judith McClure and Roger Collins, translated by Bertram Colgrave (Oxford: Oxford University Press, 2008), 146–51, 244–56, 260.

17 Gavin Wakefield and Nigel Rooms, eds, *Northern Gospel, Northern Church: Reflections on Identity and Mission* (Durham: Sacristy Press, 2016), 20.

18 David Goodhew, 'The Secularization and Resacralization of the North: New Churches in the North East', in *Northern Gospel*, 161–74, 172.

19 The history of the early Methodist Church in England is well-documented. For one good summary see Richard P. Heitzenrater, *Wesley and the People Called Methodists* (Nashville, TN: Abingdon Press 1995).

20 See Peter Norman, *St. Joseph's Parish Cardiff: The Early Years 1913–1936* (Cardiff: self-published, 2013), 16; William Morris, *On the External Coverings of Roofs* (London: Society for the Protection of Ancient Buildings, 1890).

21 For a good overview of the dynamics of Victorian Church Planting see Francis (Frog) Orr-Ewing, *Victorian Church Planter, Thomas Gaster and Church Missionary Society, India 1857–1904*, PhD thesis (Oxford: University of Oxford, 2017).

22 'The Commission for Building Fifty New Churches' in London and the surrounding area (sometimes called 'Queen Anne's churches') was an organization established by the *New Churches in London and Westminster Act* (of Parliament) in 1710.

23 For example, Rex Walford has highlighted the Church of England's effectiveness in reaching out to new residents in Middlesex, in the interwar years, through new churches and church-linked leisure institutions such as sports clubs and drama groups. See his *The Growth of 'New London' in Suburban Middlesex (1918–1945) and the Response of the Church of England* (Lewiston, NY: Edwin Mellen Press, 2007), 373–78.

24 In this context, the term 'Resource Church' was first proposed by Ric Thorpe, the Bishop of Islington, as a development of an earlier classification of 'hub church', to describe a church plant which is designated by a bishop as a locus for future church planting. This terminology began to gain popular use around 2012. See Ric Thorpe, *Resource Churches: A Story of Church Planting and Revitalisation Across the Nation* (London: The Gregory Centre for Church Multiplication, 2021), at www.ccx.org.uk.

25 European examples of church planting movements include Acts 29 Europe, Avant, City to City Europe, Exponential Europe, M4 Europe, and NewThing Europe. British examples include Church Revitalisation Trust (Holy Trinity Brompton), Co-Mission, Gregory Centre for Church Multiplication, Hillsong, Newfrontiers, New Wine Church Planting, Salt and Light, St Hild Centre for Church Planting, and Vineyard Churches UK & Ireland.

26 Note that only 90 church plants were included in *Statistics for Mission 2019* and the report clarifies that, 'Information has not been collected from these new churches for long enough to make an assessment of their attendance trends'.

27 Bob Jackson suggests that Church of England Sunday attendance figures per head of the population peaked in 1904 and church attendance has been in both relative and absolute decline since that date. See Bob Jackson, *Hope for the Church: Contemporary Strategies for Growth* (London: Church House Publishing, 2002), 17.

28 One recent development is 'Simpler, Humbler, Bolder', a vision and strategy for the Church of England which was adopted at the General Synod of the Church of England in July 2021. Among other goals, this initiative proposed establishing 10,000 new, mostly lay-led, churches and action to double the number of children and youth in the Church over the next decade. See *Simpler, Humbler, Bolder: A Church for the Whole Nation Which is Christ Centred and Shaped by the Five Marks of Mission* (GS2223), at https://www.churchofengland.org/media/24449 (accessed 28.1.2022). A parallel project was launched by the Gregory Centre for Church Multiplication in June 2021. The project is 'Myriad', named after the Greek word that means 'a large and diverse number' and the metric prefix for 10,000, at https://ccx.org.uk/myriad (accessed 28.1.2022).

29 I love small churches, but defending the small can be a form of misdirection.

30 *Anecdote to Evidence* said that 'grouping multiple churches together under one leader has in general had a detrimental effect on church growth', although this conclusion was disputed when the report was presented at General Synod in 2014. See Church Growth Research Programme, *From Anecdote to Evidence: Findings from the Church Growth Research Programme 2011–2013* (London: Archbishops' Council of the Church of England, 2014), 8.

31 One example of a trend I have noticed over the last ten years is a progression from talking about 'evangelism', to 'mission', to 'influence'.

32 Timothy Keller suggests that we need both faithfulness and fruitfulness to thrive in ministry. He terms the combination a 'theological vision'. See *Center*

Church: Doing Balanced, Gospel-Centered Ministry in Your City (Grand Rapids, MI: Zondervan, 2012), 13–26.

33 I am deeply committed to research and theological study; however, in some situations, calling for them can be an escape activity.

34 A quotation from the minutes of Bradford Diocesan Board of Finance in 1946, cited in an email on 13 May 2021 from the Diocesan Secretary and Bishop of Leeds to clergy and church officers in the Diocese of Leeds.

35 The Diocese of Bradford was dissolved in 2014 to allow the formation of the new Anglican Diocese of Leeds, which was initially known as the Diocese of West Yorkshire and the Dales.

36 A better-known equivalent is the Stockdale Paradox, named after James Stockdale, a former United States vice-presidential candidate and onetime Vietnam prisoner of war whose story was popularized by Jim Collins in *Good to Great*. See James C. Collins, *Good to Great: Why Some Companies Make the Leap – and Others Don't* (New York: HarperBusiness, 2001), 85.

37 J.B. Phillips, *New Testament in Modern English* (New York: Touchstone, 1995), 474.

38 This text is from the preface to the Declaration of Assent, an oath sworn by deacons, priests and bishops in the Church of England when they are ordained or take up a new appointment. See *Common Worship: Services and Prayers for the Church of England* (London: Church House Publishing, 2000), xi.

39 This phrase ('to proclaim afresh in each generation') was the inspiration in *Mission-Shaped Church* for the term 'fresh expression of church'. See Graham Cray *et al.*, editors. *Mission-Shaped Church: Church Planting and Fresh Expressions of Church in a Changing Context* (London: Church House Publishing, 2004), 34.

40 Quoted in https://www.churchofengland.org/news-and-media/news-and-statements/bishops-set-out-principles-church-planting (accessed 28.1.2022).

41 The House of Bishops of the Church of England. *Church Planting and the Mission of the Church: A Statement by the House of Bishops*. HB(18)05, House of Bishops of the Church of England, May 2018, para 6, at https://www.churchof england.org/media/10519 (accessed 28.1.2022).

42 *Mission of the Church*, para 9.

3

The Craft of Church Planting

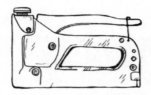

According to the grace of God given to me, like a skilled master builder I laid a foundation.

The Apostle Paul (1 Corinthians 3.10)

What type of work is church planting?

How should we describe a church planter and what do they do? To which other professions or roles might we liken the ministry of church planting? Are church planters managers, teachers, or carers; is their job like that of a community worker, a civic leader, or the CEO of a business? Using a biblical categorization, are they apostles, prophets, pastors, teachers or evangelists? In short, what type of work is church planting?

Although church planters share many roles in common with other church ministers, the work they do has distinctive elements that set their ministry apart from those who lead churches that already exist. The defining aspect of a church planter's work is that they found new churches – they dream about, plan and create new Christian communities that proclaim the gospel of Jesus Christ and make disciples. So, church planters are pioneers and innovators, and many church planters would say that their work requires creativity, especially if we understand creativity as the process of contextualization. How might this affect how we understand their role? For example, if church planters are creatives might it be better to think of them as artisans? How do we best describe someone who utilizes established skills but applies them with creativity?

In this book, the term adopted for this practice is 'craft', a description used in the medieval ages to refer to practical work that was creative or craftwork.[1] This book considers the practice of church planting and the training of church planters from the perspective of ancient craftwork – where church planting is understood as an art form and a craft activity and where creativity is considered to be an essential part of the ministry. The initial inspiration for this model are the practices of apprenticeship training in the English medieval guilds.

The city where I live

York, the city where I live, has a long heritage of apprenticeship training associated with groups of small business known as craft guilds. The first record of a guild in York appears in 1163 in the *Acta of Henry II*, which lists the granting of the King's confirmation of the 'weavers' guild and customs' in exchange for an annual payment of ten pounds.[2] Although the guilds have all but disappeared, two institutions still practising craft skills with elements of the historic craft guild model are located within a hundred metres of a building that was my office for many years. These are the Minster Stoneyard, a workshop for stonemasons and lead workers, and the York Glaziers' Trust, a conservation studio for historic stained glass. I have walked past these two workshops innumerable times and made many personal visits, when I have seen craftwork in operation. Over time this has led me to consider how the current methods of training ministers in the church might be informed by the venerable approaches of craft guilds through artisan training and historic approaches to apprenticeship.[3]

Apprenticeship

Apprenticeship training is ancient – it has probably existed as a pedagogical model since at least the Neolithic Agricultural Revolution when humans began to live in settled communities and the earliest proto-cities, more than 10,000 years ago.[4] In past generations, apprenticeship-style training has been key to the effective transformation of a novice into a master through the acquisition of craft skills and the development of the worker's personal creativity and distinct style.[5] This mode of learning is significantly different to the didactic classroom training model which is ubiquitous in modern formal learning systems and central to most models of Christian ministerial formation in the Western world.

For more than 600 years, up to the beginning of the British Industrial Revolution, medieval craft guilds trained most English youths and young adults. This was achieved through a specific form of guided apprenticeship which involved hands-on training, evidence-based education progression, community learning, and the creative development of a worker's craft skills. Through the workshops of the guilds, explicit, tacit and embedded knowledge was passed from one generation to another through training delivered by expert 'masters' who personally tutored apprentices.

A craft approach to church planting

Before we move too far with the idea of a craft approach to church planting, we need to acknowledge that the present-day usage of the word craft is quite different from the meaning of the word in the Middle Ages. Here's how the Merriam-Webster Dictionary defines craft:

> The word 'craft' comes from the Middle English word for 'strength' or 'skill' derived from the Old English word *cræft* which comes from Old High German *kraft*, for strength, and means 'skill in planning, making, executing' and, by extension, 'an occupation or trade requiring skill' and crafts, then, being those objects resulting from the application of that skill.[6]

This might not be what we first imagine when we consider craft. Perhaps we think of 'arts and craft', activities with children, or home-made commodities made by hobbyists. The contemporary concept of craft is of small-scale manufacturing of luxury or hand-made products, or an amateur and do-it-yourself approach to practical tasks. However, in the context of the guilds, craftworkers are highly experienced practitioners – people who can plan, execute and make with strength and skill. Guild craftworkers are the best at what they do, they are expert in understanding and making their products, skilled workers who have mastered the core skills of their trade with creativity.

Just as in past-times trades and professions – such as goldsmith, stonecutter, glassmaker, armourer, woodworker, saddler, baker, etc. – were learned and practised as crafts, I suggest that contemporary church planting is best learned and practised as a craft. And that apprenticeship-style training should be the preferred approach to training such modern ministry craftworkers or artisans. The argument, evidence and implications of this unfold through this book but let me briefly suggest four reasons why this approach might be preferable.

First, the craft approach fits well with pioneering methods. Just like many types of artist, church planting pioneers bring tried and tested ingredients together in original ways to form a unique piece of work – in this case, a new church. When done well, church planting produces a contextualized expression of the timeless gospel through strong skills and a creative approach. Second, the guilds made masters of ordinary people. Rather than being trained according to academic methods and standards, as Church of England ordinands are today, the craft approach found ways to develop expertise in anyone.[7] Next, the guild approach proposes that training can and should take place in the local church, the equivalent of the medieval workshop. One recent example of this is St Mellitus College, which was started to restore an ancient pattern of 'theological education [which is delivered] ... at the heart of the local church',[8] an approach that was common in Celtic monasteries and the churches established as a result of the Gregorian mission.[9] Last, as demand for church planting continues to increase, we will need methods of training that can accommodate significantly larger numbers. The guild approach to training has the replicability of a viral model – each master trains several apprentices and journeymen, many of whom become masters and train new apprentices.

About this book

This book is based on study which formed part of my Doctor of Ministry research at Asbury Theological Seminary. The purpose of my research was to

> explore how the pedagogical practices of English medieval craft guilds might inform methods of training for the next generation of church planters in the Church of England.[10]

My research had three areas of focus: masters and apprentices (the relationships that establish a craft approach), guild-type communities (the communities that support ongoing practice), and creativity (the process of experimentation in a local context). These three areas repeat as themes throughout this book and form some of the structure for my concluding thoughts in the final chapters. In this book I use the term 'master-apprentice' as a shorthand for the interaction between experts and trainees in the context of apprenticeship-style training.

This book is not a textbook for training church planters. Such a book would need to offer clear proposals for tightly defined practices. In applied theology terms, this book is a pre-intervention discussion, rather than the defence of a proposed method. My aim here is to present a set of valuable resources which stimulate the Church to new thinking and offer some creative leads for other practitioners. Or, put another way, I see this book as Green Paper, not a White Paper.[11]

Who is this book for?

This book is written for the contemporary church planting equivalents of the principal actors in the guilds: apprentices, journeymen (itinerant learners), and masters, roles that are unpacked in Chapter 6. These are women and men who are at different stages of learning about church planting, testing out and honing their skills, planting churches, and training and sending others. Perhaps you are an apprentice (or a prospective apprentice) looking to learn the basics of church planting – which means you need a master to teach you and a workshop where you can learn. Or maybe you are a journeyman – an apprentice who has graduated by demonstrating you have learned the basics and you are looking to develop your skills through self-directed learning from other masters, journeymen and new contexts. Or you are a master – an established practitioner who is now also training the next generation.

If I can stretch the guild overview a little more, there are two other characters in view: patrons and guild masters. Patrons are not necessarily practitioners, but they do open and close doors of opportunity for those who are; patrons appoint people to roles, they lend credibility and support, they are someone to look to in challenging times, and they hold the overall vision for the ministry. Today these are our bishops, archdeacons, area deans, diocesan staff and leaders in the national institutions of the Church of England. Our patrons need a vision for church planting and – as most don't have first-hand or primary experience of church planting – they also need the humility to cherish the practitioners who do.

Guild masters are senior masters in the extended guild community who have a role that is wider than their own workshop. So, in addition to being practitioners and trainers, they are network leaders who are investing in the future of their guild through vision and strategic leadership, safeguarding the culture of their guild, and appointing new masters. Church planting guild masters today are usually operating either in non-denominational networks that work alongside the denominational churches, or they are leading informal networks of church plants and planting churches within denominations. The latter are often networks of their own creation – typically made up of churches and leaders they have sent out.

The term 'master'

The term 'master', which is used throughout this book, is retained from its historic usage despite the obvious gender bias. When I use the term, I am simply repeating the title used ubiquitously in medieval examples; it is an aspect of history that virtually all guilds were overseen by masters who were men.[12] When I report the findings of interviews, and in my conclusions and recommendations, I continue with this same term; however, I am using it there with a gender-inclusive intent.

Despite my own convictions – that both women and men are called to lead in God's church – I have resisted the temptation to relabel 'master' with an alternative term, such as coach, chief, expert, mentor, etc. These are all good labels, but none quite captures the richness of the historic identity of the term. Also, I have resisted using the archaic feminine form 'mistress', because of its obvious sexual and moral connotations in contemporary use – although I did consider making use of an obsolete form of this word, 'mastress', which might have resolved the problem noted above.

On balance – for accuracy, clarity and consistency – I have used the term 'master' throughout. I have taken a similar view with the word 'journeyman' (which is introduced in Chapter 6); however, for this label I am able to offer a useful calque (wanderer) and helpful alternative descriptors used by recent commentators. Likewise, I have retained the word 'father' in most biblical quotations, although in some passages that I have translated myself I have used 'parent' to convey a gender-inclusive view of ministry. Nevertheless, I hope women readers will know that this book is as much about them and their ministry in the church today as it is about the historic role of men in craft guilds.

Old lessons, new context

A book of this length can't possibly do justice to the rich, diverse and 700-year-long history of the English guilds. Moreover, as with any summary of history, there is a danger of nostalgia and romanticism that could have the undesired effect of presenting the guilds as an idealistic example or perfect world. While looking to the guilds for inspiration, we should also acknowledge significant concerns in the way people were treated at the time. Perspectives we recognize and support today – such as 'Me Too', 'Black Lives Matter', safeguarding from abuse, preventing child and worker exploitation, and ensuring equal opportunities – would certainly highlight the inadequacies of the guilds. It is important to acknowledge that the guilds were institutions of their time and were far from perfect. This creates the conditions for our current challenge: to learn from their history, receiving what is good and leaving what is not.

I suggest that training structures for church planting today might be modelled on fresh contextualizations of historic guild practice, powerfully formational yet locally flexible, rooted in invitational and contextual learning but reflecting the full inclusivity of the gospel. This is the vision that drives the proposal of this book.

Summary

This book is divided into five parts, each of which gathers wisdom from an important source that will enable us to rediscover the importance of craft and apprenticeship for church planting. In this first part I have set the scene, highlighting the urgency of this conversation, my personal interest, and setting out my approach. In Part 2, I consider selected biblical and theological foundations for craft apprenticeship. To do this I use eight Scripture passages to explore apprenticeship in the Bible and then I consider three texts which help us develop a theology of craft and creativity. These two chapters open up the themes of apprenticeship, guilds and creativity, with additional questions included to help with making these connections. Part 3 considers the wisdom embedded in tradition and practice. I begin with an overview of the English medieval craft guilds; next, I summarize the contemporary understanding of apprenticeship, which is followed by a select history of ministerial formation; and last, I offer a basic theory for craft church planting. Part 4 builds on the two preceding sections with further wisdom from a study of experts involved in church planting and training. This section concludes with four simple ethnographic reports from contemporary examples of craft apprenticeship that ground some of the concepts explored. Finally, Part 5 offers some conclusions and recommendations for the Church of England and other groups involved in church planting today.

For readers who are not Anglican, I acknowledge that almost all the illustrations, terminology and data in this book are from the Church *of* England; however, some of the historical material predates the establishment of the Church of England and so forms part of the common history of all in the Church *in* England. Nevertheless, I am confident that the ideas in this book will translate well to other church networks and traditions and will encourage the training of the next generation of church planters and the re-evangelization of our nation, *Deo volente*.

So, let's begin, with the craft of church planting.

Notes

1 For an alternative to the term 'craft', medieval writers, such as Hugh of St Victor, used the term 'mechanical arts' to refer to activities that apply artistic skills to practical work. The mechanical arts brought together the beauty and purity of art with the practicality of human creation. See Anya Burgon, *The Mechanical Arts and Poiesis in the Philosophy and Literature of the Twelfth-Century Schools*, PhD thesis (Cambridge: University of Cambridge 2018), at https://core.ac.uk/download/pdf/222832421.pdf (accessed 28.1.2022).

2 See Nicholas Vincent, *Acta of Henry II and Richard I: Handlist of Documents Surviving in the Original, in Repositories in the United Kingdom* (London: List and Index Society, 1996); and Sarah Rees Jones, *York: The Making of a City 1068–1350*, 1st edn (Oxford: Oxford University Press, 2013).

3 For a separate part of my Doctor of Ministry studies I completed an ethnographic study of the craft workers at York Glaziers' Trust.

4 Stephen Billett, 'Apprenticeship as a Mode of Learning and Model of Education', *Education + Training*, Vol. 58, No. 6, 2016, 613–628, doi:10.1108/ET-01-2016-0001, 618.

5 Stuart Russell estimates that 'since the dawn of humanity, we have spent roughly a trillion person-years just passing on what we know to the next generation'. See 'AI: A Future for Humans?' lecture 4 of 4 in *Living with Artificial Intelligence*, The Reith Lectures (BBC: 2021), first broadcast on 22 Dec. 2021, at https://www.bbc.co.uk/programmes/m001216k (accessed 28.1.2022).

6 This definition is taken from *Merriam-Webster's Unabridged Dictionary*, at https://unabridged.merriam-webster.com/unabridged/craft (accessed 28.1.2022).

7 Bishop Jill Duff makes this point when she contrasts Paul with Peter, saying 'I'm not convinced that Peter – the rock on who Jesus built his church – would easily navigate his way through selection and ordination training in the Church of England.' See Jill Duff, 'Estates and the Gospel', a paper delivered at the Urban Estates Evangelism Conference in 2017. For an example from English history, the Wesley brothers and the early British Methodists made leaders of uneducated people. See Howard A. Snyder, *The Radical Wesley and Patterns for Church Renewal* (Westmont, IL: InterVarsity Press, 1982), 53.

8 St Mellitus College was established in 2007, see Jonathan Aitken, *The St Mellitus Story* (Private publication, 2017), 3–4. Other institutions following this approach include St Hild College and Emmanuel Theological College.

9 Although, the dissolution of the monasteries (1536–1541) disbanded monasteries, priories and convents, and made way for a distinctive English church and parish model.

10 A shortened form of my purpose statement. See Christian Selvaratnam, 'The Craft of Church Planting: Guild Training Models for Apprenticing Church Planters' (DMin dissertation, Wilmore, KY: Asbury Theological Seminary, 2020), 11.

11 In the British Government, White Papers are debated as final statements of new or revised policy, whereas Green Papers are for discussion of proposals at a formative stage.

12 An interesting story about one female master was related to me during a guided tour of the wine caves of Veuve Amiot in Saumur, France. In 1871, Armand Amiot set up a company trading wine in the region and later bought a business which made sparkling wines; however, his wines were not good. In 1882 Armand

died, but his widow Elisa concealed his death (keeping his body in their bedroom) and she started running the business in his name. Within two years the wines were good, the business was growing, and she was able to take over the role of mistress of the business, which she renamed Veuve Amiot (widow Amiot). Not only was Elisa better at making wine than her husband, she was also a much better employer: she provided gardens and allotments for her workers, child benefits and a school and crèche for her employees' children – all unusual benefits for that time, at https://www.veuveamiot.fr (accessed 28.1.2022).

PART 2

Wisdom from Scripture and Theology

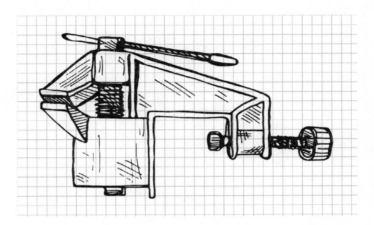

Keep these words that I am commanding you today in your heart. Recite them to your children and talk about them when you are at home and when you are away, when you lie down and when you rise. Bind them as a sign on your hand, fix them as an emblem on your forehead, and write them on the doorposts of your house and on your gates.

Moses (Deuteronomy 6.6–9)

4

Apprenticeship Training in the Bible

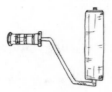

Let your house be a meeting place for the wise; be covered in their dust; and, with thirst, drink in their words.

Yose ben Yoezer, third century BC rabbi[1]

Poor is the apprentice who does not surpass his master, poorer is the painting which does not excel the sketch.

Leonardo da Vinci[2]

The Old and New Testaments give many instances of training interactions between established leaders and novices – where, typically, an older leader prepares, trains and mentors a younger student through on-the-job instruction. This process of apprenticeship-style training usually involved a student accompanying a master in a practice of close discipleship over a period of years. Through a process of instruction, students are first enabled to minister under supervision and then, in time, either to succeed their teacher or to work independently. In a well-known example, after several years of master-apprentice training, Jesus said to his disciples: '[you will] do the works that I do and, in fact, will do greater works' (John 14.12), that is, Jesus apprenticed his disciples to succeed him in ministry.

With more than 3,000 people named in the Old and New Testaments,[3] we can reasonably estimate that there are many hundreds (or more) of training relationships between explicitly named parties in the Bible, and many thousands (or more) where the participants are not directly documented. To take one well-known figure, Paul; the New Testament documents 36 named missionary travel companions, co-workers, fellow prisoners, or close supporters of the Apostle – these are all people we know, or can presume, received training from Paul.[4]

This chapter seeks to develop the biblical background to apprentice-ship training, particularly focusing on masters and apprentices, guild-type communities and creativity. To focus this investigation, I have selected eight pericopes (four from each Testament) to explore these themes from diverse perspectives. Each text resonates with at least one of the focus areas, most with two. In addition, there are questions at the end of each section – 18 in total – to assist with making these connections.

Multi-generational apprenticeship training in Deuteronomy 6

Deuteronomy 6 offers the first biblical image of the practice of disciple-ship and family-apprenticeship in ancient Israel. Verses 5.32–6.9 bring to a close the section that introduces the giving of the Decalogue (5.6–21) which is received as the basis for Israel's faith-covenant with Yahweh.[5] In particular, what the New Testament refers to as the first and second commandments (Deut. 5.6–10 and Lev. 19.18) stand at the heart of all that follows in Deuteronomy – commands that are further highlighted for their primacy by Jesus (Matt. 22.36–40) and James (James 2.8) in the New Testament.[6]

In Deuteronomy 6, verses 4–9 are known in Judaism as 'The Shema': a daily prayer which is titled after the first word of the text, 'hear' (shema). The Shema is Judaism's pre-eminent declaration of faith.[7] It is said by some to be of equivalent liturgical importance to The Lord's Prayer in Christianity,[8] and it has been called by others the 'Magna Carta of the home'.[9] It is important to note that the basic unit of Israelite society was not the conjugal family. The smallest domestic unit documented in the Old Testament is bayith (Hebrew, 'father's house'), a multi-generational household living in a single location, such as that mentioned in the tenth commandment in Exodus (Exod. 20.7). Larger groups were local 'clans' (Hebrew, mishpachah) comprising kinship bayith, and lastly 'tribes' (Hebrew, shevet) of associated clans.[10] The Shema was instruction to be passed on to the following generations by all members of society, the latter part (6.4–9) being in the form of a doxology which would have been memorized by children. As one of the earliest examples of training in the Bible, Deuteronomy 6 provides a helpful illustration of an inter-generational pattern of training that was foundational to ancient Jewish practice.

In Deuteronomy 6.1–9, the community of Israel, and in particular bio-logical parents, are given foundational instructions on how to transfer the teaching and faith inheritance they have received to the next gen-eration in a repeating pattern that continues through the generations.

Verses 6.2 and 6.7 enjoin parents and others to be personally involved in training their children through constant reminders of God's story with his people, encouraging memorization of promises, answering questions, and catechistic teaching of God's commandments. The key verbs used in this section are hear, fear (or revere), keep, teach and do. A similar collection of themes is seen in the Wisdom Literature, especially Proverbs chapters 1–9.

This passage offers one of the earliest references in Scripture to a master-apprentice type training relationship, where parents personally nurture their children through verbal instruction and tactile interaction: the responsibility is with the parent (master) to train the child (apprentice). The extended family, the clans and the tribes operate as a self-perpetuating community of learning, for training, holding knowledge and passing on oral tradition to the next generation. Expressions of creativity and artistry are seen in the exhortation to make religious jewellery, reminder symbols and devotional calligraphy. These principles and practices, which are integral to God's people in the Old Testament, offer insight into God's people now, especially those dedicated to passing on the faith through discipleship and family-apprenticeship in creative ways.

Questions

1 Where do you see family apprenticeship practices in the church? What are the obstacles to embedding intentional intergenerational training in the church?

2 What role could there be for renewed forms of 'catechesis' (Greek, 'to teach orally'), where doctrine is often memorized and taught in question-and-answer forms?[11]

3 How might expressions of creativity, religious jewellery, reminder symbols and devotional calligraphy assist in passing on the Christian faith?

Bezalel and Oholiab gifted in craft skills by the Holy Spirit

Exodus 31 introduces a curious story of two artisans who are 'filled ... with ability and intelligence, with knowledge and all craftsmanship' (Exod. 31.3 ESV) by the Spirit of God. The craftworkers are Bezalel and Oholiab who, although there is no description that they received a ceremonial anointing with priestly oil, are described as having received the reality of it, direct from the Spirit of God. Their anointing equipped them with a variety of craftwork skills (Exod. 31.2–5; 35.30–35), the ability to teach others (Exod. 35.34), and the ability to manage other craftworkers (Exod. 31.6).

Although no master-apprenticeship relationship between Bezalel and Oholiab is explicitly described, it is implied in Exodus 35.34 which says that the Spirit of God 'has inspired him to teach, both him and Oholiab' (Exod. 35.34 ESV; cf. Exod. 31.6, 36.1–2, 38.23). As spirit-filled skilled labours, Bezalel, Oholiab and their assistants receive a spiritual anointing to enhance their natural abilities and skills that have already been cultivated in the usual ways. Bezalel, whose name means 'in the shadow of God', was called by God and appointed by Moses as the chief artisan overseeing the construction of the Tabernacle. As an instructor and manager of apprentices, he was also a master-workman (Exod. 35.30–35). According to rabbinic tradition, Bezalel is said to have been aged only 13 years when he began the construction of the Tabernacle.[12] This perhaps explains another rabbinic tradition that God asked Moses if Bezalel was acceptable for this task.[13]

The unusual description of how Bezalel and Oholiab are trained and gifted in their artisan, teaching and management skills highlights God's involvement in the practical activities of human life and raises interesting questions about the interplay between natural abilities, the common work of the Spirit, and possible additional or special anointing. Probably both had already been apprenticed in craftwork by human trainers; but what is not clear is whether this text describes the general or a selective work of the Holy Spirit. Are the events in the passage a special case or an illustration of the universal work of God? What the passage does suggest is that it is the Spirit's anointing that enables Bezalel and Oholiab to train others through apprenticeship methods, thereby communicating their human and divinely received craft talents to others (Exod. 35.34).

Questions

1 If Bezalel was only 13 years old when he started as a craft worker, what might that teach us about training and involving young people in and through the church?
2 What is the Holy Spirit's role in nurturing creativity in people, and how can the church invite, support and bless this gift of God among His people?

The mentoring of Elisha by Elijah in 1 and 2 Kings

Old Testament prophets have typically been seen as solo agents who work on their own. When commenting on this idea, Rick D. Moore acknowledges that 'there is a long-standing stereotype of the Old Testament prophet as an [independent] "lone ranger" figure'.[14] Associated with this viewpoint is the notion that prophets are not humanly trained but rather receive equipping directly from the Spirit of God.[15] For example, Karl Heinrich Rengstorf believes that the patterns of producing leaders in the Hebrew scripture are limited to either those of direct impartation from God, or faithful re-communication of established instruction to a servant by a reliable teacher.[16] Others, however, think that leadership training, discipleship training and mentoring occur frequently in the Bible.

Martin Hengel notes that Josephus uses the Greek word for disciple (*mathetes*) when describing Elisha's relationship to Elijah.[17] Moreover, Hengel believes Elisha's call to Elijah is analogous to Jesus' calling of his own disciples, saying: 'Elijah and Elisha ... are frequently used among the rabbis to exemplify the teacher-pupil relationship.'[18] This view is shared by Richard Calenberg, who believes that the verb 'to walk', which may be used with reference to following after a teacher, illustrates the Elijah-Elisha relationship (cf. 1 Kings 19.21).[19] Likewise, Michael Wilkins sees master-apprentice type relationships among the prophets.[20] Calenberg, in particular, views the relationship between Elisha and Elijah as the definitive master-disciple model in the Old Testament.[21] He believes this is in part due to the language used to describe Elisha following after Elijah. The Hebrew phrase, which is used in 1 Kings 19.21 for example, includes the verb *yalak* (to walk), which may be used with reference to following after a teacher (cf. 1 Kings 19.21).[22] From studying Moses, Elijah and Isaiah, Moore concludes that 'mentoring is ... arguably one of the constitutive facets of the Old Testament prophetic vocation'.[23] With this in mind, this section is an exploration of the dynamics of the mentoring relationship between Elijah and Elisha.

As the leading figure of the former prophets, Elijah's mentoring relationship with his protégé Elisha is therefore significant. Walter Brueggemann notes that the narrative concerning Elijah and Elisha occupies over 20 per cent of the Books of Kings concluding that 'this must mean that the editors wished to accent their work'.[24] Moore believes the Elijah-Elisha mentoring relationship is all the more significant because it has 'long-noted Moses-Joshua parallels' with 'numerous indications of the [same] mentoring relationship'.[25]

The Books of Kings (1 and 2 Kings) are rich in the language of fathers and sons, with over 400 references to those words across the two books.

The father-son terminology is also particularly evident in the Elisha-Elijah descriptive within those books, especially in 2 Kings 2 where the narrative of the chapter highlights Elisha inheriting from Elijah the role of 'father' to the 'sons of the prophets' (2 Kings 2.15). This idea is reinforced by an earlier event in 1 Kings 19 where, in a moment of great despair, Elijah cries out, '[T]ake away my life, for I am no better than my fathers' (1 Kings 19.4 ESV). Moore believes this comment points to a 'fathering deficit' in Israel, one that Elijah is perhaps divinely called to address in his engagement with younger men.[26] At their parting, Elisha calls Elijah '[m]y father, my father' (2 Kings 2.12) – a statement which is repeated verbatim by Joash at Elisha's death (2 Kings 13.14) – perhaps highlighting Israel's fatherless state at the time. Whether or not Israel or Elisha felt fatherless, it is evident that both Elijah and Elisha acted as fathering-prophets to a small group of disciples who are referred to as the 'sons of the prophets'. The 'sons of the prophets' are referred to ten times in the last chapter of 1 Kings and the first nine chapters of 2 Kings, and also in the New Testament by Peter in his speech at Solomon's Portico (Acts 3.25). The Elisha-Elijah account highlights the importance of relationship in the apprenticeship process. In this case, Elijah operates in a fatherly way to Elisha, delivering a holistic and socially comprehensive training experience, rather than being a dispassionate or professionally detached trainer.

When reflecting on Moore's commentary on the Elisha-Elijah relationship, Walter Brueggemann agrees with Moore that the prophets of Israel are at the centre of the process of mentoring emerging prophetic leaders. Furthermore, Brueggemann supports the idea that there were schools in ancient Israel for the 'subversive mentoring' of elite young leaders.[27] Some of these schools may have been 'schools of prophets' – groups which receive occasional, fleeting and ambiguous mention in the Old Testament historical and prophetic books (e.g. 1 Sam. 10.5–6, 10.10–13, 19.19–24; 2 Kings 2.3, 2.15, 4.1, 4.38, 6.1–4, 9.1–3; Ezra 5.2).

The absence of detailed description of these groups makes it hard to draw strong conclusions, though from an extensive survey of 1 Samuel and Kings, Ira M. Price believes their role was significant. Price observes that there were schools of the prophets in at least six locations – some with buildings that functioned as permanent teaching centres – comprising a hundred or more members (1 Kings 18.4). They received input or oversight from Samuel, Elijah and Elisha and, in this role, Samuel is titled their 'father' (1 Sam. 10.10), Elijah their 'father and master' (2 Kings 2.3, 5, 12, 16), and Elisha their 'master' (2 Kings 6.5). They received instruction in prophecy with worship, sacred music and practical matters; they spent their time in study, worship, doing errands for their masters, and the 'regular duties of a prophet' in the local community.[28] The existence of these schools adds an interesting second dimension to the mentoring relationship between Elisha and Elijah. Alongside his mentoring, Elisha also benefits from his membership of a school of prophets which is 'fathered' by Elijah as their 'master', a role which passes to Elisha on Elijah's departure.

Questions

1 In what ways might father-son or mother-daughter type relationships be important in developing the next generation of leaders in the church, especially in a society with fathering deficit?

2 What might the story of Elijah and Elisha show us about the importance of mentoring relationships that exist outside of biological family structures?

3 Where do we see other Elijah-Elisha type relationships in the Bible?

4 What can we learn from the 'schools of prophets' – occasional gatherings of emerging leaders, some of whom are being mentored by established leaders?

Theological education by extension in Nehemiah 8

Nehemiah 8 is a noteworthy example of community discipleship training in the early Second Temple period. In the section 8.1–8, the whole community of adults, including 'children old enough to understand' (Neh. 8.2 NIV), gather to receive theological discipleship training through the public reading of Scripture, explanation in smaller groups, and spontaneous worship. In the subsequent section, 8.9–12, there are worshipful responses and, in 8.13–18, within the families further dissemination and application of the teaching is given over the course of a week. In addition to Ezra, who reads the Law to the whole assembly, at least three distinct groups of people are involved in the training process: trained Levites who help the people to translate and understand what they are hearing, local communities who gather to celebrate 'the words that were declared to them' (Neh. 8.12 NIV), and the heads of the ancestral families who meet to study the text, apply the teaching and later pass on their application decisions to their families.

Community is a theme common to the teaching and learning methods seen in the passage. Children who can understand are included in the gathering (Neh. 8.3). The phrase 'all the people' occurs ten times in the chapter and the statement 'both men and women' is also repeated. The involvement of the community is also clearly key in the spontaneous worship that occurs during the reading of the Law, and is an implicit part of the celebrations and application responses that follow.

The educational methods illustrated in Nehemiah 8 are termed by Kenneth Mulholland and F. Ross Kinsler as 'decentralized theological education', which they define as 'a field-based approach', which 'does not interrupt the learner's productive relationship to society'.[29] Kinsler also notes it is an education method that enables people to 'develop their gifts and ministries without leaving their homes, jobs, communities, and local congregations'.[30] David J. Shepherd and Christopher J. H. Wright believe the Nehemiah 8 event is the first example of theological education by extension in the Bible.[31] The term 'theological education by extension' (TEE) was first conceived in 1963 in Guatemala as an alternative to seminary education and has since been applied, retrospectively, to teaching models as diverse as John Wesley's 'on the job' training for lay preachers and the methodology of The Open University.[32] Key traits of TEEs are local learning groups and training in context. Shepherd and Wright may be over-interpreting the Nehemiah passage when they conclude that theological education is taking place; however, the direct evidence of the passage certainly suggests that discipleship and basic instruction are occurring.

Questions

1 What are the advantages of learning together as a whole community of faith, including children old enough to understand?
2 How can we value the role of scholarship and teaching gifts in the process of community-based learning and training?
3 What are the advantages of a field-based approach or on-the-job training?

The training priorities of Jesus

A common assumption is that Jesus was a rabbi who taught his disciples according to rabbinic methods. This supposition is problematic for two reasons. First, it is not clear from the biblical text or other evidence whether Jesus was a formal rabbi, or if his disciples addressed him using the title 'rabbi' (teacher) merely as a title of honour. Second, beyond the canonical Gospels, the only extant evidence of rabbinic methods comes from after the destruction of the Second Temple, in the Talmudic Period. Commentators disagree over how closely those assessments can be read back into Jesus' relationship with his disciples. I conclude that, although Jesus' practices described in the Gospels resemble those of a rabbi, it is more likely that he functioned as what N. T. Wright and others term a 'renewing prophet of Israel'. For this reason, there is no further discussion about Jesus' teaching as a rabbi, beyond the direct evidence of the four canonical Gospels.[33]

The evidence of the Gospels suggests that Jesus spent a significant proportion of the time between his baptism and crucifixion with groups of close disciples. For example, reading simply from the text of the Gospel accounts, Jesus attended 46 events with the few and 17 events with the masses, meaning Jesus spent nearly three-quarters of his documented events with his closest disciples.[34] While little is said explicitly about the details, we can surmise that Jesus' ministry involved ongoing teaching relationships with his disciples, as implied for instance by John's account of 'the disciple Jesus loved' (John 19.26 ESV). The smallest group he trained was three (Peter, James and John). In his study of the gospel accounts of the ministry of Jesus, Clark Macaulay observes that Christ's training was principally delivered to five groups which ranged in size from thousands to three people.[35]

Macaulay provides a useful analysis of the groups whom Jesus taught, which is utilized here to understand the dynamics of these different units in Jesus' ministry.[36] The largest group engaged by Jesus were the crowds that came to hear him speak and perform miracles in public places. Macaulay calls this group the 'curious followers'. Following the miracle at the wedding in Cana, some of these followers 'believed in him' (John 2.11 ESV), but when his teachings became difficult, in John 6, some of his followers 'turned back and no longer walked with him' (John 6.66 ESV; cf. John 6.64–69). The second group are those whom Macaulay calls 'believing disciples', though John P. Meier argues that only those who were personally and directly called by Jesus should be termed disciples.[37] Of the thousands who listened to Jesus, many believed in him, and some of those followed him as he travelled (John 2.23, 4.39–41, 7.31, 8.30).

The 70 others, who are sometimes referred to as the Seventy-Two, are only described in chapter 10 of Luke's Gospel and not in any other New Testament book. They are chosen by Jesus from the believing disciples and sent out in pairs as emissaries to do preparatory evangelism in the towns to be visited by him (Luke 10.1). They are properly referred to as disciples because they are selected by Jesus, but in the Eastern tradition this group is termed apostles. The Seventy-Two are the largest group that receive direct training from Jesus.

Helen Bond, Professor in Christian Origins and Head of the School of Divinity at The University of Edinburgh, and Joan Taylor, Professor of Christian Origins and Second Temple Judaism at King's College London, believe that half of this group were female.[38] In *Jesus's Female Disciples: The New Evidence* (2018), Bond and Taylor suggest that the description of The Seventy being sent 'two by two' (Luke 10.1 ESV) is presented as a deliberate echo of the story of Noah, where mixed-gender pairs of animals are sent into the ark (Gen. 7.9, 7.15). They further argue that if the Seventy were to anoint people with oil or baptize with water, actions requiring bodily contact or speaking at small intimate gatherings, it was essential that the company include women as well as men.[39] This opinion is supported, but not proved, by the references to the 'many women' who closely followed Jesus (Matt. 27.55; Mark 15.41). Examples include Joanna, Susanna and 'many others' who 'provided for [Jesus and The Twelve] out of their means' (Luke 8.3 ESV) and Mary of Bethany who 'sat at the Lord's feet' (Luke 10.39 ESV), a phrase also used by Paul to describe his rabbinic education by Gamaliel (Acts 22.3). Bond and Taylor conclude that the canonical accounts illustrate – but fail to fully name – the many women, some of whom had significant standing in society, who were chosen and sent out by Jesus.

In addition to the Seventy, for three years Jesus personally mentored 12 men, who are commonly referred to as the Twelve. In summarizing a 'broad spectrum of modern Jesus studies' Scot McKnight concludes that most scholars believe that Jesus chose 12 *men* for this role with 'fundamental intention' as part of a symbol of renewal and restoration.[40] In addition to being 'special companions' who were sent out as an extension of Jesus' mission, McKnight proposes the common scholarly view that the Twelve represented 'the restoration and reunification of the 12 tribes as promised in ancient Jewish traditions, most notably in Isaiah and Ezekiel'.[41] To accomplish this they needed to symbolize the original group of 12 male tribe-heads, thereby requiring Jesus' Twelve to be: 12 in number, Jewish and male.[42] The appointment of the Twelve is recorded by Luke and Mark (Mark 3.13–19; Luke 9.1–2) who note that they are called to be in close proximity to Jesus, to preach and proclaim the kingdom of God, to have power and authority over all demons, to cure diseases and heal the sick. Moreover, as part of their training, they are sent on short ministry expeditions in pairs when they were to discern whom to meet and to trust for the supply of provisions and accommodation (Luke 9.3–6). After the death of Jesus, the Twelve apostles form the initial team of senior leaders of the early church. Russell L. Huizing notes the significance of this group: 'Jesus took a band of relatively untrained individuals and within a short period had qualified them to lead his mission to change the world.'[43]

Lastly, Jesus worked most closely with Peter and the two sons of Zebedee, James and John. These were selected from the Twelve and were included in longer discussions and selected meetings, such as the healing of Jairus' daughter (Mark 5.37), the transfiguration (Matt. 17.1–2), and in the garden of Gethsemane (Mark 14.33). Following the death and resurrection of Jesus, this inner group were three of the leading apostles of the early church and later referred to by Paul as 'pillars of the church' (Gal. 2.9 NLT).

In summary, Jesus engaged with different groups of people, in public and private. He worked more directly with some groups of emerging leaders whom he personally selected, although we note that the gospel writers are varied in how they identify and describe these groups and their relative importance.

Jesus spoke publicly to large numbers of people who were curious about his teaching and works. Many of those became believers, and some became followers. Some travelled with Jesus, sharing meals and day-to-day life. This extended contact is likely to have afforded them the opportunity for comprehensive discussions and closer observation of Jesus' life: they would have learned from Jesus in a fuller and more holistic way than the crowds. Others received more personal contact with Jesus and were developed through more practical experiences during their travels, such as baptizing new believers (John 3.22) or casting out demons (Matthew 17.14–21). Some enjoyed privileged access to personal discussions with Jesus, for example, being able to ask Jesus 'Teach us to pray' (Luke 11.1 NIV). The limited descriptions in the gospels of Jesus' training methods highlights an approach that focuses on small groups of novices who are developed through an interactive blend of instruction, shared life-experiences, and practical ministry-experiences. Moreover, rather than being selected because they were accomplished students or those from high-status families, some of Jesus' trainees were described as 'unschooled' and 'ordinary' (Acts 4.13). Perhaps the training methods utilized by Jesus were particularly appropriate for realizing the potential of these women and men.

Questions

1 How does your church do discipleship and leadership development? Are the 'unschooled' and 'ordinary' included?
2 Although we can't prove that Jesus included women in the Seventy-Two, we do know he took a radical approach in recognizing women as disciples and honouring women in traditionally male spaces of power (e.g. Mary of Bethany).[44] In what ways does church leadership need to change to follow Jesus in this area?
3 What did the disciples learn from short ministry expeditions in pairs when they were to discern whom to meet and to trust for the supply of provisions and accommodation?

The phases of Paul's mentoring of Timothy

Given that the apostle Paul is one of the most significant leaders of the Apostolic Age, his training interactions with emerging leaders are clearly important to any biblical understanding of this subject. Paul was a second-generation Pharisee (Acts 23.6), educated under the supervision of Gamaliel in Jerusalem (Acts 22.3), who in his own words 'was advancing in Judaism beyond many of my own age among my people, so extremely zealous was I for the traditions of my fathers' (Gal. 1.14 ESV). Paul was probably from a group that the author of *Kohelet Rabbah* had in mind, when commenting on Ecclesiastes 7.28, saying

> out of a thousand people who study Sacred Scripture normally a hundred attain the readiness for the study of the Mishnah; out of these, ten attain the readiness for the Talmud, and out of these, only one will achieve mastery and becomes a master.[45]

Commenting on this quotation, Reinhard Neudecker believes the purpose of this demanding process of selection and training was to produce exceptional teachers who could pass their learning on to key disciples.[46]

The New Testament contains numerous references to key acquaintances or ministry colleagues of Paul, who would have received his instruction. Edward Earle Ellis suggests that the book of Acts and the Pauline letters cite as many as 95 co-workers (or people with similar roles) associated with the apostle, the most common designations being co-worker (*synergos*), brother (*adelphos*), minister (*diakonos*), and apostle (*apostolos*).[47] For example, Paul's companions during his missionary journeys include Aristarchus, Barnabas, Epaphras, Gaius, Jason, Sopater, John Mark, Luke, Onesimus, Silas, Sosthenes, Trophimus, Tychicus and Timothy.[48] At least 11 people are identified in the book of Acts as people whom he personally trained or with whom he travelled. It is reasonable to assume that a travelling companion would gain a significant amount of informal instruction. Of these people, Timothy is perhaps Paul's most trusted companion and student – someone he knew and invested in for nearly 20 years.[49] Timothy, more than any other pupil, would have witnessed the detail of Paul's personal life and public ministry and experienced his mentorship as he became Paul's disciple, and later his travelling-companion and partner in ministry.

Rick Warren suggests that Paul's relationship with Timothy follows three key phases, which he describes as parenthood, pacesetting and partnering.[50] I'd suggest one final stage: promotion. This four-stage process is utilized in the analysis below, although it is in danger of being an imposed structure; nevertheless, it is helpful in highlighting aspects of Timothy's development relationship with Paul.

Timothy's biological father was Greek, and it is assumed he was a Gentile since there is no explicit evidence in the New Testament that Timothy's father was a follower of Jesus. Also, since Timothy had not been circumcised (Acts 16.3), it is unlikely that either Timothy or his father were Jewish proselytes. Little is said of Timothy's father in the New Testament, suggesting that Timothy's mother was either a widow or, for some other reason, his sole or principal parent. This argument is strengthened by the credit Paul gives to Timothy's mother and grandmother as the family line through which Timothy received his Christian faith (2 Tim. 1.5). Because Timothy's grandmother and mother, Lois and Eunice, were some of Paul's first converts from the Jewish community in Lystra, it is probable that Timothy became a follower of Jesus between Paul's visits to that area. In addition to being Timothy's teacher, Paul was a spiritual father to him. This relationship is acknowledged in Paul's first letter to the Corinthians when he addresses him as 'my son whom I love' (1 Cor. 4.17 NIV; cf. Phil. 2.22; 1 Tim. 1.2).

It is interesting to note that as a single man (1 Cor. 7.7–8), presumably without natural offspring, Paul was happy to describe a younger man he was training as a son. Possibly Paul did this because of his longstanding relationship with Timothy's mother and grandmother, or because he had an undocumented involvement in Timothy becoming a follower of Jesus, thus feeling like a 'spiritual father'. Elsewhere, Paul does call Onesimus his son, stating this is because he led him to faith while in prison

(Philem. 1.10). Paul also calls Titus his son in Titus 1.4. It seems that Paul saw his connection through the gospel to younger men as the cause of his parental relationship with the people he trained. In 1 Corinthians 4, he sums this up by saying, 'I write not these things to shame you, but as my beloved sons' (1 Cor. 4.14–15 KJV). He goes on, 'For though you have countless guides in Christ, you do not have many fathers. For I became your father in Christ Jesus through the gospel' (1 Cor. 4.15).

Another factor in Paul's use of parental language may be that he was actively training Timothy as an apprentice. At Paul's first meeting, Timothy is referred to as a disciple (Acts 16.1–3) and only later is he termed a son. The imperative of apprenticeship-style training is illustrated in Paul's statement to the church in Corinth when he says, '[Y]ou had ten thousand teachers in Christ, but you do not have many fathers' (1 Cor. 4.15 NIV). Philippians 2 seems to suggest that Paul saw Timothy as 'a son with his father' because he had 'served with me in the work of the gospel' (Phil. 2.22). This brings together parental terminology and apprenticeship in its most common expression of the day: father-son-apprenticeship. While it is not known for certain exactly why Paul favours calling his mentees sons, it is clear that it is a description used with great affection.

Warren's second key phase of the Paul-Timothy relationship is pacesetting, which he defines as 'being the example of what mature ministry looks like'.[51] Paul's model of pacesetting is to be an exemplar model of public ministry and private living for Timothy to replicate a principle that he describes in 1 Corinthians 11 in the maxim, 'imitate me as I imitate Christ' (1 Cor. 11.1 ESV). In his second letter to Timothy, he observes this process explicitly when he says, you 'know what I teach, and how I live, and what my purpose in life is. You know my faith, my patience, my love, and my endurance' (2 Tim. 3.10–11 NLT).

Warren's last phase of ministry is partnering.[52] By the time that Paul writes the book of Romans, he is happy to describe Timothy as 'my fellow worker' (Rom. 16.21 ESV), completing Timothy's journey from disciple, to a son, to a partner. Timothy has grown from spiritual infancy to the stage where he is a spiritual parent to others. This is best summed up in 2 Timothy 2, where Paul says, '[W]hat you have heard from me in the presence of many witnesses entrust to faithful men who will be able to teach others also' (2 Tim. 2.2 ESV).

The final stage, promotion, is unpacked by Perry L. Stepp, who suggests that, although Paul does not make Timothy into an apostle in his stead, there is evidence of 'varying degrees of replacement' including what he terms 'strong succession' and 'weak succession'.[53] In 1 Timothy, Stepp sees evidence of succession from Jesus to Paul (1.11–12) and weak succession from Paul to Timothy where he is 'entrusted' with a charge (1.18), 'authorized' to confront false teachers (1.3–4), 'solemnly charged' (5.21), and instructed to 'guard what has been entrusted' (6.20). In 2 Timothy, Stepp believes Timothy receives strong succession. Timothy is instructed to 'rekindle the gift' (1.6), hold to sound teaching that has been 'entrusted' to him (1.13–14), entrust good teaching to others (2.2), and to re-join Paul (4.9–13). Stepp concludes, 'In 1 Timothy, the succession from Paul to Timothy was limited to a single task' and 'In 2 Timothy, Timothy is to suffer as his predecessor suffered and teach as his predecessor taught. He is even responsible for training and appointing successors ... following the model of his predecessor.'[54] Although Timothy is not appointed as an apostle, Paul makes him his full successor in the administration of the gospel and care of churches.[55]

Questions

1 In your church context, are leaders treated like sons and daughters, with great affection? What role could you have/play in changing the culture of leadership training?

2 What are good examples you have seen of parenthood, pacesetting, partnering and promoting in the development of Christian leaders? Where are the gaps?

3 How do you respond to the idea of Paul asking Timothy to imitate him (as he imitated Christ)? Would you be willing to do the same? How important is it for Christian leaders to be open about the way they live, not just what they teach?

4 How can we avoid the dangers of paternalism and misogyny in mentoring relationships?[56]

5 If you are in Christian leadership, are you training people to be your supporters or successors? How would you feel if the person you are training became more effective than you?

Training in the Hall of Tyrannus

The account in Acts 19 of Paul teaching in the Hall of Tyrannus offers an interesting example of large-scale training for church planters.[57] The apostle Paul's usual custom when entering a city was to teach about the kingdom of God in local Jewish synagogues. In Ephesus, Paul was able to do this for three months before he was forced to stop because of lack of engagement and direct opposition (Acts 19.8–10). He and his disciples relocated to a local public space to deliver daily lectures, which probably engaged with a larger and more diverse audience. Martin Hengel conjectures that the contents of Paul's letters, and especially Romans and parts of 1 and 2 Corinthians, contain 'brief summaries of [these] lectures' and the 'much reduced quintessence' of what Paul taught in the Tyrannus lecture theatre.[58] Similarly, John Stott concludes that Paul's curriculum and delivery was serious, well-reasoned, thorough and persuasive.[59] The suggestion is that Paul's lectures in the Hall of Tyrannus represented a substantial and comprehensive delivery of theological material focused on evangelism and mission. Ben Witherington III notes that Acts 19.8–10 represents Paul's longest stable period of ministry without trial or expulsion and it is 'a lasting model of what universalistic Christian mission ought to look like'.[60]

Not much is definitively known about the Hall of Tyrannus. Tyrannus may have been the name of a Greek rhetorician or a wealthy Jewish rabbi. A hall (Greek, *schole*) was the public auditorium or teaching-room of a philosopher, orator or poet; such lecture halls, often located in gymnasia, were commonplace in Greek cities. The Western text adds that Paul's daily meetings ran, 'from the fifth hour to the tenth', meaning 11 o'clock in the morning until four in the afternoon.[61] In the Mediterranean world, these timings equate to the hottest hours of the day, when most workers would be resting. Perhaps this meant the Tyrannus hall was vacant for free use or available for a lower price. Either way, this arrangement would have allowed Paul to follow his usual practice of self-support (Acts 20.34; 1 Cor. 4.12) and to offer large-scale theological lectures at times when working people were free.

It may be that Paul's teaching model included the direct participation of the disciples who came with him to Ephesus. Nothing is explicitly stated in the passage, though it is quite possible that his disciples assisted with discussion, answering questions, sharing their faith, memorizing Paul's talks, and even deputizing for Paul. David J. Williams speculates that the disciples may have been sent on short mission-trips to local towns and the surrounding province and may have accompanied Ephesian converts as they returned home.[62] Though not directly attested to in the text, it is possible that Paul's disciples, who were with him in Ephesus, were apprenticed by direct ministry participation in this model, which is similar to that of Jesus when he sends out his disciples (Luke 10.1–9).

The account of the Hall of Tyrannus is relevant to this study because of the distinctiveness of the training model and the ensuing establishment of new churches. In 19.10, Luke notes – probably hyperbolically

– that, 'all the inhabitants of Asia, Jews and Greeks, heard the word of the Lord Jesus' (Acts 19.10 my translation) which is later confirmed by Demetrius who says, 'Paul has convinced and led astray large numbers of people here in Ephesus and in practically the whole province of Asia' (Acts 19.26 NIV). Since Demetrius' evidence is reported by Luke, the claim is not necessarily impartial. However, C. K. Barrett believes that the seven churches established in the leading cities of Asia Minor, which are described in Revelation 2 and 3, are some of the results of Paul's Tyrannus co-workers' mission.[63] Likewise, Jerome Murphy-O'Connor and James D. G. Dunn believe it is likely that most, if not all, of the towns and cities located within 120 miles of Ephesus had churches planted by people trained by Paul at Tyrannus.[64] In summary, the impact of daily theological training over two years in a large cosmopolitan trading port was that an entire region was exposed to the gospel through the natural travel of traders who passed through Ephesus and then spread the ideas they had heard to the communities of the surrounding region. Paul's lectures raised up missionaries – which might have included disciples who were travelling with him – who travelled the region spreading the Tyrannus teaching. The result was that new churches were planted.

Questions

1 What do you imagine Paul would have taught in the Hall of Tyrannus that equipped 'ordinary people' to become effective church planters after two-years of part-time training?[65]

2 In what ways do you imagine Paul's travelling companions might have been involved in the training process (for example, leading discussion, answering questions, sharing their faith, memorizing Paul's talks, deputizing for Paul and participating in short mission-trips)?

The imagery of children, youth and parents in 1 John 2

The section 2.12–14 in John's first epistle offers a poetic illustration of occupational development in a community of faith presented in mnemonic form. The section forms a self-contained unit, with little logical connection to the surrounding text, and is structured as two sets of three statements on the theme of maturity and growth. Although written anonymously, all three of the books that have come to us as 1, 2 and 3 John are traditionally believed to have been authored by the apostle John who was one of Jesus' chosen Twelve.[66]

It was common for early Christian leaders to address their followers using family labels,[67] and John does this frequently (1 John 2.28, 3.7, 3.18, 4.4, 5.21). In this section, he uses the terms 'children' (*teknia* and *paidia*), 'young men' (*neaniskoi*) and 'fathers' (*pateres*). The gender-inclusive term 'children' was, at the time, a common figure of speech for a teacher addressing a pupil and – other than the obvious dynamics of the teacher-pupil relationship – its use does not imply any condescension. John uses this term a further ten times in the letter as his preferred way of addressing the whole community and probably has in mind the development and care that a parent offers to a child.[68] In this passage, young men are described as those who are growing in strength through the training they are receiving. Unlike in the modern Western world, where young people are usually still engaged in education, these young men were likely to be at work learning their trade. The label 'fathers' is probably a reference to the community's more experienced leaders, who have either structural seniority or spiritual maturity because of their seasoned wisdom, evidenced in a steadfast faith.[69] Karen H. Jobes notes that in using the masculine terms of 'young men' and 'fathers', John is following the Jewish custom of his age and is unlikely to be excluding women, although in the Greco-Roman society of the time only men were public agents.[70]

Whether this passage represents three conversations with the same audience or separate intercourse with distinct groups with different levels of Christian maturity, is debated by commenters. The latter opinion is favoured by ancients such as Clement of Alexandria and Origen and by modern authors, such as John Stott.[71] Ignatius of Antioch equated the three labels with the three-fold ministries of deacons, presbyters (priests) and bishops, though there is no direct evidence that this ordering was in existence at this time.[72] Raymond E. Brown suggests that the most popular view among modern scholars is for two groups as part of the whole. In his summary, 'children' is a term that applies to all, and 'young men' and 'fathers' are subdivisions of the whole community.[73] Whatever structure or connection between the three categories John intended, this three-fold ordering does leave room for parallels of equivalence with the apprentice-journeyman-master model being explored in this project.

Questions

1 How might this three-stage approach be used in training church planters; are there fruitful parallels between the three labels in John and the apprentice-journeyman-master model being explored in this project?
2 What difference would it make to training if it was offered with the care with which a parent nurtures a child?

Notes

1 A Maccabean period instruction for students to accompany masters (*Pirke Avot* 1.4). In the fifteenth century Ovadiah ben Abraham (Bertinoro) extended this saying: 'by walking after them [wise sages/scholars], you will be covered by their dust'. See Leonard Kravitz and Kerry M. Olitzky, *Pirke Avot: A Modern Commentary on Jewish Ethics* (New York: UAHC Press, 2004), 4.

2 Said to have been written by Da Vinci in his notebook when painting 'Lady with an Ermine' – an oil painting that did not show as much life as his original sketch. See Jean Paul Richter, *The Notebooks of Leonardo Da Vinci* (Mineola, NY: Dover, 1970), 169.

3 Ruth A. Tucker has identified 3,237 named people in the Bible. See, *The Biographical Bible: Exploring the Biblical Narrative from Adam and Eve to John of Patmos* (Ada, MI: BakerBooks, 2013).

4 Andonichus, Apphia, Archippus, Aristarchus, Barnabas, Carpus, Demus, Epaphras, Epaphroditus, Erastus, Gaius, Jason, Junia, Justus, Lucius, Luke, Lydia, Marcus, Nymphus, Onesimus, Onesiphorus, Phebe, Philemon, Priscilla and Aquila, Secundus, Silas, Sopater, Tertius, Timothy, Titus, Trophimus, Tychicus, Tyrannus, Urbane.

5 J. G. McConville, *Deuteronomy* (Westmont, IL: IVP Academic, 2002), 133.

6 Chris Wright, *Deuteronomy* (Milton Keynes: Paternoster Press, 1996), 72.

7 John Dupuche et al. 'Three Prayers in Dialogue: The Shema, the Lord's Prayer, and al-Fatiha', *Journal of Ecumenical Studies*, Vol. 52, No. 4, Fall 2017, 587–609, doi:10.1353/ecu.2017.0054, 590.

8 Dupuche, 'Three Prayers', 587–89.

9 *Words on Cassette*, Vol. 1 (New Jersey: R. R. Bowker Publishing, 1999), 1437.

10 Lawrence Boadt, *Reading the Old Testament: An Introduction* (Mahwah, NJ: Paulist Press, 1984), 255–56; Dearman, J. Andrew. 'The Family in the Old Testament', *Interpretation: A Journal of Bible and Theology*, Vol. 52, No. 2, Apr. 1998, 117–29, doi:10.1177/002096430005200202, 117–18.

11 Oxbrow, Mark and John Kafwanka, eds., *Intentional Discipleship and Disciple-Making: An Anglican Guide for Christian Life and Formation* (Anglican Consultative Council, 2016), available at https://www.anglicancommunion.org/media/220191/intentional-discipleship-and-disciple-making.pdf

12 Adin Steinsaltz, et al., editors, *Koren Talmud Bavli, Noé ed.* 1st Hebrew/English edn (Jerusalem: Shefa Foundation: Koren Publishers, 2012), *Sanhedrin*, 69b.

13 Steinsaltz, *Koren Talmud, Brachot*, 55a.

14 Rick D. Moore, 'The Prophet as Mentor: A Crucial Facet of the Biblical Presentations of Moses, Elijah, and Isaiah', *Journal of Pentecostal Theology*, Vol. 15, No. 2, Apr. 2007, 155–72, doi:10.1177/0966736907076334, 121.

15 Moore, 'The Prophet as Mentor', 158.

16 Karl Heinrich Rengstorf, 'Mathētēs', *Theological Dictionary of the New Testament*, edited by Gerhard Kittel et al., Vol. 4 (Grand Rapids, MI: Wm. B. Eerdmans, 1976, 415–41, 427–30.

17 Martin Hengel, *The Charismatic Leader and His Followers* (New York: Crossroad, 1981), 16.

18 Hengel, *Charismatic Leader*, 17.

19 Richard D. Calenberg, *The New Testament Doctrine of Discipleship* (Winona Lake, IN: Grace Theological Seminary, 1981), 51–63.

20 Michael J. Wilkins, *Discipleship in the Ancient World and Matthew's Gospel*, 2nd edn (Eugene, OR: Wipf and Stock, 2015), 90–91.

21 Wilkins, *Discipleship*, 60.

22 Calenberg, *Discipleship*, 50.

23 Moore, 'The Prophet as Mentor', 157.

24 Walter Brueggemann, 'A Response to Rickie Moore's "the Prophet as Mentor"', *Journal of Pentecostal Theology*, Vol. 15, No. 2, Apr. 2007, 173–75, doi:10.1177/0966736907076335, 174.

25 Moore, 'The Prophet as Mentor', 161.

26 Moore, 'The Prophet as Mentor', 162.

27 Brueggemann, 'A Response to Rickie Moore's "the Prophet as Mentor"', 174.

28 Ira M. Price, 'The Schools of the Sons of the Prophets', *The Old Testament Student*, Vol. 8, No. 7 (Chicago: University of Chicago Press, 1889), 244–49.

29 Kenneth Mulholland and F. Ross Kinsler, *Adventures in Training the Ministry: A Honduran Case Study in Theological Education by Extension* (Phillipsburg, NJ: Presbyterian and Reformed Publishing, 1976), 66.

30 F. Ross Kinsler, *The Extension Movement in Theological Education: A Call to the Renewal of the Ministry* (Pasadena, CA: William Carey Library, 1981), 30.

31 David J. Shepherd and Christopher J. H. Wright, *Ezra and Nehemiah* (Grand Rapids, MI: Wm. B. Eerdmans, 2018), 126

32 Harley Atkinson, 'Theological Education by Extension: An Alternative in Christian Education', *Christian Education Journal*, Vol. IX, No. 2, Winter, 1990, 25–37, 25.

33 The principal challenge is that there is no relevant extant biblical or extra-biblical written description of rabbinic life or Jewish traditions before the Talmudic Period, which begins at the destruction of the Second Temple in AD 70; so, Jesus could have been modelling distinct practice, or critiquing rabbinic teaching methods as easily as embodying them. For more on this discussion see Hengel, Martin, *The Charismatic Leader and His Followers* (New York: Crossroad, 1981), 42–50; Köstenberger, Andreas J., 'Jesus as Rabbi in the Fourth Gospel', *Bulletin for Biblical Research*, 8 (1998), 97–128, 98–101, 102n22; Neudecker, Reinhard, 'Master-Disciple/Disciple-Master Relationship in Rabbinic Judaism and in the Gospels', *Pontificia Universitas Gregoriana*, 80.2 (1999), 245–61, 246; Neusner, Jacob, 'Pharisaic-Rabbinic Judaism: A Clarification', in *Early Rabbinic Judaism:*

Historical Studies in Religion, Literature and Art (Leiden: Brill, 1975), 50–51; Riesner, Rainer, *Jesus Als Lehrer*, 3rd edn (Tübingen: Mohr Siebeck, 1988), 246–76; Wilkins, Michael J., *Discipleship in the Ancient World and Matthew's Gospel*, 2nd edn (Eugene, OR: Wipf and Stock, 2015), 202.

34 This analysis is by Ferguson and Bird, *Hero Maker*, 61–62. However, the self-acknowledged selectivity of the Gospel accounts suggests that counting verses is of very limited value, we may simply be seeing the focus of the Gospel writers.

35 Macaulay, Clark. 'The Training Methods of Jesus', *Biblical Ministries Worldwide*, 31 Mar. 2014, at https://www.biblicalministries.org/see/blog/2014/03/31/the-training-methods-of-jesus (accessed 28.1.2022).

36 We should note, however, that Luke places more emphasis on distinct groups, such as the Twelve and the Three, than John, for example, who focuses on a community of friends. There is a temptation for some here to see a ridged model comprising a strategic grid of ministry groups. Nevertheless, this is at least illustrative of different types and stages of apprenticeship at work in the ministry of Jesus.

37 Meier, John P. 'The Circle of the Twelve: Did It Exist During Jesus' Public Ministry?' *Journal of Biblical Literature*, vol. 116, no. 4, 1997, pp. 635–72, https://doi.org/10.2307/3266551.

38 Helen K. Bond and Joan Elizabeth Taylor, 'Jesus's Female Disciples: The New Evidence', *Minerva Media Film and Television for Channel 4 Television* (8 April 2018), 00:57–02:08; Joan E. Taylor, '"Two by Two" The Ark-Etypal Language of Mark's Apostolic Pairings', in *The Body in Biblical, Christian and Jewish Texts* (London: Bloomsbury T&T Clark, 2014), 58–82, doi:10.5040/9780567659149.ch-004, 59–66.

39 Bond and Taylor, 'Jesus's Female Disciples', 25:30–26:00, 27:20–27:35; Taylor, '"Two by Two"', 64–65.

40 Scot McKnight, 'Jesus and the Twelve', *Bulletin for Biblical Research*, Vol. 11, No. 2, 2001, 203–31, 203.

41 McKnight, 'Jesus and the Twelve', 212.

42 McKnight, 'Jesus and the Twelve', 217.

43 Russell L. Huizing, 'Leaders from Disciples: The Church's Contribution to Leadership Development', *Evangelical Review of Theology*, Vol. 35, No. 4, Oct. 2011, 333–44, 344.

44 For one perspective on women in leadership in the church, see N. T. Wright, 'The Biblical Basis for Women's Service in the Church', Pricilla Papers, CBE International, October 30, 2006, at https://www.cbeinternational.org/resource/article/priscilla-papers-academic-journal/biblical-basis-womens-service-church (accessed 28.1.2022).

45 *Kohelet Rabbah* 7.41 quoted in Reinhard Neudecker, 'Master-Disciple/Disciple-Master Relationship in Rabbinic Judaism and in the Gospels', *Pontificia Universitas Gregoriana*, Vol. 80, No. 2, 1999, 245–261, 248.

46 Neudecker, 'Master-Disciple', 248.

47 E. E. Ellis, 'Paul and His Coworkers', *Dictionary of Paul and His Letters*, edited by Gerald F. Hawthorne, Ralph P. Martin and Daniel G. Reid (Westmont, IL: InterVarsity Press, 2005), 183–89, 183.

48 Christian Pilgrimage Journeys, 'Apostle Paul Life, Teaching & Theology: The Companions of Paul & Biblical Persons Related to Paul', *Christian Pilgrimage Journeys*, at https://www.christian-pilgrimage-journeys.com/biblical-sources/apostle-paul-life-teaching-theology/companions-of-paul/, sec. 1 (accessed 28.1.2022).

49 Paul Jeon, *1 Timothy: A Charge to God's Missional Household* (Eugene, OR: Pickwick Publications, 2017), 17.

50 Rick Warren, '3 Phases of a Paul and Timothy Relationship', *Pastors. Com*, 6 February 2014, at https://pastors.com/paul-timothy/, para. 2 (accessed 28.1.2022).

51 Warren, '3 Phases', para. 6.

52 Warren, '3 Phases', para. 8.

53 Perry L. Stepp, 'Succession in the New Testament World', *Evangelical Journal of Theology*, Vol. 10, No. 2, Biblijski institut, Dec. 2016, 161–75, on pp. 162, 165, 171–73.

54 Stepp, 'Succession in the New Testament', 173.

55 Stepp, 'Succession in the New Testament', 173.

56 For a recent example of an exposé of paternalism in Christian leadership, see the podcast *The Rise and Fall of Mars Hill*, produced by Christianity Today in 2021 and hosted by Mike Cosper, at https://www.christianitytoday.com/ct/pod casts/rise-and-fall-of-mars-hill (accessed 28.1.2022), which highlights the allegedly abusive leadership style of Mark Driscoll. In another example, the 'Billy Graham Rule', a practice where senior male leaders avoid spending time alone with women, has been suggested to be misogynistic because it limits development and mentoring opportunities for women leaders and encourages a view that women are a potential threat to men's leadership integrity.

57 For a more detailed exploration of the missional and church planting focus of Acts 19.8–10 see Daniel M. McGinnis, *Missional Acts: A Call to Action* (Eugene, OR: Pickwick Publications, 2022), 205–206.

58 Martin Hengel, *Acts and the History of Earliest Christianity* (Philadelphia, PA: Fortress Press, 1979), 11.

59 John R. W. Stott, *The Message of Acts: To the Ends of the Earth*, 2nd edn (Westmont, IL: InterVarsity Press, 1991), 312.

60 Witherington, Ben. *The Acts of the Apostles: A Socio-Rhetorical Commentary* (Milton Keynes: Paternoster Press, 1998), 572–73.

61 Stott, *Message of Acts*, 313.

62 David J. Williams, *Acts* (Ada, MI: BakerBooks, 1990), 332.

63 Charles K. Barrett, *A Critical and Exegetical Commentary on the Acts of the Apostles: In Two Volumes*, Vol. 2: Introduction and Commentary on Acts XV – XXVIII, original edn 2004, reprinted (Clark, 2010), 906.

64 Jerome Murphy-O'Connor, *Paul: A Critical Life* (Oxford: Oxford University Press, 1997), 173–75; James D. G. Dunn, *The Acts of the Apostles* (Grand Rapids, MI: Wm. B. Eerdmans, 2016), 253.

65 Might considering the Tyrannus example provide fresh insight into training and deployment for bi- or co-vocational ministry? Bi-vocation and co-vocational have similar meanings: both derive from the Latin word *vocatio*, meaning 'a call or summons'; the prefix 'bi' means two and the prefix 'co', together. In current usage, a bi-vocational church planter or minister has temporary or supplemental paid income, whereas a co-vocational minister holds two callings concurrently, either reducing or eliminating the need to be paid by the church. For more on this, see Brad Brisco, *Covocational Church Planting: Aligning Your Marketplace Calling & The Mission of God* (Nashville, TN: Missional Press, 2021). Also available as a free ebook from SEND Network (2018), at https://www.namb.net/send-network/resource/ebook-covocational-church-planting (accessed 28.1.2022).

66 Karen H. Jobes, *1, 2, and 3 John* (Grand Rapids, MI: Zondervan, 2014), 22.

67 Gary M. Burge, *John* (Grand Rapids, MI: Zondervan, 2000), 112.

68 Burge, *John*, 112; David Rensberge, *The Epistles of John* (Louisville, KY: Westminster John Knox Press, 2001), 30.

69 Thomas E. Johnson, *1, 2 and 3 John* (Milton Keynes: Paternoster Press, 1995), 49; Jobes, 102–04; Burge, 113.

70 Jobes, *1, 2, and 3 John*, 105.

71 Raymond E. Brown, *The Epistles of John* (New York: Doubleday, 1982), 297.

72 Brown, *Epistles*, 297–98.

73 Brown, *Epistles*, 298.

5

Towards a Theology of Craft and Creativity

Sing clear-voiced Muse, of Hephaestus famed for skill. With bright-eyed Athena he taught men glorious crafts throughout the world – men who before used to dwell in caves in the mountains like wild beasts. But now that they have learned crafts through Hephaestus famous for his art they live a peaceful life in their own houses ...

Homer, Hymn to Hephaestus[1]

Craftsmen are all poets ... they are not all called poets: they have other names

Plato, Symposium[2]

Creativity is a significant part of the culture of both the craft guilds and of church planting. As we will see in the next chapter, the craft guilds existed in a pre-industrial and pre-secular era – an age when all work was considered artistic and when religious and working life enjoyed a rich symbiotic relationship. In part, creativity is a lost legacy of the medieval mindset. Before modernity, machines and modern manufacturing, training and work in guild-life was characterized by creativity. The decline of the guilds in the eighteenth century paralleled the rise of modernity, which corresponded to a shift from an age of artistry to an industrial era. In this transition, much of the understanding of creativity as a normal part of work was lost.

So, to understand a craft approach, we need to explore creativity and understand its connection to work and ministry. This chapter explores some resources for a theological understanding of craft and creativity by reviewing contributions from three selected authors, each of which brings fresh wisdom to our exploration. As in the previous chapter, there are questions at the end of each section to help make connections with training methods and church planting.

Introducing the authors

Richard Sennett is Professor of Sociology at the London School of Economics and former Professor of the Humanities at New York University. In *The Craftsman* (2008) Sennett explores creativity, artistry and learning by making connections to craft and craftwork. He particularly considers the role that materials, tools and the human body play in helping modern creative people find their identity in post-industrial society. Although not a theologian, Sennett offers a perceptive and distinctive contribution which connects strongly with the purpose of this project and the thoughts of the other two authors.

The second author is the late Pope, John Paul II, the former head of the Roman Catholic Church. In his *Letter of His Holiness Pope John Paul II to Artists* (1999), he explores the relationship between the church and artists, and the part they play in the mission of the church.

The third voice is Trevor Hart, an Anglican priest and Professor of Divinity at St Andrews University, Scotland. In *Making Good: Creation, Creativity, and Artistry* (2014) Hart considers creativity and *poesis* (Greek, making), which are explored as human participation in God's supreme role as creator-artist.

Richard Sennett – *The Craftsman*

In *The Craftsman*, Richard Sennett states that he dislikes the term 'creativity', considering it overused, particularly by modern people. The word creativity, he says 'carries too much Romantic baggage – the mystery of inspiration, the claims of genius'.[3] He prefers to talk about the processes involved in craft and art, thereby reducing the mystery associated with the creative method. For example, Sennett suggests that creative leaps happen through reflection on the physical action of using tools. The enemies of creativity, in his eyes, are mindless machines like James Watt's steam engine or the factories they produced.[4] The friends of creativity are 'mirror-tools' that empower the work of the human hand[5] and 'material awareness' that triggers imagination and exploration.[6] Sennett's embodiment of craft and art is 'the craftsman', a term that is more inclusive than 'artisan' because he believes there is a craftsman in each of us.[7]

Animal Laborans and Homo Faber

Fifty years ago, Sennett was a student of the German-American philosopher and political theorist Hannah Arendt, who is the author of *The Human Condition* (1958). In *The Human Condition* – as part of an account of *vita activa* (active life) in the history of the Western world – Arendt develops an analysis of labour and work, for which she uses the terms *Animal Laborans* and *Homo Faber* respectively. Arendt's *Animal Laborans* is a labouring-worker producing things of necessity by an act of the body, resulting in 'consumption goods'. This 'animal worker', she proposes, is a beast of burden that creates nothing of permanence, simply a human involved in work that is routine and separated from wider life, where work is an end in itself.[8] By contrast, *Homo Faber* – which means 'man as maker' – is a term Arendt borrows from Renaissance philosophy of art. It is the idea of men and women involved in 'higher work', above the day-to-day labours of necessity. A *Homo Faber* is a maker in the collaborative 'human realm', which is above that of nature and animals. She suggests that those defined as *Homo Faber* are, for example, builders, architects, craftworkers, artists and legislators, which are roles that she associates with the Greek words *techne* (craft) and *poiesis* (making). Because of this, *Homo Faber*'s work produces things governed by the freedom of human control, rather than nature and necessity. It is also work that is inherently public, that resides in a common world of human society. Arendt presents human beings as creatures who live in one of these two dimensions, although she is clear that *Homo Faber* is superior to *Animal Laborans*. This is because *Animal Laborans* is absorbed in the utility of making necessary things with little thought, whereas *Homo Faber* collaborates intelligently with other humans to make those things that contribute to a greater society.[9]

Sennett summarizes Arendt's classification, observing that *Animal Laborans* asks 'How?' but *Homo Faber* asks 'Why?' However, he rejects Arendt's harsh division of human work into these separated terms. Sennett prefers to see *Animal Laborans* as *Homo Faber*'s guide because 'thinking and feeling are contained within the process of making'.[10] Rather dramatically, he states that he 'has sought to rescue *Animal Laborans* from the contempt with which Hannah Arendt treated him'.[11] He does this by bringing *Animal Laborans* and *Homo Faber* together in the idea of the craftsman.

The craftsman

Sennett believes the idea of the craftsman is poorly understood, in part because it is a pattern of work that declined in the industrial era.[12] He thinks that, unfortunately, modern people think craftworkers are rare individuals, either associating the term with low-skilled manual work or as a minor sub-group of manufacturing artists. Nevertheless, he believes 'there is an intelligent craftsman in most of us'[13] driven by a 'basic human impulse ... to do a job well for its own sake'.[14] In his mind, the term craftmanship applies to a wide range of activities that include the computer programmer, the doctor, the artist, the parent and others; each of these is characterized by 'the skill of making things well'.[15] He links the German word *handwerk*, the French word *artisanal*, the old-English word *statecraft*, and the Russian word *mastersvo* to build his picture of highly skilled creative artisans who feel and think deeply about their occupations.[16]

Sennett suggests one of the earliest celebrations of craftworkers in literature appears in a seventh-century BC short hymn attributed to Homer, which depicts Hephaestus, the Greek master god of craftsmen. The hymn begins:

> Sing clear-voiced Muse, of Hephaestus famed for skill. With bright-eyed Athena he taught men glorious crafts throughout the world – men who before used to dwell in caves in the mountains like wild beasts. But now that they have learned crafts through Hephaestus famous for his art they live a peaceful life in their own houses the whole year round.[17]

No doubt also aware that in Homer's *Iliad* Hephaestus forges Achilles' shield and armour, Sennett says that Hephaestus is 'a bringer of peace and the maker of civilization'.[18] The stark contrast presented between a cave-dwelling beast and a community resident living in peace suggests that Homer's craftworkers are people of good or high standing, positively connected to their community and other craftworkers. Next, Sennett cites Plato, who associated craftwork with the Greek word *poiein* (making), from which the English word 'poetry' is derived.[19] In the philosophical text *Symposium*, Plato observed that '[c]raftsmen are all poets' but 'they are not all called poets: they have other names'.[20] If craftworkers are poets, then their technical skills and creative intelligence are no doubt working in concert. Referencing Homer, Plato and others, Sennett compiles a picture of a craftsman: a high-standing intelligent worker, with creative skills, who is in harmony and peace with society, working alongside those who share the same vocation.

Sennett suggests that the learning process for craftworkers begins with the acquisition of technical skills, which he also calls 'trained practice'.[21] He rejects the idea of the untrained talent that appears *coup de foudre* – from sudden and unexpected inspiration arising from innate ability. Rather, he believes that technical skills are acquired through repetitious practice, provided that two factors are at work. The first factor, the 'Isaac Stern rule' – named after the famous violinist – is that as the student's technique improves practice sessions can get longer. The second factor is that, as the student's skills develop, the content of what they practice must develop and advance. As technical skills are mastered, the craftworkers move into a second phase, where they are freer to 'think and feel' about their activity – a liberation which releases the work of imagination.[22] One caution is offered in his observation of this process: the development of craft skill is not linear. Sennett observes that 'skill builds by moving irregularly' and 'sometimes by taking detours'.[23] In craftwork, he says 'some issues are left unresolved'[24] thereby keeping the process of learning alive as skill development meets and overcomes resistance and explores ambiguity.

Sennett uses the term 'embedding' to describe the end process that occurs as skills are learned. It is a common experience that skills once mastered become instinctive abilities, whereby the skill can be utilized with little or no conscious thought. Sennett defines embedding as the conversion of technical information and skill practices into tacit knowledge.[25] As this happens, higher stages of skills can be deployed, and the craftworker can utilize tacit habits and thereby release the use of their imagination and the creativity that emerges from a foundation of learned technical skill. The last, and most significant, process of learning observed by Sennett is play. He illustrates this with the example of a child playing with a piece of cloth, learning about the material through sensory stimulation and unstructured exploration.[26] This observation further reinforces Sennett's point that craftsmanship is for everybody, because play is universal.[27]

The workshop

Sennett says, 'the workshop is the craftsman's home'.[28] For most of human history, this has literality been the case, such as when medieval craftworkers lived, ate and slept in their workshops. The medieval workshop was a small business unit modelled on the hierarchy of the family, although not necessarily built on blood-ties. Masters in workshops stood in *loco parentis* over the apprentices and journeymen who were indentured to their household. Parents would entrust their children to the master as a surrogate parent which often included the rights to discipline misbehaviour with corporal punishment.[29] The masters were constrained by a religious oath, whereby they promised to improve the skills of their charges; in return, apprentices swore a religious or fealty oath to keep their master's secrets. These reciprocal commitments established a trust relationship between the surrogate father and the adopted apprentice-son.[30]

The effectiveness of these workshops was determined by the skills of its master, who oversaw the household, operated the business and trained the workers. As Sennett says, 'In craftsmanship there must be a superior who sets standards and who trains.'[31] In English medieval workshops, the master of a craft-trade had dignity in his profession because he was a Christian-worker: all people assumed that Jesus Christ, who was the son of a carpenter, spent his formative years training in his father's workshop. Through the workshops of the craft guilds, masters trained their workers as parents nurturing their adopted children. Thereby, guild-workshops lived out a principle of the age, *rex qui nunquam moritur* (Latin, the king never dies). Because they were places where craft skills were passed from generation to generation, through knowledge learned by 'imitation, ritual, and surrogacy',[32] the workshops were centres for the transfer of knowledge capital between workers. Workshops bound people together in learning communities of masters and apprentices, which Sennett describes as places of 'joined skill in community'.[33] It is, however, worth noting that some masters did not pass on all their wisdom; as an example, Sennett cites Benvenuto Cellini, who said in his autobiography that the secrets of his art would die with him.[34]

An important training function of every workshop was sending out journeymen to further their learning. As apprentices completed their basic training, the master would send them as journeymen for their 'wandering-years', when they were tasked to visit other masters to broaden their experience through peripatetic work-based learning. After three years the journeymen were expected to return to their sending workshop so they could teach their master new skills and ideas. The workshop was thereby refreshed in creativity and innovation. In the eyes of others, this practice was effective. One striking comment comes from Ibn Khaldûn, a Tunisian-born fourteenth-century Muslim historiographer, who writes in *The Muqaddimah* that a good master 'presides over a travelling house'.[35] Khaldûn made these comments from observing English guild goldsmith journeymen who had travelled to Andalusia in Spain as part of their wandering-years.[36]

Sennett notes that the result of training, for both the apprentice and the journeyman, was recognized through evidence of their skill demonstrated in producing an example of their craft trade. For the apprentice, a *chef-d'oeuvre* (French, masterpiece) was required as proof of their ability to imitate the basic skills they had been taught. The journeyman had to demonstrate both skill and creativity by producing a *chef-d'oeuvre élevé* (French, higher masterpiece).[37] The *chef-d'oeuvre élevé* was expected to combine evidence of learning in their first workshop, as well as new ideas from their journeyman years, and the craftworkers' own innovation and creativity. Sennett sums up the creative blend which was evidenced in the journeyman's *chef-d'oeuvre élevé* using the words of the sixteenth-century poet, John Donne. Donne imagined the craftsman 'as a phoenix rising from the ashes of received truth and tradition'.[38] Donne's craftworker has mastered the wisdom of the past and added his own innovation to produce new and fresh creativity. His poem 'An Anatomy of The World' sums up his thinking:

Prince, Subject, Father, Son, are things forgot,
For every man alone thinks he hath got
To be a Phoenix, and that then can be
None of that kind, of which he is, but he.[39]

The hand

Sennett believes that creative skills are nurtured in the human hand. He quotes Immanuel Kant, who said, 'The hand is the window on to the mind'[40] as an illustration of the significance of the link between the head and the hand in the craftworker's development of creativity.[41] He explores Charles Bell's idea of 'the intelligent hand' as a God-given limb that provides the brain with more information than any other sense[42] and Charles Darwin's atheistic theory that the brains of apes and humans evolved as they began to use their hands for more than movement.[43] Whichever path of argument is followed, he concludes that there is an intimate connection between head and hand for learning and developing creative skills. This is, he says, because 'all skills ... begin as bodily practices' (hand) and 'technical understanding develops through the powers of imagination' (head).[44]

Sennett suggests that the common criterion of 10,000 hours of practice is an accurate assessment of the input necessary for a student to acquire creative mastery. The 10,000 hours idea has been popularized by Malcolm Gladwell in *Outliers: The Story of Success* where he considers how successful people learn elite skills. This theory was first proposed in the paper 'The Role of Deliberate Practice in the Acquisition of Expert

Performance' (1993) by Anders Ericsson, which reported the discoveries of psychologists in Berlin studying the practice habits of children learning to play the violin. However, Ericsson later rejected Gladwell's simplification of his theory.[45] Nevertheless, Sennett observes that goal-directed deliberate practice establishes complex skills that through practice become deeply ingrained and readily available to a creative worker. He notes that three hours of daily practice for ten years – which is a common training span for young people in sports – or seven years of work as an apprentice working five hours a day, or a busy three-year medical internship, all produce 10,000 practice hours.[46]

Questions

1 Which model of creative work and learning appeals to you the most: *Animal Laborans* which asks 'how', or *Homo Faber* which asks 'why'?
2 Sennett suggests that technical skills are acquired through a process: repetitive practice that in time releases the work of imagination and results in skills embedded as tacit knowledge, ending with ongoing learning through play. Has this been your experience?
3 What if we were to imagine a church plant as a workshop? What are the gifts (and the limits) of this analogy?
4 What keeps us from cultivating habits and practices that nurture creative work, both in the church and outside of it?

John Paul II – *The Letter of His Holiness to Artists*

In *The Letter of His Holiness to Artists* (1999), John Paul II says that 'to communicate the message entrusted to her by Christ, the Church needs art'.[47] The association of art with the Christian church over the last 2,000 years is extensive. Church buildings are typically not just functional but also often beautiful. They might contain statues, works of art or stained glass windows with depictions of biblical stories, exemplar Saints and biblical themes. Church music, both ancient and modern, has been prolific in both sacred and secular culture, religious art, in the form of paintings and murals, has been a commonplace *Biblia pauperum* (poor-man's Bible) telling the gospel in the public space. John Paul calls these creative non-verbal representations of the Bible a 'concrete mode of catechesis',[48] a phrase which he paraphrases from a letter by Gregory the Great to Serenus, Bishop of Marseilles in AD 599.

Artists in the image of God

In the introduction to his *Letter*, John Paul defines God the Creator as the exemplar of all artists and craftworkers, an association that he sees in the lexical similarity between the words 'creator' (*stwórca*) and 'craftsman' (*twórca*) in Polish, which is his first language,[49] and in the history of the church. Art which is created by humans then is inspired by the 'sole creator of all things' as an 'echo'[50] or a 'mirror'[51] of the whole of God's creation. Although the creator and the craftworker are associated, John Paul notes that the creator creates out of nothing (Latin, *creatio ex nihilo*) whereas the artist and craftworker use 'something that already exists', to which they give 'form and meaning'.[52] In this respect, artistic creativity is an evidentiary trait of beings who are made 'in the image of God'.[53] Although not everyone is called to be an artist, John Paul affirms that 'all men and women are entrusted with the task of crafting their own life' as 'a work of art, a masterpiece'.[54] Those who are called to be artists have 'a special relationship to beauty'[55] which is empowered by a 'divine spark which is the artistic vocation'.[56]

Whether society needs artists is a moot point. Artists have been part of societies since the beginning of civilization. Unlike engineers, who make practical things, or, say, physicians, who bring healing, artists find their role in bringing inspiration, imaginative thinking and wellbeing to their communities. The work of the artist has the potential to display beauty, enrich culture and contribute to the common good.[57] And the 'higher good' of an artist can become a 'spiritual service' which contributes to the renewal of people and their community. John Paul quotes the Polish poet, Cyprian Norwid, who wrote that 'beauty is to enthuse us for work, and work is to raise us up'.[58] The same idea is also found in the Deutero-canonical book of Ecclesiasticus, which describes the importance of craftsmen in the welfare of a town:

> So it is with every artisan and master artisan who labours by night as well as by day ... All these rely on their hands, and all are skilful in their own work ... [T]hey maintain the fabric of the world, and their concern is for the exercise of their trade. (Ecclesiasticus 38.27, 31, 34)

God as the subject of art

Although the Old Testament prohibits the representation of God in any 'graven or molten image' (Deut. 27.15 KJV), artists, says John Paul, are expressing the 'mystery of the Incarnation' which is now the central manifestation of the God who has been revealed in Jesus Christ (Gal. 4.4). Borrowing terms from Paul Claudel and Marc Chagall, John Paul says that Scripture becomes an 'immense vocabulary' (Claudel) and an 'iconographic atlas' (Chagall) from which artists can draw their inspiration.[59] This can be seen, for example, in an icon, which is not adored for its own sake, but because it points beyond itself to the subject that it represents.[60] Like a sacrament, an icon 'makes present the mystery of the Incarnation in one or other of its aspects'.[61] In this respect, all artists are limited in their ability to convey the mysteries they are glimpsing,[62] fulfilling what Paul observed when he says:

> The God who made the world and everything in it ... does not live in temples made by man ... as though he needed anything, since he himself gives to all mankind life and breath and everything ... Yet he is actually not far from each one of us, for
> 'In him we live and move and have our being'
> as even some of your own poets have said,
> 'For we are indeed his offspring.'
> Being then God's offspring, we ought not to think that the divine being is like gold or silver or stone, an image formed by the art and imagination of man. (Acts 17.24–29 ESV)

Artists in the Church

In recognizing that the church needs art, John Paul quotes the 1966 Pastoral Constitution *Gaudium et Spes* which said to the Church, 'This world ... needs beauty in order not to sink into despair. Beauty, like truth, brings joy to the human heart and is that precious fruit which resists the erosion of time, which unites generations ...'[63] He also quotes from the Constitution on the Sacred Liturgy *Sacrosanctum Concilium* from Vatican II, which sought to honour the role of 'sacred art' as 'a noble ministry' in enabling that 'the knowledge of God [to] be better revealed and the preaching of the Gospel [to] become clearer to the human mind'.[64] He concludes, 'In order to communicate the message entrusted to her by Christ, the Church needs art'[65] noting, as a minor point, that 'Christ made extensive use of images in his preaching.'[66]

In his closing thoughts, John Paul reminds us that the Spirit of God is vital to the form of art he has been considering. He quotes the Pentecost hymn from Vespers, *Veni, Creator Spiritus*: 'Come, O Creator Spirit, visit our minds, fill with your grace the hearts you have created' as a reminder of the Spirit's role in bringing inspiration.[67] The involvement of the Holy Spirit is the necessary part of the beauty that is conveyed in sacred art. Without the Spirit there can be no true transcendence or revelation of mystery. Created things, he says, 'can never fully satisfy' but they can 'stir ... hidden nostalgia for God'.[68] His last word is from Augustine: 'Late have I loved you, beauty so old and so new: late have I loved you!'[69]

Art and the New Evangelization

In summary, John Paul's *Letter* is an extensive appeal, based on the teaching and history of the Church, to embrace the role of art in the ministry of the Christian church. As such, it is part of the strategy of 'New Evangelization' – popularized by John Paul – which is a call in the Roman Catholic Church to commit fresh energy to the evangelization of society. As an artist himself, John Paul is certainly qualified to speak into this discussion. While at university, he was an amateur actor; as a young priest, he wrote poetry and plays. No doubt these formative experiences allowed him to understand the interconnection of art and the ministry and mission of the Christian church. His *Letter* is a call to all artists, including painters, poets, musicians, playwriters, film-makers, sculptors, architects, musicians and actors who are all mentioned explicitly. His call is to everyone, even though – as in the Parable of the Talents (Matt. 25.14–30) – some have been given more gifts than others.

Questions

1 Does the church *need* art to communicate Christ's message?
2 In what ways might art and artists in the church bring fresh energy to the evangelization of society?
3 Is church planting an art form?

Trevor Hart – *Making Good: Creation, Creativity, and Artistry*

In his introduction to *Making Good: Creation, Creativity, and Artistry* (2014), Trevor Hart describes theology as a human activity 'in which the quotient of imagination is set extraordinarily and necessarily high'.[70] Because Christian theology has its focus on the God who is revealed in Jesus Christ and is a response which is shaped by engagement with that revelation, it is, in Hart's opinion, inseparable from what he calls 'imaginative *poesis*' (Greek, making). More specifically, Hart sees 'imaginative *poesis*' as a two-way dynamic engagement between the self-revealing God, and imaginative human discovery.[71]

Hart believes the 'imaginative stretch' implied and required by his approach can be helpfully progressed by the notion of a metaphor.[72] He develops this idea by citing David Brown who describes a metaphor in this context as when 'some sense of what is promised is grasped ... but the mystery remains'[73] and Sallie McFague, who draws on Paul Ricoeur to present the idea of theological discovery as 'a whisper, "it is, *and it is not!*"'[74]

In concluding his introduction, he also notes the challenges arising from a modern outlook on artistry, specifically the association of art with play and leisure, rather than with work. In the modern world, Hart suggests, true artists are unhelpfully considered to be rare characters who are born with a gift that most others do not have. This perspective, he believes, is opposite to the views of the biblical, patristic and medieval eras.[75] In their historic use, Hart believes the terms 'artist' and 'craftworker' can be used interchangeably to describe both God the creator and the human beings who engage in the 'imaginative *poesis*' of theological discovery.[76]

God the master craftsman

Beginning with the biblical account of the creation of human beings (Gen. 2.7), Hart describes God as the original craftsman. Like a divine potter, God shapes and moulds the first people from 'lumps of clay' into which he breathes life.[77] Hart prefers to render the Hebrew verb *yatser*, which is typically translated as 'formed', as 'potter' when used in this verse, and as 'craftsman' or 'artist' when used generically.[78] Developing this theme, Hart cites Terence Fretheim, who believes there are approximately 20 different images of God as a creative in the first two chapters of Genesis alone. He suggests the ones most used are 'God as King' and 'Sovereign Lord'.[79] When considering the further usage of *yatser* in Exodus 25–31 and 35–39, Hart concludes that the first two books of the Hebrew Bible present God as a master craftsman.

In the Prophets and Wisdom books, Hart demonstrates that God in his external actions is depicted as one who does the things associated with the activities of a master craftworker and artist. Hart cites more than 24 biblical descriptions of God operating or being described as a craftworker,[80] and he later refers to 'a thousand scattered references' in the canon to God the artist.[81]

Creativity through covenant

In covenant with his created order, Hart believes that God is not only the 'creative maker' but also the 'creative manager' who continues with his created order, 'fashioning it ever more fully into the likeness of his artistic vision'.[82] He presents the idea of God as a 'divine artist' who is as involved in his ongoing covenant with his created order as he was in first making it. From the New Testament, he cites Romans 9.20–24, which begins 'Who are you, O man, to answer back to God? Will what is moulded say to its moulder, "Why have you made me like this?"' (Rom. 9.20 ESV). This depicts the divine potter continuing his work. Hart cites Edward Lucie-Smith, who notes that under the Roman empire – although the social standing of artists and craftworkers had declined – craftsmanship in building and architecture were recognized and acclaimed.[83] He observes that the New Testament's most consistent description of God as a craftworker is drawn 'from the vocabulary of architecture and the building trade'.[84] For example, in Hebrews 3.4, God is 'the builder of everything' (NIV).

Creativity is like jazz

There is a tension between the creativity of human beings, who are limited to making use of things that already exist, and the creativity of God, who is the true creator. Hart states, 'Where human artistry is concerned, no art comes out of nothing.'[85] All human artistic creations stand on their material and non-material antecedents from which new creations are made.[86] To achieve this, Hart proposes that the artisan brings 'creative freedom' as the quality that makes something new, from ideas and examples that already exist. Hart believes that this result can be achieved if 'creativity arises and flourishes in the form of imaginative response'.[87] Hart proposes that the idea of tradition is a productive way to progress the understanding of how creativity can arise from extant components and creative freedom.[88] To develop this idea, he suggests that when humans learn skills they always do so in a social context, where they also acquire associated 'social practices'.[89] This means that learned practices are inherently social, in that they typically involve a community of practice. He summarizes his idea by saying that 'the work of the individual artist is therefore beholden in one way or another to the community of practitioners which granted it birth and nurture'.[90]

Hart offers a vivid illustration of how creativity can make new things from extant ingredients by following 'social' rules, in a community context. The illustration is of a jazz musician playing 'free jazz' with other musicians. If successful, the musicians produce something new which is made from extant things, such as chords and snippets of music and which is constructed using the 'social rules' of jazz in dynamic concert with the other musicians. This produces something that is new and recognizable as jazz, made possible because the musicians have spent time practising scales, arpeggios and musical pieces with the accompanying 'social practices' of jazz music.[91]

Art and craft

Craftsmanship and creativity are not the same – the former describes a skill and the latter the work of imagination. Hart has already established that in the pre-modern world, the concepts of art and craft are essentially the same and creativity is effectively the application, or outworking, of imagination. He cites Howard Becker, who defines craft as 'a body of knowledge and skill which can be used to produce useful objects'.[92] So, craft has more to do with the quality and method of production than with imagination.

Hart also cites Dorothy L. Sayers, who believes that all work can be seen as creative if it is for 'the making of something'.[93] She suggests that women and men are truly themselves when they are creating (making) something. She explains:

> a seemingly uninspired and uninspiring task can become 'a sacrament and manifestation of man's creative energy,' if only it is approached and undertaken with a clear vision of the intrinsic worth of the work ... and out of a desire and a love that longs only to see it done and done to the highest achievable standard – that it may be all that it is capable of being and becoming.[94]

Sayers is saying that if 'work' is undertaken in a purposeful manner and with a love for the end result and the process of making, it is creative in the fullest sense. She adds the observation that 'he [God] is in love with his creation for its own sake'.[95] From the faith-perspective of the pre-modern world, God is creative in his creation-work and human beings are true to their God-given identity when exercising human creativity in their work through making.

Questions

1 Do you agree with Dorothy L. Sayers that creativity lies in whether women and men are being truly themselves when they are making something?

2 What is the significance of God as not only the creative maker of the world but also an ongoing creative manager continuing his work? How does God's ongoing involvement in creation change the church's missional orientation to the world?

3 How might Hart's jazz analogy help with developing creativity in the church and among church planters? Where might we need more or better improvisation: where might we need more consistent practice of set pieces?

Notes

1 'Homeric Hymn to Hephaestus,' in H. G. Evelyn-White, trans., *Hesiod, the Homeric Hymns, and Homerica* (Cambridge, MASS: Harvard Loeb Classical Library, 1914), 447, quoted in Richard Sennett, *Craftsman* (London: Penguin, 2009), 298.

2 Plato *Symposium* 205b–c, quoted in Sennett, *Craftsman*, 298.

3 Sennett, *Craftsman*, 290.

4 Sennett, *Craftsman*, 83.

5 Sennett, *Craftsman*, 84.

6 Sennett, *Craftsman*, 145.

7 Sennett, *Craftsman*, 144–45.

8 Sennett, *Craftsman*, 6.

9 Sennett, *Craftsman*, 6.

10 Sennett, *Craftsman*, 7.

11 Sennett, *Craftsman*, 286.

12 Sennett, *Craftsman*, 9.

13 Sennett, *Craftsman*, 11.

14 Sennett, *Craftsman*, 9.

15 Sennett, *Craftsman*, 8–9.

16 Sennett, *Craftsman*, 20.

17 Quoted in Sennett, *Craftsman*, 21.

18 Sennett, *Craftsman*, 21.

19 Sennett, *Craftsman*, 24.

20 *Symposium* 205b–c quoted in Sennett, *Craftsman*, 298.

21 Sennett, *Craftsman*, 37.

22 Sennett, *Craftsman*, 20–21.

23 Sennett, *Craftsman*, 238.

24 Sennett, *Craftsman*, 263.

25 Sennett, *Craftsman*, 50.

26 Sennett, *Craftsman*, 273.

27 Sennett, *Craftsman*, 273.

28 Sennett, *Craftsman*, 53.

29 Sennett, *Craftsman*, 63.

30 Guilds had, of course, many imperfections including issues of power-abuse. For a balancing view see Sheilagh Ogilvie, 'The Use and Abuse of Trust: Social Capital and Its Deployment by Early Modern Guilds', *Jahrbuch Für Wirtschaftsgeschichte / Economic History Yearbook*, Vol. 46, No. 1, Jan. 2005, doi:10.1524/jbwg.2005.46.1.15; Steven R. Smith, 'The Ideal and Reality: Apprentice-Master Relationships in Seventeenth Century London', *History of Education Quarterly*, Vol. 21, No. 4, 1981, 449, doi:10.2307/367925; Steven R. Smith and Jonathan Zeitlin, 'The London Apprentices as Seventeenth-Century Adolescents', *Past and Present*, Vol. 61, No. 1, 1973, 149–161, doi:10.1093/past/61.1.149.

31 Sennett, *Craftsman*, 54.

32 Sennett, *Craftsman*, 65.

33 Sennett, *Craftsman*, 51.

34 Quoted in Sennett, *Craftsman*, 74.

35 *Muqaddimah* 6.40.1, quoted in Sennett, *Craftsman*, 59.

36 Sennett, *Craftsman*, 59–60.

37 Sennett, *Craftsman*, 58.

38 Quoted in Sennett, *Craftsman*, 78.

39 Quoted in Sennett, *Craftsman*, 78.

40 Quoted in Sennett, *Craftsman*, 149.

41 Sennett, *Craftsman*, 149.

42 Sennett, *Craftsman*, 149–50.

43 Sennett, *Craftsman*, 150.

44 Sennett, *Craftsman*, 10.

45 See K. Anders Ericsson, 'The Danger of Delegating Education to Journalists: Why the APS Observer Needs Peer Review When Summarizing New Scientific Developments', *Radical Eyes for Equity*, 2014, at https://radicalscholarship.wordpress.com/2014/11/03/guest-post-the-danger-of-delegating-education-to-journalists-k-anders-ericsson (accessed 28.1.2022).

46 Sennett, *Craftsman*, 172.

47 Pope John Paul II, *Letter of His Holiness Pope John Paul II to Artists* (Pauline Books and Media, 1999), 12.1.

48 John Paul, *Artists*, 5.5.

49 John Paul, *Artists*, 1.3.

50 John Paul, *Artists*, 1.1.

51 John Paul, *Artists*, 1.3.

52 John Paul, *Artists*, 1.4.

53 John Paul, *Artists*, 1.5.

54 John Paul, *Artists*, 2.1.

55 John Paul, *Artists*, 3.3.

56 John Paul, *Artists*, 3.4.

57 John Paul, *Artists*, 4.1.

58 Quoted in John Paul, *Artists*, 3.1.

59 John Paul, *Artists*, 5.3.

60 John Paul, *Artists*, 7.4.

61 John Paul, *Artists*, 8.1.

62 John Paul, *Artists*, 6.1–2.

63 Quoted in John Paul, *Artists*, 11.2.

64 Quoted in John Paul, *Artists*, 11.2.

65 John Paul, *Artists*, 12.1.

66 John Paul, *Artists*, 12.2.

67 John Paul, *Artists*, 15.1.

68 John Paul, *Artists*, 16.3.

69 *Confessions* 10.27, quoted in John Paul, *Artists*, 16.3.

70 Trevor A. Hart, *Making Good: Creation, Creativity, and Artistry* (Waco, TX: Baylor University Press, 2014), 11.

71 Hart, *Making Good*, 11.

72 Hart, *Making Good*, 14.

73 Hart, *Making Good*, 14.

74 Hart, *Making Good*, 14, emphasis in original.

75 Hart, *Making Good*, 22.

76 Hart, *Making Good*, 22.

77 Hart, *Making Good*, 31–32.

78 Hart, *Making Good*, 32.

79 Hart, *Making Good*, 21.

80 Hart, *Making Good*, 32–33.

81 Hart, *Making Good*, 41.

82 Hart, *Making Good*, 34.

83 Hart, *Making Good*, 36.

84 Hart, *Making Good*, 36.

85 Hart, *Making Good*, 250.

86 Hart, *Making Good*, 250.

87 Hart, *Making Good*, 251.

88 Hart, *Making Good*, 252.

89 Hart, *Making Good*, 254.

90 Hart, *Making Good*, 254–55.

91 Hart, *Making Good*, 245.

92 Hart, *Making Good*, 292.

93 Hart, *Making Good*, 298.

94 Quoted in Hart, *Making Good*, 299.

95 Hart, *Making Good*, 299.

PART 3

Wisdom from Tradition and Practice

... the effective church planter sees themselves as a craftsman who understands how God has worked creatively in the area where the church is being planted. The many different models of church planting are then not seen as fixed procedures for producing churches, but rather as tools in the church planting craftsman's toolbox ...

Ron Anderson

Note: Ron Anderson, 'Creative Church Planting Involving Lay People', in *Church Planting in Europe: Connecting to Society, Learning from Experience*, edited by Evert Van de Poll and Joanne Appleton (Eugene, OR: Wipf and Stock, 2015), 216–26.

6

Craft Guilds

The 'tramping years' were at one time the university of the craft system, a sort of degree in the free school of life.

Rudolf Wissel, Des alten Handwerks Recht und Gewohnheit[1]

A good master presides over a travelling house.

Ibn Khaldûn, The Muqaddimah[2]

Having drawn on the Scriptures and theology, our first source of traditional and practical wisdom for the craft of church planting is the English medieval craft guilds. The guilds are the principal historical foundation of this book and the inspiration for the model that is being explored.[3] They give us not only a carefully-worked precedent for craft apprenticeship but also an invaluable outline for a structure of formation, from apprentice to guild-master.

Origin of the guilds

For approximately 700 years, spanning the High and Late Middle Ages, occupational guilds were the most important example of apprentice-style training in England.[4] Through these guilds, youths and young adults in England were trained in skills, ethical behaviour, community life and the complexities of their chosen profession. This training was delivered under the supervision of a master-worker, who personally tutored apprentices. Master-workers had been trained the same way themselves. Guilds enabled the transfer of working skills through apprenticeship,[5] so much so that nearly all urban craftworkers in the Middle Ages were guilded.[6]

A guild is a group of people who do the same work or who affiliate around a common interest. Though the spelling 'guild' is most used, it can also be written as 'gild' as it is derived from the Anglo-Saxon 'Gildan' meaning 'to pay'. Gabriel La Bras suggests that 'gild' in the Germanic languages has the ancient meaning of 'fraternities of young warriors practising the cult of heroes' and is used in literature to refer to any group connected by rites, friendship and some shared financial resource.[7] Anthony Black identifies the earliest documented use of the word in AD 450, where 'gilda' was a sacrificial meal associated with religious liberation and the cult of the dead. The common threads suggest that guilds are a group of people, often with subscription membership, who are connected in common purpose and relationship.

There were four main kinds of medieval guild: religious guilds, for pious devotion and good works; frith guilds, for the promotion of peace, friendship and the establishment of law and order; merchant guilds, for trade and commerce; and craft guilds.[8] Each craft guild focused on a specific artisan trade, such as candle making, weaving, bookbinding or printing. A large city in the Middle Ages might have as many as 100 different types of guild, each providing a means for trade and craft skills to be passed to the next generation.

Craft guilds were associations and confraternities of artisan craft workers organized in workshop small business units which were overseen by an owner-master. The earliest English craft guilds began in London, Oxford and York.[9] The first record of a trade guild in York appears in 1163 in the *Acta of Henry II*, which lists the granting of the King's confirmation of the 'weavers' guild and customs' in exchange for an annual payment of ten pounds. By 1180, the same record lists guilds of glovers, saddlers, hosiers and cordwainers (shoemakers) as established bodies.[10] By the thirteenth century guild training in York had become prolific: for example, in 1415 there were 96 craft guilds in York,[11] a time in which the population of the city was no more than 15,000 people.[12]

Usually, masters recruited youth as apprentices, who were indentured to work for seven years in return for basic provisions, lodging and the opportunity to learn a trade. Admittance to guilds was not uniform and was at the whim of the local master, who functioned like a self-employed small business owner. In their simplest form, guilds were a natural extension of family work, training and business; some see them as the antecedents of modern professional groups and unionized models of work. For example, Lujo Brentano believes that the earliest guilds must have evolved from family and neighbourhood community work that in time became a more formalized working-family for business and education.[13]

The structure of guilds

The basic unit of a guild was a workshop: a small financially independent business unit, usually located in the master's home. A typical guild would have comprised a three-part hierarchy of livery, freemen and apprentices. The livery consisted of masters who had been inducted into that guild. Freemen were senior journeymen who had completed their journeyman-years and were now liberated from their contract to their master; and apprentices were indentured workers in training. In some cities, journeymen who had completed their wandering-years could apply to become freemen of the city; in all cities, such journeymen could apply to become masters recognized by their guild if they could prove their skills and had the means to set up a workshop. Other journeymen, who were neither livery nor freemen, were travelling away from their master's workshop as part of a three-year self-guided internship. Last, apprentices were the most junior members of guilds. They were recruited by masters and served under a contract where they received basic training, board and keep.[14]

Masters were established craftworkers with proven abilities, who had been recognized and admitted into their guild. Masters held a great deal of power, particularly over their apprentices who were like adopted children because they were under the masters' legal and moral oversight.[15] The term 'master' has the common meaning of 'expert'. For example, guilds are the origin of the name of master's degrees awarded by universities,[16] and from the late twelfth century, mastery in arts was recognized in university education, tracing its origin to the *Licentia docendi* (teaching license) of the University of Paris.[17]

Apprenticeship was the most basic element of the craft guild structure. Typically, apprentices would be inducted in their teens and would train with their master for between five and nine years. A good apprenticeship was highly desirable, and parents may have paid to have their sons admitted to sought-after workshops. Sheilagh Ogilvie notes that gaining an apprenticeship was not always easy because most guilds excluded 'Jews, bastards, migrants, laborers, farmers, propertyless men, former serfs and slaves, gypsies, members of other guilds, adherents of minority religions, men of 'impure' ethnicity, and those who couldn't afford the admission fees.'[18] Ogilvie cites a Spanish author who says, perhaps hyperbolically, that 'those without funds "called in vain at the door of the guild, for it was opened only with a silver key"'.[19] On joining a workshop apprentices would be trained in craft skills and learn the specialist – and sometimes highly guarded – knowledge of their trade. This trust requirement is illustrated by an early modern apprentice-oath, which states: 'his said master faithfully his secrets keep'.[20]

Once apprentices had completed their apprenticeships, they could become journeymen. The term derives from the French word *journée*, which means 'day'. Accordingly, journeymen were skilled workers who could receive a daily wage for their labour. The journeyman-years functioned as the second stage of training, in the form of self-guided learning that lasted for three years and a day.[21] During that time, the journeymen could not return to their masters' workshop; instead, they had to travel and work in short bursts for different masters to learn a wider range of skills. After the journeyman-years, they could apply to be recognized as masters in the guild, which would allow them to open a workshop and train their own apprentices.

Many guilds had additional roles that members could hold: some were tied to the hierarchical structure of the guild, and others could be held by any member. In most guilds, the group of masters would elect a senior, called the guildmaster. A pageant-master, who did not need to be a master, played a leading role in the organization of community plays. A searcher was a public office that could be held by any craftworker. Searchers were typically nominated to serve for a year by their predecessors, subject to the approval of the group of masters. They were sworn to maintain and enforce the standards of their craft trade. They also called guild meetings, managed guild finances and 'searched' articles made by guild members to ensure they were of genuine materials and sufficient quality. Keepers fulfilled a supervisory role in the internal running of guilds, registering details in town records and supervising subscription payments.[22] Many larger guilds employed chantry priests to celebrate masses and to conduct funerals as chaplains for the members.[23] Last, wardens were senior office-holders who were elected to manage the day-to-day affairs of the guild and the welfare of members. In some cities, guilds played a significant role in the administration of the city, so much so that their officers might be considered quasi-public officials.[24]

The demise of the guilds

The economist and philosopher Adam Smith, who is referred to as 'the father of economics',[25] was highly critical of the guild model. In his seminal work, *An Inquiry into the Nature and Causes of the Wealth of Nations*, which was published at the turn of the British Industrial Revolution in 1776, Smith censured guilds as 'a conspiracy against the public'.[26] Smith thought guilds were a financial conspiracy against the working-classes; moreover, he theorized that guilds had a detrimental effect on society and the economy because they limited the ability of a worker to thrive.[27]

The controversial revolutionary Karl Marx was equally critical of the guilds, which he thought prevented the development and implementation of the technological changes associated with the Industrial Revolution. In the opening of Chapter One of the *Manifesto of the Communist Party,* Marx expresses the root of his frustration, when he says '[the] guild-master and journeyman, in a word, oppressor and oppressed'.[28] Anna Vaninskaya summarizes a communist perspective on the decline of the guilds when she observes that 'guilds met their end as a result of industrialization and capitalist monopolistic excess'.[29] However, it should be noted that, typical to his focus on workers' welfare, Marx's criticism was directed towards the system and hierarchy of the guilds, not the workers and their craft.

The revolution in France caused an abrupt abolition of its guilds in 1791, and this institutional reform quickly spread to the other nearby European countries.[30] However, it is worth noting that English guilds had been in decline since the late 1500s; for example, only a quarter of the guilds in existence in the sixteenth century survived to the seventeenth.[31] Causes of this decline included the effects of the European Reformation, external pricing and trade restrictions, and the growth in power of centralized national governments. Governments were changing the landscape of work through legislation, access to new markets, and greater central capital resources – all changes conspired to weaken the influence of guilds. Ogilvie believes that the selfish practices of the guilds – such as price-fixing, labour restrictions and blocking innovation – weakened their position, leaving them vulnerable to these external changes in society.[32] Ogilvie sums up her thoughts on this subject by quoting Adam Smith's observation on urban guilds: '[P]eople of the same trade seldom meet together, even for merriment and diversion, but the conversation ends in a conspiracy against the public, or in some contrivance to raise prices.'[33] No single factor was responsible for the demise of the guilds, the contributing forces were technological, international, social, economic, political and cultural which 'came together in the mid-18th century to provide the stimulus for industrial advance'.[34]

The demise of the guilds was probably inevitable, and the evidence of decline was already evident. The final blow to the dominance of the British guilds was the advent of the Industrial Revolution, fuelled by, among other things, the development of James Watt's steam engine. Céline Dauverd notes the transition: '[E]arly modern craft guilds formed the backbone of industrial production before the rise of the steam engine.'[35] The Industrial Revolution initiated a transition from agrarian and handicraft production to new industry and machine-based manufacturing. As a result, first, manual labourers were replaced by machines; but second, jobs became machine-work and workers themselves became machines. Most people who were previously considered artists became operators or workers in the new factory economy. Despite Marx's hope that the ending of the guilds would result in workers being set free from oppression, Antony Black summarizes the result: '[T]he guild system recognized the human value of labour and had to be abolished before labour could be treated as a mere commodity' and the result was that 'after the abolishment of the guild system, labour could be treated as a mere commodity'.[36] Although some might see the new opportunities provided by industrialization – such as designing a steam engine or making cloth on a mechanized loom – as creative acts, nevertheless, Black observes that the demise of the guilds actually diminished the value of human labour. Industrialization had a dramatic impact on the social cohesion of England.[37] Although Marx hoped for something better to replace the guilds, which he believed were oppressive, the new factory economy shifted working-life away from villages and towns into cities, which, in places, quickly became crowded slums of a new working poor.[38]

Training in the guilds

Although guilds were first and foremost commercial and political associations that existed principally for promoting their social enterprise, training was nevertheless a significant part of their identity and activity. When considering the period between 1400 and 1800, Stephan R. Epstein and Maarten Roy Prak suggest that 'probably their single most important contribution to innovation and the pre-industrial economy generally was the guilds' involvement in the training of human capital'.[39] Anthony Black concurs, '[T]he real significance of the guild was that it enabled people to develop through social contact with their fellows.'[40]

Training in guilds was achieved through an on-the-job model, where work and learning occurred at the same time. Patrick Wallis observes that, 'most training was through observation, imitation and practice by apprentices that occurred while they were engaged in useful work – thus even apprentices' learning could even be productive' [sic].[41] He concludes that, '[i]n short, an apprentice's training occurred in *parallel* with their engagement in work'.[42] Apprentices in medieval guilds typically served for between five and seven years before they could advance to become journeymen. In London in 1556, the authorities determined that 'until a man grows unto the age of 24 he has not grown into the full knowledge of the art that he professeth', meaning that some journeymen would have trained for 12 years or more before they could become masters.[43]

Apprentices would usually be required to pass an examination or produce a piece of work as evidence of their learning.

Pieces and masterpieces as evidence of training

An interesting aspect of training in craft guilds is the distinctive evidence-based learning progression of the model. For both apprentices and journeymen to advance to the next stage of learning and status in the guild, they must produce evidence of their learning in the form of 'pieces' which are assessed by their superiors. For an apprentice, the confirmation is in the form of one or more 'pieces', and for a journeyman, typically in the form of a single piece referred to as a 'master's piece' (masterpiece). In literature, this is variously described using the terms *magnum opus* (Latin, great work), *chef-d'œuvre élevé* (French, high masterpiece), master's piece, masterpiece, and masterwork.[44]

It is thought that the earliest documented example of this requirement is in Etienne Boileau's *Livre des Métiers* (Book of Trades), which are the written regulations for Parisian trades and crafts, published somewhere between 1261 and 1271.[45] For example, Boileau's statutes for *chapuiseurs* (carpenters employed in the making of frames for saddles) stipulate that

> as soon as an apprentice is able to make a masterpiece (*chef-d'œuvre*), his master may take another one in his employ, because when an apprentice knows how to do this, it is reasonable that he should ply his trade, be active in it and receive greater honour for it than he who cannot do it.[46]

In some guilds, a Court of Assistants was responsible for ensuring that apprentices received proper treatment from their master. At the end of their apprenticeship period, workers would submit their pieces directly to the wardens. The pieces would be craftwork made entirely by the apprentice that would typically incorporate all of the techniques of their craft trade, as evidence of competency. If accepted the apprentice would receive 'papers', the equivalent of a modern-day diploma, and would become a freeman of the guild. In some guilds, journeymen were only allowed one attempt at submitting a masterpiece. If accepted they could join the masters of the guild, be permitted to start a workshop, and recruit apprentices; if they were not accepted, they could never join that guild as a master.

Pieces and masterpieces were required in all kinds of craft guilds, not just from workers in trades that might be considered artisanal.

For example, goldsmiths and weavers would submit pieces, but so also would apothecaries, carpenters and rope makers.[47] For instance, barbers in fifteenth-century Reims who wished to become masters would be required to demonstrate:

> a wet well and shave in a competent manner; [they had to be able to] comb, trim, and thin a beard; prepare lancets suitable for the bleeding of the ill, and be knowledgeable enough in this operation to be able to distinguish between a vein and an artery ... and know also the appropriate time to carry out a bleeding.[48]

Painters, sculptors and glaziers might likewise be required to produce a painted panel, a small statue, or a panel of stained glass, respectively. The subject of their piece would be determined by their master. For example, Walter Cahn notes that a fifteenth-century master might typically require a depiction of the Virgin Mary, of Christ on the Cross, or of a local saint.[49]

Creativity and artistry in guilds

One aspect of the creative life of Craft Guilds is illustrated in their involvement in Mystery and Miracle plays. These community theatre productions, which are among the earliest plays in medieval Europe, focused on the representation of biblical stories or the lives of Christian saints, in street drama, typically presented with accompanying antiphonal song. Adolphus William Ward clarifies that 'properly speaking, *Mysteries* deal with gospel events only ... *Miracle-plays*, on the other hand, are concerned with incidents derived from the legends of the Saints of the Church'.[50] Robert Ignatius Letellier notes that 'the plays originated as simple tropes, verbal embellishments of liturgical texts, and slowly became more elaborate'.[51] Plays were typically evangelistic in focus and often apocalyptic in style and they covered subjects such as creation, Adam and Eve, the murder of Abel, the fall of Lucifer, Noah and the flood, the nativity and the Resurrection.

Letellier notes that '[t]he nomenclature derives from "mystery" used in its sense of miracle, but another derivation is from *ministerium*, meaning craft, as the "mysteries" or plays were often played by the craft guilds'.[52] The Latin *ministerium* meaning 'occupation', that is, the occupation of the guilds. In this respect, the Mystery and Miracle plays were an integral extension of the occupational work-identity of the guild.

Plays came to be sponsored by the emerging medieval craft guilds, for example, in 1433 the York Mercers sponsored the Doomsday pageant. Each guild might present scenes that linked to their particular trade, such as carpenters presenting the building of Noah's Ark or bakers acting the miracle of the loaves and fishes.

The engagement of the guilds with Mystery and Miracle plays is a small window into the collaborative creativity of these organizations. It highlights the natural association between creativity, training, trade skills and local commerce. The culture of the guilds was such that they were naturally places of artistry and work.

Conclusion

For nearly 700 years, the methods and culture of the guilds shaped almost all examples of training in England. They bequeath to us crucial structures for church planting: the workshop for immersive on-the-job training; the key role of the master near the very beginning of the training process; the wider practical experience of the journeyman years; and through it all the importance of creativity. Some of the language, and even some of the artefacts, endure from the period of domination of the craft guilds, but arguably their greatest contribution are just these structures which can still foster deep and creative learning today.

Questions

1 What is the equivalent of the journeyman-years (the second stage of training: self-guided learning) for those training to be church planters?

2 How important is an on-the-job model (where work and learning occur together and through social contact) for training pioneers and church planters?

3 What might an evidence-based method of assessment and progression look like for different stages of church planter training? What might a 'master's piece' be for a church planter?

4 What are the advantages and disadvantages of a master taking the leading role in the recruitment, selection and initial training of future church planters? Is it appropriate for masters alone to choose their apprentices?

Notes

1 Wissel has a romanticized view of the journeyman life, which he refers to as being 'on the tramp', Rudolf Wissel, *Des alten Handwerks Recht und Gewohnheit* (Berlin, Wasmuth, 1929), I: 301 translated and quoted by Sheilagh Ogilvie, *The European Guilds: An Economic Analysis* (Princeton, NJ: Princeton University Press, 2018), 448.

2 Paraphrased by Richard Sennett, *The Craftsman* (London: Penguin, 2009), 59–60, from *Muqaddimah* 6.40. Khaldûn was a fourteenth-century Arab sociologist, philosopher and historiographer.

3 The key scholarly commentators on medieval guilds are Anthony Black, Walter Cahn, Stephan R. Epstein, Robert Ignatius Letellier, George Unwin, Sheilagh Ogilvie, Geoffrey Gowlland, Eamon Duffy, Steven R. Smith, Patrick Wallis and Sylvia L. Thrupp. Their extensive study of the primary data is invaluable to understanding the guilds.

4 Although other countries (such as Japan, Ireland and North America) have historic apprenticeship systems, I only consider English examples in this book, though reference is made to their European antecedents where it is relevant to understanding the history of the English guilds. For an overview of Japanese apprenticeship in traditional crafts, which has origins before the common era, see Francis W. Wolek, 'The Managerial Principles Behind Guild Craftsmanship', *Journal of Management History*, Vol. 5, No. 7, Nov. 1999, 401–13, 410, Doi: 10.1108/13552529910297460. The Irish guilds, which developed in parallel to the English model, date back to 'fosterage' in seventh-century Brehon Laws, see J. G. Ryan, 'Early Irish Crafts and Apprenticeships: An Historical Background', in *Prometheus's Fire: A History of Scientific and Technological Education in Ireland*, edited by Norman McMillan (Carlow, Ireland: Tyndall Publications, 2000), 25–50. The North American model was derived from British examples immediately preceding the Industrial Revolution. For an overview of craft apprenticeship in the United States, which begins with the apprenticeship experiences of Benjamin Franklin, see W. J. Rorabaugh, *Craft Apprentice: From Franklin to the Machine Age in America* (Oxford: Oxford University Press, 1988).

5 Stephan R. Epstein, 'Craft Guilds, Apprenticeship and Technological Change in Preindustrial Europe', *The Journal of Economic History*, Vol. 58, No. 03, Sept. 1998, 684–713, doi:10.1017/S0022050700021124, 684.

6 Sheilagh Ogilvie, 'The Economics of Guilds', *Journal of Economic Perspectives*, Vol. 28, No. 4, 2014, 169–92, 169.

7 Gabriel le Bras, 'Les Confréries Chrétiennes: Problèmes et Propositions', *Revue Historique De Droit Français et Étranger* (Sirey, 1940), 310–63, 316.

8 Edwin Burton and Pierre Marique. 'Guilds', *The Catholic Encyclopedia*, Vol. 7 (New York: Robert Appleton Company, 1910), 67–68.

9 Wolf-Dietrich Greinert, *Mass Vocational Education and Training in Europe: Classical Models of the 19th Century and Training in England, France and Germany during the First Half of the 20th Century* (Office for Official Publications of the European Communities, 2005), 23.

10 Simon D. Smith, et al., *The Merchant Taylors of York: A History of the Crafts and Company from the Fourteenth to the Twentieth Century*, edited by R. B. Dobson and D. M. Smith (York: Borthwick Institute Publications, 2006), 14; Sarah

Rees Jones, *York: The Making of a City 1068–1350*, 1st edn (Oxford: Oxford University Press, 2013), 112.

11 Clifford Davidson, 'York Guilds and the Corpus Christi Plays: Unwilling Participants?', *Early Theatre*, Vol. 9, No. 2, 2006, 11–33.

12 Jones, *York*, 236.

13 *Brentano* ix quoted in Anna Vaninskaya, 'The Middle Ages', *William Morris and the Idea of Community: Romance, History, and Propaganda, 1880–1914* (Edinburgh: Edinburgh University Press, 2010), 115–36, 117.

14 J. G. Ryan, 'Early Irish Crafts and Apprenticeships: An Historical Background', in *Prometheus's Fire: A History of Scientific and Technological Education in Ireland*, edited by Norman McMillan (Carlow, Ireland: Tyndall Publications, 2000), 25–50, 31.

15 Stephan R. Epstein, 'Craft Guilds, Apprenticeship and Technological Change in Preindustrial Europe', *The Journal of Economic History*, Vol. 58, No. 03, Sept. 1998, 684–713, doi:10.1017/S0022050700021124. 691; E. Lipson, *Economic History of England*, Vol. 1, *The Middle Ages* (London: Adam & Charles Black, 1966), 312–13.

16 Stephan R. Epstein and Maarten Roy Prak, eds, *Guilds, Innovation, and the European Economy, 1400–1800* (Cambridge: Cambridge University Press, 2008), 7.

17 Charles George Herbermann, 'Master of Arts', in *The Catholic Encyclopedia: An International Work of Reference on the Constitution, Doctrine, Discipline, and History of the Catholic Church*, edited by Robert C. Broderick (New York: Robert Appleton Company, 1913), 312–13.

18 Sheilagh Ogilvie, 'The Economics of Guilds', *Journal of Economic Perspectives*, Vol. 28, No. 4, 2014, 169–92, 173.

19 Ogilvie, 'Economics of Guilds', 173.

20 Epstein, 'Craft Guilds', 694.

21 In modern language: a minimum of three years.

22 K. J. Allison et al., 'Medieval Beverley: The Guilds and Their Plays', in *A History of the County of York East Riding (the Borough and Liberties of Beverley)*, edited by P. M. Tillott, Vol. 6 (Victoria County History, London: The Institute of Historical Research, 1989), 42–49, 42.

23 Eileen White, *The St. Christopher and St. George Guild of York* (York: Borthwick Institute, 1987), 7–8; Eamon Duffy, *The Stripping of the Altars: Traditional Religion in England 1400–1580*, 2nd edn (New Haven, CT: Yale University Press, 2005), 141–43.

24 Sylvia L. Thrupp, 'The Gilds', in *The Cambridge Economic History of Europe from the Decline of the Roman Empire*, edited by M. M. Postan et al., Vol. 3 (Cambridge: Cambridge University Press, 1963), 230–280, doi:10.1017/CHOL9780521045063.006, 232.

25 Jesse Norman, *Adam Smith: What He Thought, and Why It Matters* (London: Allen Lane, 2018), xi.

26 Adam Smith, *The Wealth of Nations: Books I–III* (Kiribati: Penguin Publishing Group, 1982), 232; Sheilagh Ogilvie, 'The Economics of Guilds', *Journal of Economic Perspectives*, Vol. 28, No. 4, 2014, 169–92, 177.

27 Smith, *Wealth of Nations* 1.10.2; Adam Smith, *The Theory of Moral Sentiments*, edited by D. D. Raphael and A. L. Macfie (Oxford: Clarendon Press, 1976), 139–44.

28 Quoted in Harold J. Laski, *Communist Manifesto: Socialist Landmark* (Abingdon, Oxon: Routledge, 2014), 120.

29 Vaninskaya, 'The Middle Ages', 118.

30 Ogilvie, 'Economics of Guilds', 172.

31 Craig Muldrew, 'Interpreting the Market: The Ethics of Credit and Community Relations in Early Modern England', *Social History*, Vol. 18, No. 2, May 1993, 163–83, doi:10.1080/03071029308567871, 172–73.

32 Sheilagh Ogilvie, 'The European Guilds: A Lecture by Sheilagh Ogilvie' (London: King's College London, 2019), 02:57–04:46.

33 Sheilagh Ogilvie, *The European Guilds: An Economic Analysis* (Princeton, NJ: Princeton University Press, 2018), 2.

34 Melvin Kranzberg, 'Prerequisites for Industrialization', in *Technology in Western Civilization*, edited by Melvin Kranzberg and Carroll W. Pursell, Vol. 1 (Oxford: Oxford University Press, 1967), 217–29, 228–29.

35 Kranzberg, 'Prerequisites for Industrialization', 228–29.

36 Antony Black, *Guilds and Civil Society in European Political Thought from the Twelfth Century to the Present*, 1st edn (London: Methuen Young Books, 1983), 10.

37 One well-known and emotive commentary on those times comes from William Blake in the preface to his poem *Milton: A Poem in Two Books* written between 1804 and 1810. The text is popularly known as the hymn 'Jerusalem', which was set to music by Sir Hubert Parry in 1916. In the poem and hymn, Blake imagines Jesus Christ returning to 'England's green and pleasant land' to create a new heaven, in contrast to 'dark Satanic Mills' (see William Blake, 'Milton a Poem', edited by Morris Eaves, Robert N. Essick and Joseph Viscomi, *Blake: An Illustrated Quarterly*, Vol. 29, No. 3, Winter 1996, 91–92, 91). A literal interpretation would suggest dark satanic mills are the new factories of the Industrial Revolution; however, most commentators imagine them to be the institutions of society, possibly including the Church of England.

38 Paul Schlicke, 'Popular Culture and the Impact of Industrialization', *The British Library*, 2–3.

39 Epstein and Prak, *Guilds*, 7.

40 Antony Black, *Corporatism, Medieval and Modern* (Dundee: University of Dundee, Department of Political Science & Social Policy, 1992), 6.

41 Patrick Wallis, 'Apprenticeship and Training in Premodern England', *The Journal of Economic History*, Vol. 68, No. 3, Sept. 2008, 832–61, *Cambridge Core*, doi:10.1017/S002205070800065X, 24.

42 Wallis, 'Apprenticeship and Training', 24.

43 Ogilvie, 'Economics of Guilds', 181.

44 Walter Cahn, *Masterpieces: Chapters on the History of An Idea* (Princeton, NJ: Princeton University Press, 1979), 3.

45 Cahn, *Masterpieces*, 4.

46 Étienne Boileau, *Les métiers et corporations de Paris : XIIIe siècle. Le livre des métiers (Book of Trades) d'Étienne Boileau (1879)* (Hachette Livre-BNF, 2012), 4.

47 Boileau, *Book of Trades*, 5.

48 Boileau, *Book of Trades*, 5.

49 Cahn, Walter, *Masterpieces: Chapters on the History of An Idea* (Princeton, NJ: Princeton University Press, 1979), 5.

50 Ward, Adolphus William, *History of English Dramatic Literature to the Death of Queen Anne* (Macmillan and Co., 1875), 23.

51 Letellier, Robert Ignatius, *The Bible in Music* (Cambridge Scholars Publishing, 2017), 2.

52 Letellier, Robert Ignatius, *The Bible in Music*, 2.

7

Contemporary Apprenticeship

Tell me, and I will listen; teach me, and I'll remember; involve me, and I will learn.

Unknown Chinese apprentice (third century BC)[1]

Contemporary apprenticeship training

Apprenticeship in the medieval guilds has been described in the previous chapter; this section brings this analysis up to date, exploring the dynamics of apprenticeship training in the contemporary era. As in the guilds, the specific focus is a form of apprenticeship known as 'guided apprenticeship learning,' which is characterized by guided-learning from experts, through participation in authentic workplace tasks.[2] Areas considered include situated learning and the related theories of communities of practice and legitimate periphery participation, the practical model of situational leadership training, and short summaries of the dynamics of mimetic learning, tacit knowledge and scaffolding.

History of apprenticeship

Apprenticeship has existed as a pedagogical model since at least the Neolithic Agricultural Revolution, when humans began to live in settled communities and the earliest proto-cities, more than 10,000 years ago.[3] For example, apprenticeship forms of vocational education are known to have existed before 3000 BC in the ancient Sumerian city of Mesopotamia and apprenticeship was an established element of society at the time of the Pharaohs in ancient Egypt and ancient Greek and Roman civilizations.[4]

For most of human history, apprenticeship-style training has been the core method of developing novice workers through a mode of teaching and participatory learning which is rooted in work-related activities and 'dependent on participation of the learner in work-related activities'.[5] Through apprenticeship training, a novice develops into a full participant in a community of practice through direct guidance and the informal learning afforded by the workplace.[6] As a mode of learning, apprenticeship is significantly different to the didactic classroom training which is ubiquitous in modern formal learning systems. The pre-eminence of the apprenticeship mode of training is noted by researchers, such as Brigitte Jordan, who observes, 'Whatever the origins of the didactic mode, it has always been a minor mode of knowledge acquisition in our evolutionary history.' Likewise, Joan Lane believes that apprenticeship in British and European training heritage was one of the most important means by which occupational training was supplied in pre-modern Europe: 'Apprenticeship is part of the social history of England.'[7]

The English word 'apprentice' developed in the fourteenth century as a contraction of the Latin word *apprehendre*, which is an imperative for learners to apprehend or seize knowledge from what was being enacted around them.[8] Stephen Billett, Professor for Adult Vocational Education in the School of Education and Professional Studies at Griffith University in Australia, notes this distinctive characteristic of the historic apprenticeship mode of education when he observes, '[B]efore [modernity] individuals *learnt*, rather than being *taught*.'[9] This learning, says Billett, occurred through processes of observation, imitation and practice: a process that is termed mimetic learning.[10]

Apprenticeship is a method of training in which a beginner develops to occupational proficiency through on-the-job learning. It characteristically includes an emphasis on training through real-work and on-the-job assignments, which are typically overseen by experienced supervisors who learned in the same manner themselves. In some contexts, an apprentice may receive bespoke training that has a focus on the development of individual skill, resulting in an experienced practitioner with a distinctive and personal style. Apprentices may receive additional didactic instruction, as well as learning together in peer-community.[11]

Situated learning

According to social anthropologist Jean Lave and educational theorist Étienne Charles Wenger, who co-formulated the theory of situated cognition, situated learning is an example of apprenticeship where learning takes place as a function of the context, culture and social situation in which it occurs.[12] As such, situated learning is a theory about how human minds develop in a social context, using tools from that culture to learn, remember and understand.[13]

Lave and Wenger argue that learning is necessarily situated through a process or participation in communities of practice and that newcomers join such communities through a 'process of legitimate peripheral participation', or learning by immersion in the new community and absorbing its modes of action and meaning as part of the process of becoming a full community member.[14]

In situated learning theory, thinking and acting cannot be separated from the sociocultural context in which they arise, because knowledge is not decontextualized, abstract or general. Because of this, says Billett, '[the] learning activities of vocational practitioners are derived from a culture of practice which has developed over time.'[15]

Lave and Wenger argue that apprenticeship modes of learning can be found in communities of practice where novices are progressively exposed to the skills and activities of experts and where social interaction is a vital component of the accumulation of skills and ideas. For novices to join such communities, they need to adopt a 'legitimate' yet 'peripheral' participatory role in the community, termed legitimate peripheral participation.[16]

As a methodology, situated learning assists an apprentice to learn, acquire and integrate the different types of knowledge and experiences required for the mastery of vocational practice. Workplaces offer rich environments where learners can observe, participate and be guided by local experts within an existing culture of practice.[17]

Billett suggests there are three important aspects to the cognitive activities which are utilized when an individual engages in thinking or learning in an apprenticeship context. The first is propositional knowledge, comprising facts, abstract ideas, concepts and propositions; the second is procedural knowledge, which comprises methods, skills and the ability to achieve goals. These are colloquially termed 'knowledge that' and 'knowledge how' respectively, and form that base of an individuals' knowledge. Because the answer to the questions, 'What is important?' and, 'Why is it important?' in a workplace requires more than propositions and procedures, these knowledge types are conditional on Billett's third aspect, attributes and values. These are associated work skills, such as personal values, attitudes and social values. Attributes and values assist the practitioner in a learning journey by answering questions such as, 'Is this worth doing?' and, 'If so, how well?'[18]

From the perspective of the instructor, the situated learning apprenticeship model of instruction involves four phases: modelling, coaching, scaffolding and fading. In the apprentice's activity, the first three correspond to observation, training and practice respectively.[19] Modelling occurs when a learner observes an expert execute a task. From these types of experience, a beginner can build a conceptual model of the processes required to complete a task well.[20] This process requires experts to verbalize their internal thinking to assist the learners to gain procedural and cognitive knowledge. Just as modelling occurs when a learner observes an expert at work, coaching follows when an expert observes a learner as he or she attempts new activities. Experts can provide hints, suggestions, supportive comments, clues, 'tricks of the trade' and feedback to assist the learner to achieve the desired outcome; and coaching may require repeated demonstrations of a task, or parts of a task, before the learner has gained the new skill.[21] Learners might connect with several experts, and through this gain exposure to a variety of models of expertise. This variety of modelling helps apprentices to understand that there may be multiple ways of carrying out a task and to recognize that no one trainer embodies all knowledge or expertise.[22] Scaffolding refers to the range of support that experts can provide for learners as they progress towards being experienced workers. This can include opportunities to learn which are within the learner's ability, ongoing reminders and suggestions, assisting with part of the task, and cooperative problem-solving. The concept of scaffolding was devised by Jerome S. Bruner in 1976 as 'a process whereby the teacher helped students by doing what the child could not do at first, and allowing students to slowly take over parts of the ... process as they were able to do so'.[23] A requisite for effective scaffolding is a diagnostic of the learner's current level of skill and the difficulty of the task.[24] Fading consists of the gradual removal of support until the learner can function autonomously. At this stage, the expert may switch to a mode of passive support, where support is only provided at the apprentice's request.

Communities of practice

Jean Lave and Étienne Wenger (Wenger-Trayner) coined the term 'community of practice' while studying apprenticeship as a learning model in the late 1980s and early 1990s. Communities of practice describe the learning interactions of an apprentice beyond the student-master relationship. Wenger defines communities of practice as 'groups of people who share a concern, a set of problems, or a passion about a topic, and who deepen their knowledge and expertise in the area by interacting on an ongoing basis'.[25] In Wenger's words, the term was coined to describe a community that acts as 'a living curriculum for the apprentice'.[26] In this section, I am indebted to the paper 'Communities of Practice – A Brief Introduction' (2015) by Étienne and Beverly Wenger-Trayner, which is the most recently published summary of communities of practice.

From their research, Wenger-Trayner and Wenger-Trayner have shown that communities of practice bring together several different aspects of training that take place within apprenticeship communities. They say, 'People usually think of an apprenticeship as a relationship between a student and a master, but studies of apprenticeship reveal a more complex set of social relationships through which learning takes place mostly with journeymen and more advanced apprentices.'[27] If their observations are correct, then learning in a community of practice benefits – and is dependent on – the involvement of learners at different stages of development.

A community of practice is a group of people who have a shared interest in a craft. Because of their mutual passion for something they love and do, they continue to learn about their craft through their regular interaction,[28] and create a set of relationships over time.[29] A community of practice is more than a network of informal relationships because it is focused on 'something' beyond the relationships themselves. Consequently, it continues to exist because it produces a 'shared practice as members engage in the collective process of learning'.[30]

Communities of practice may well be known by other names, such as learning communities, networks, or thematic groups. They can be a small group of committed people or a large group, with a core and a periphery of members; they might meet in-person, or online, or both. Such groups have 'existed for as long as human beings have learned together'.[31] Through connections in home-life, at work, at school and recreational activities, people all belong to numerous communities of practice. Wenger says, 'in some we are core members[:] in many, we are merely peripheral'.[32]

Wenger-Trayner and Wenger-Trayner distinguish communities of practice from other kinds of community or group by three critical elements. First, a community of practice has a defined shared domain of interest, which imparts identity to the community and determines an implicit membership, defined by a commitment to the activity of the domain. Second, a community of practice is self-evidently an intentional community of members who engage in joint activities, mutual help, and who share information. Members of the community build relationships within the community that facilitate learning from each other. Because of this, communities of practice innovate, solve problems, invent new practices, create new knowledge and define new territory.[33] Third, members of communities of practice are 'practitioners with a shared competence or practice'.[34] As a community, they produce a shared repertoire of experience, techniques, resources, vocabulary and ways of addressing recurring problems, which can be summarized as a shared practice.[35] Using research conducted through the IBM Institute for Knowledge Management, E. L. Lesser and J. Storck have shown that communities of practice can help develop and maintain a long-term organizational memory.[36]

Legitimate peripheral participation

The term 'legitimate peripheral participation' describes the experience-journey of an apprentice into a community of practice through engagement with activities that enable the novice to become acquainted with the practices of the community's existing members. Lave and Wenger summarize their understanding:

> Learning viewed as situated activity has as its central defining characteristic a process that we call legitimate peripheral participation. By this we mean to draw attention to the point that learners inevitably participate in communities of practitioners and that the mastery of knowledge requires newcomers to move toward full participation in the socio-cultural practices of a community.[37]

Through participation in activities and a process of social learning, newcomers work their way towards full inclusion in the community of practice and the mastery of the skills, knowledge and cultural practices of the group. New apprentices initially participate by engaging with tasks that are peripheral to the activity of expert members. Through engagement with these activities, novices become acquainted with the tasks, vocabulary and organizing principles of the community's existing practitioners. Additionally, the social inclusion of newcomers allows them to participate in activities, albeit ones of lower importance, that provide them with the 'legitimacy' of being up-front members of these communities, thus establishing the basis for fuller future participation.

Wenger suggests that the characteristics of 'peripherality' can include lessened intensity, lessened risk, close supervision and lessened production pressures. He also identifies aspects of legitimacy as including: being useful, being sponsored, being feared, being the right kind of person, and having been born into the right social class.[38] Legitimate peripheral participation provides a way to describe the relationship between the novices and experts in a community of practice through an understanding of training that focuses more on learning than institutional instruction, and learning from a social rather than a cognitive perspective.

Situational leadership theory

Situational leadership theory was developed by Paul Hersey and Ken Blanchard in the 1960s from their research into the management of organizational behaviour. The authors set out their model in the article 'Life Cycle Theory of Leadership' (1969) and book *Management of Organizational Behavior: Utilizing Human Resources* (1969). A defining principle of the situational leadership model is that effective mentors adjust their training style to fit the current needs of the learner and the task being attempted. Both authors subsequently developed their variants of the initial model, and their concepts were also popularized by various authors.

In their model, Hersey and Blanchard categorize the behaviour of trainers using a four-box grid, with axes of 'task behaviour' and 'relationship behaviour'. The resulting segments each describe a training-style and are labelled S1 to S4, where S1 is directing, S2 is coaching, S3 is supporting and S4 is delegating (see Figure 7.1).

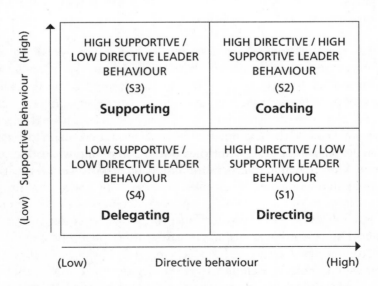

Figure 7.1: Hersey-Blanchard situational leadership training-styles

In Blanchard's model, these leadership-styles are matched to the maturity levels of the learner which are described using a matching four-box grid with axes of confidence and competence. These learner-styles are labelled M1 to M4, where M4 is very capable and confident; M3 is unable but confident; M2 is capable but unwilling; and M1 is unable and insecure.

'The Square' is a popularized application of situational leadership theory produced by Mike Breen and Walt Kallestad.[39] It is one of eight discipleship tools, called LifeShapes, which are based on simple geometric shapes and used as a rule of life for The Order of Mission and churches in the 3DM Network. Breen and Kallestad's Square is a four-stage process to develop an apprentice into master, visualized as a square. Each side of the square maps to a Hersey-Blanchard leadership-style and learner-style, identifying the stage of the learner and the preferred leadership-style of the trainer. In colloquial language, the steps are: 'I do: you watch', 'I do: you help', 'you do: I help', and 'you do: I watch' (see Figure 7.2).

Figure 7.2: Breen-Kallestad 'The Square'

Situational leadership is an example of master-apprentice training and legitimate peripheral participation, where the four training-styles match the modelling-coaching-scaffolding-fading phases of the situated learning apprenticeship model.[40]

Mimetic learning

In concluding this section two final concepts are briefly considered: mimetic learning and tacit knowledge. Mimetic learning is learning by imitation or mimicry.[41] It constitutes one of the most important processes of learning, one that has existed for as long as human beings have worked together. In family life, for example, children instinctively mimic the actions and behaviour of their parents, and in so doing learn by mimesis. In *Things Hidden Since the Foundation of the World* (1978), René Girard makes the bold claim that all human behaviour is based upon mimesis.[42] Stephen Billett agrees with Girard on this point but notes that the observation is not apparent to modern society, because mimetic learning is less obvious in 'schooled societies'.[43] Brigitte Jordan makes the same point:

> In the West, however, the didactic mode of teaching and learning has come to prevail in our schools to such an extent that it is often taken for granted as the most natural, as well as the most efficacious and efficient, way of going about teaching and learning. This view is held despite the many instances in our own culture of learning through observation and imitation.[44]

Christoph Wulf builds on Girard's claim, saying that mimetic learning is related to the whole body, by which he means that it is a multisensory and bodily process, not just an intellectual one. His corollary is that 'to a large extent, cultural learning is mimetic learning'.[45] Wulf summarises: '[Mimetic learning] establishes a connection between the individual and the world as well as other persons; it creates practical knowledge, which is what makes it constitutive of social, artistic, and practical action.'[46]

Tacit knowledge

Propositional knowledge consists of information that is factual, theoretical, logical and explicit. As such it can be recorded and learned from printed sources. By contrast, tacit knowledge – a term coined by Michael Polanyi – consists of information that is difficult to pass to another person using writing or verbal communication.[47] John Seely Brown and Paul Duguid believe knowledge that is tacit is intuitive and hard to define information that is colloquially referred to as 'know-how'.[48] Because it cannot be articulated, Polanyi says, 'We can know more than we can tell.'[49] This latent nature of tacit knowledge leads some to see it as the most valuable kind of knowledge. For example, Jerry Wellman says, 'Although tacit knowledge is the most difficult to recognize and handle, it is often the tacit knowledge that leads to significant breakthroughs and is of more value to the organization.'[50] Because tacit knowledge is located within the relationships between people, Stephan R. Epstein and Maarten Roy Prak believe that 'tacit knowledge happens most effectively in "communities of practice", like craft guilds'.[51]

Scaffolding

Instructional scaffolding (which has already been mentioned in this chapter) is a method of on-the-job training where an expert instructor accelerates and enhances the learning experience for a student through direct support. The theory was first explored in the late 1950s by Jerome Bruner when studying language development in children, although it was inspired by Lev Vygotsky's sociocultural theories about community learning and development, expert assistance, and the zone of proximal development.[52] The zone of proximal development is defined as the gap between what a student can do without assistance and what they can do with the support of a more knowledgeable peer or instructor.[53]

Scaffolding includes at least four elements. First, the instructor and the student need to be working collaboratively on a shared task. Second, support should be tailored to each student. Third, learning should take place within the student's zone of proximal development. And last, as the student becomes more competent, the support and guidance provided by the instructor is progressively reduced.[54] The goal is that the student gains a deeper and accelerated learning journey towards independent ability. In Vygotsky's words, 'what the [student] is able to do in collaboration today he will be able to do independently tomorrow'.[55]

Examples of scaffolding can include 'modelling behaviours, coaching and prompting, thinking out loud, dialogue with questions and answers, planned and spontaneous discussions, as well as other interactive planning or structural assistance'.[56] Scaffolding can be provided by expert instructors or what Vygotsky terms 'More Knowledgeable Others', who might be more advanced students.

Conclusion

Apprenticeship is the most natural form of training: a more experienced person models skills to another and nurtures them in their learning. Almost every human society has examples of this type of learning by mimicry, which usually occurs in a shared working context that can be termed a 'Community of Practice'. Though the historic guilds have passed, modern theories of situated learning have in fact validated many of the key elements that we have identified in the apprenticeship process. At the same time, modern learning theories offer models of learning that are not strictly hierarchical but also communal, they encourage not only mastery of 'styles' but highly original responses to unpredictable situations. These too are vital insights for training today's church planters in their craft.

Questions

1 How might we facilitate 'legitimate peripheral participation' for emerging leaders in churches? What would need to change in our practice for churches to be 'communities of practice' for immersive training?

2 If tacit knowledge ('know-how' and organizational memory) is held and transferred in communities of practice what does that mean for how we train church planters?

3 How might we apply the concepts of scaffolding and fading to accelerate the training of church planters?

4 How might a church or theological college be a living curriculum for apprentices in training?

5 How might we recover mimetic learning – especially in the 'schooled societies' of the West – to create multisensory learning for practitioners?

Notes

1 This aphorism is often attributed to Benjamin Franklin; however, Eric L. Hutton suggests there is no evidence for this and attributes the original saying to Xun Kuang, a Confucian philosopher who lived in the third century BC. Hutton's translation reads: 'Not having heard of it is not as good as having heard of it. Having heard of it is not as good as having seen it. Having seen it is not as good as knowing it. Knowing it is not as good as putting it into practice. Learning arrives at putting it into practice and then stops ...' See Hutton, *The Achievements of the Ru* (Princeton, NJ: Princeton University Press, 2014), 64. Several versions in English exist, the version quoted was first published in 1986. See Jack C. Richards and Theodore S. Rodgers, *Approaches and Methods in Language Teaching: A Description and Analysis* (Cambridge: Cambridge University Press, 1986), 100.

2 Stephen Billett, 'Situating Learning in the Workplace – Having Another Look at Apprenticeships', *Industrial and Commercial Training*, Vol. 26, No. 11, Dec. 1994, 9–16, doi:10.1108/00197859410073745, 11.

3 Stephen Billett, 'Apprenticeship as a Mode of Learning and Model of Education', *Education + Training*, Vol. 58, No. 6, 2016, 613–28, doi:10.1108/ET-01-2016-0001, 618.

4 Stephen Billett, 'Apprenticeship as a Mode of Learning', 618.

5 Geoffrey Gowlland, 'Apprenticeship as a Model for Learning in and Through Professional Practice', in *International Handbook of Research in Professional and Practice-Based Learning*, edited by Stephen Billett et al. (New York: Springer, 2014), 759–79. 760.

6 Gowlland 'Apprenticeship as a Model for Learning', 760, 776.

7 Joan Lane, *Apprenticeship in England, 1600–1914* (London: UCL Press, 1996), 1.

8 'Apprentice', *Oxford Dictionary of English*, third edn (Oxford: Oxford University Press, 2010), 77.

9 Billett, 'Apprenticeship as a Mode of Learning', 618, emphasis added.

10 Stephen Billett, *Mimetic Learning at Work: Learning in the Circumstances of Practice.* (New York: Springer, 2014).

11 Jean Lave and Etienne Wenger, *Situated Learning: Legitimate Peripheral Participation* (Cambridge: Cambridge University Press, 1991), 59–83.

12 Lave and Wenger, *Situated Learning*, 15.

13 Lave and Wenger, *Situated Learning*, 11.

14 Lave and Wenger, *Situated Learning*, 14.

15 Billett, 'Situating Learning in the Workplace', 9.

16 Andrew Parker, 'Lifelong Learning to Labour: Apprenticeship, Masculinity and Communities of Practice', *British Educational Research Journal*, Vol. 32, No. 5, 2006, 687–701. Wiley Online Library, doi:10.1080/01411920600895734.690.

17 Billett, 'Situating Learning in the Workplace', 9.

18 Billett, 'Situating Learning in the Workplace', 10.

19 Allan Collins et al., 'Cognitive Apprenticeship: Teaching the Crafts of Reading, Writing, and Mathematics', in *Knowing, Learning, and Instruction: Essays in Honor of Robert Glaser* (New Jersey: Lawrence Erlbaum Associates, Inc., 1989), 453–94, 456–57.

20 Billett, 'Situating Learning in the Workplace', 11.

21 Billett, 'Situating Learning in the Workplace', 11.

22 Collins et al., 'Cognitive Apprenticeship', 457.

23 Trevor H. Cairney, *Pathways to Literacy* (London: Continuum International, 1995), 36; David Wood, et al., 'The Role of Tutoring in Problem Solving', *Journal of Child Psychology and Psychiatry*, Vol. 17, No. 2, Dec. 2006, 89–100, doi:10.1111/j.1469-7610.1976.tb00381.x, 90, 98.

24 Billett, 'Situating Learning in the Workplace', 12.

25 Etienne Wenger et al., *Cultivating Communities of Practice: A Guide to Managing Knowledge* (Brighton, MA: Harvard Business School Press, 2002), 4.

26 Wenger et al., *Cultivating Communities*, 38.

27 Etienne Wenger-Trayner and Beverly Wenger-Trayner, *Communities of Practice: A Brief Introduction*, 2015, at http://wenger-trayner.com/introduction-to-communities-of-practice/, Para. 4 (accessed 28.1.2022).

28 Wenger-Trayner and Wenger-Trayner, *Communities of Practice*, 1.

29 Lave and Wenger, *Situated Learning*, 98.

30 Etienne Wenger, *Communities of Practice: Learning, Meaning, and Identity* (Cambridge: Cambridge University Press, 1998), 4.

31 Wenger, *Communities of Practice*, 4.

32 Wenger, *Communities of Practice*, 4.

33 Wenger-Trayner and Wenger-Trayner, *Communities of Practice*, 6.

34 Barbara Slater Stern, ed., *Curriculum and Teaching Dialogue* (Charlotte, NC: Information Age Publishing, 2008), 274.

35 Wenger-Trayner and Wenger-Trayner, *Communities of Practice*, 2.

36 E. L. Lesser and J. Storck, 'Communities of Practice and Organizational

Performance', *IBM Systems Journal*, Vol. 40, No. 4, 2001, 831–41, doi:10.1147/sj.404.0831.832, 832.

37 Lave and Wenger, *Situated Learning*, 29.

38 Wenger, *Communities of Practice*, 101.

39 Mike Breen and Walt Kallestad, *The Passionate Life* (Eastbourne, East Sussex: Kingsway Publications, 2005), 109–33.

40 Collins et al., 'Cognitive Apprenticeship', 456–57.

41 Christoph Wulf, 'Mimésis et Apprentissage Culturel', *Le Télémaque*, Vol. 45, No. 1, 2014, 123–36, doi:10.3917/tele.045.0123, 123.

42 René Girard, et al., *Things Hidden Since the Foundation of the World*, translated by Stephen Bann and Michael Leigh Metteer (London: Bloomsbury Academic, 1978), 7, 26, 307.

43 Stephen Billett, *Mimetic Learning at Work: Learning in the Circumstances of Practice* (New York: Springer, 2014), 2.

44 Brigitte Jordan, 'Cosmopolitical Obstetrics: Some Insights from the Training of Traditional Midwives', *Social Science & Medicine*, Vol. 28, No. 9, Jan. 1989, 925–37, doi:10.1016/0277-9536(89)90317-1, 932.

45 Wulf, 'Mimésis', 123.

46 Christoph Wulf, 'Mimetic Learning', *Designs for Learning*, Vol. 1, No. 1, Mar. 2008, doi:10.16993/DFL.8, 56.

47 Michael Polanyi, *Personal Knowledge: Towards a Post-Critical Philosophy* (London: Routledge, 1997), 96.

48 John Seely Brown and Paul Duguid, 'Organizing Knowledge', *California Management Review*, Vol. 40, No. 3, 1998, 90–111, doi:10.2307/41165945.

49 Michael Polanyi, *The Tacit Dimension* (New York: Doubleday, 1966), 4.

50 Jerry Wellman, 'Introduction', in *Organizational Learning: How Companies and Institutions Manage and Apply Knowledge* (Reston, VA: AIAA, 2009), 1–26, 21.

51 Epstein and Prak, *Guilds*, 6.

52 See D. Wood and H. Wood, 'Vygotsky, tutoring and learning', *Oxford Review of Education*, Vol. 22, No. 1, 1996, 5–16.

53 E. Ellis and L. Worthington, *Research Synthesis on Effective Teaching Principles and the Design of Quality Tools for Educators* (Eugene, OR: University of Oregon, 1994), at http://people.uncw.edu/kozloffm/ellisressynth.pdf (accessed 28.1.2022).

54 P. Beed, M. Hawkins, and C. Roller (1991), 'Moving Learners Towards Independence: The Power of Scaffolded Instruction', *The Reading Teacher*, Vol. 44, No. 9, 648–55.

55 L. S. Vygotsky, 'Thinking and Speech', in L. S. Vygotsky, *Collected works*, Vol. 1, 39–285, edited by R. Rieber and A. Carton, translated by N. Minick (New York: Plenum), 211 (original works published in 1934, 1960).

56 'Instructional Scaffolding', *Wikipedia*, Wikimedia Foundation, 2 Sept. 2021, at https://en.wikipedia.org/wiki/Instructional_scaffolding (accessed 28.1.2022).

8

Ministerial Formation

Jesus said, 'I will build my church,' but he has equipped church planters to be master craftsmen to help him.

Ron Anderson[1]

May God grant me to speak with judgement,
and to have thoughts worthy of what I have received;
for he is the guide even of wisdom
and the corrector of the wise.
For both we and our words are in his hand,
as are all understanding and skill in crafts.

Solomon's prayer for wisdom, Wisdom 7.15–16

This section considers the subject of ministerial formation, especially as it applies to future church planters.[2] Through the select examples in this chapter a picture of formation emerges which, at points, is flexible, practical, radically holistic and character-focused. There are significant resources here for our reimagination of training today. In exploring the development of ministerial formation over nearly two millennia, it is a challenge to document all the significant developments. This section focuses on only four areas that illustrate something of the development through time, diversity of approaches and practical focus of models of training.

Ministerial formation in the early centuries of Christianity

There is very little extant extra-biblical evidence of instruction from the earliest centuries of the Christian church on the spiritual formation and education of Christian leaders. The ancient text, *Training of the Twelve Disciples: The Lord's Teaching Through the Twelve Apostles to the Nations*, which is commonly referred to as *The Didache*, is a first-century Christian treatise that offers probably the first reflection from the Apostolic Fathers on sacerdotal training. For example, it says, 'Appoint, then, for yourselves bishops and deacons worthy of the Lord, ... for they themselves are your honoured ones with the prophets-teachers.'[3] *The Didache* was rediscovered in 1873 by Philotheos Bryennios, the Greek Orthodox Metropolitan of Nicomedia. It is mentioned by Eusebius of Caesarea as a pre-canon text that is useful, alongside the books of Scripture, for understanding Christian living and ministry. He says,

> Let there be placed among the spuria the writing of the Acts of Paul, the so-called Shepherd and the Apocalypse of Peter, and besides these the Epistle known as that of Barnabas, and what are called the Teachings of the Apostles [Didache], and also ... the Apocalypse of John, if this be thought fit.[4]

The material of *The Didache* functioned as an early pre-canon ministry guide for first-century Christian novices looking to follow the 'Way of Life'.[5] The text was written between AD 65 and AD 80 and was likely to have been compiled and edited by several redactors.[6] Vernon Bartlet suggests that the beginning of the document, which focuses on the 'two ways: one of life and one of death,' may have an oral Jewish catechesis as its source;[7] however, most of the remaining material either parallels or quotes New Testament writing, especially the Sermon on the Mount, Acts, the pastoral epistles and Matthew, as well as Malachi from the Old Testament.[8]

The 16 chapters of *The Didache* are organized in three parts. The first part (Chapters 1–6) consists of catechetical lessons and the 'two ways'; the second (Chapters 7–10) concerns the liturgy of Christian rites including baptism, prayer and fasting and the Eucharist; the third part (Chapters 11–16) discusses aspects of ministry and church leadership including the role of itinerant ministers of apostles and prophets, as well as the local ministers who are identified as bishops and deacons. However, Claudia Rapp notes that 'with its omission of presbyters, the Didache reflects a time before the development of the tripartite hierarchy of deacons-presbyters-bishop'.[9]

Polycarp, the second-century Bishop of Smyrna, outlined the importance of the Christian minister's witness in life as an authentic disciple of Christ; his good character and practical skills in pastoral ministry are also listed as being important. Polycarp (d. AD 155), who was a disciple of

John the Apostle, writes, 'The presbyter must be tender-hearted, merciful toward all, turning back the sheep that has gone astray, visiting the sick, not neglecting the widow or orphan or poor man.'[10] Consistent with the teaching of the New Testament, these two ancient sources outline the character and implied education requirements needed by early Christian ministers.

Not all clergy and bishops in the early church were educated or suited to academic study. The *Apostolic Constitutions*, compiled in the fourth century, are a collection of treatises on early ecclesiastical law, ethics, clergy duties and liturgy. Book Two, which is a rewording of the *Didascalia Apostolorum*, comments on the appointment of illiterate bishops in Chapter one, verse one.[11] Claudia Rapp translates this verse as 'Let him [bishop or priest] be educated, if that is possible. But even if he is illiterate, let him be experienced in scripture, having the proper age.'[12] Rapp also notes Eusebius' observation of a priest called Malchion, who was the head of a school of rhetoric in Antioch, who owed his appointment to the priesthood to 'the surpassing sincerity of his faith in Christ', and not to his education or intellectual ability.[13] Rapp concludes that prospective bishops and clergy in the early church might be unsuited to study, and even illiterate; however, they can be appointed, if their character matches the descriptions in 1 Timothy, especially the responsibility to keep their households in order.[14]

Patterns of formation in monasticism

The advent of the Monastic age saw the emergence of a new pattern of formational training that comprised study, asceticism and a common life in community. John Tracy Ellis notes that 50 years before Augustine of Hippo (d. AD 430), Eusebius of Vercelli (d. AD 371) 'combined the monastic discipline with a common life for the parochial clergy with whom he lived personally'.[15] Not long after Augustine became the Bishop of Hippo in AD 396, says Ellis, 'his [Augustine's] episcopal residence at Hippo was the school for the superiors of a good many monastic houses as well as for a considerable number of diocesan bishops, and in this way clerical community became a model for imitation elsewhere'.[16] Ellis notes that these early examples of monastic training emphasized education and training in the community, as well as the involvement of bishops in receiving and, presumably, giving training to others.[17] In monastic life, clerical training becomes a community experience where postulants learn alongside, and under, the supervision of bishops. The human, spiritual and intellectual formation modelled by Augustine was experienced through living in community in his Hippo residence,[18] where common life was of such importance that Augustine had a rule that no one would be ordained a priest unless he had lived in community for some time.[19] Augustine's legacy was an educated clergy who were formed in the community.

The monasteries founded by Benedict of Nursia (d. AD 543) trained priests in addition to their other work. However, according to Benedict's Rule, his *opus Dei* (work of God) was to be undertaken by everyone, of whom only some were priests, and these were admitted in to the community as a discrete body.[20] That said, Clark notes that in the monasteries, 'there can be little doubt the ablest candidates were accelerated towards ordination'.[21] Priests in training were developed in community, as Clark says, 'The pedagogic link between the novitiate and ordination was underpinned by the efforts of convents whenever possible to progress their candidates together as a cohort.'[22]

The motto of the Benedictine Confederation, *ora et labora* (pray and work), speaks of the value of reflective learning, where every experience in life is an opportunity to learn. Learning through experience is highlighted several times in Benedict's Rule and monks would have spent several hours each day in silent private prayer and reading Scripture provided daily opportunity for reflective learning.[23] Columba Stewart suggests that the three distinctive aspects of monastic training are: community living, a monastic rule, and a superior or monastic leader.[24] Bede (d. 735) gives an insight into the monastic formation in his day:

> I have spent all the remainder of my life in this monastery and devoted myself entirely to the study of the Scriptures. And while I have observed the regular discipline and sung the choir offices daily in church, my chief delight has always been in study, teaching, and writing.[25]

The combination of study, teaching and writing was called the *trivium* (the meeting of three roads) which included Latin grammar, logic and rhetoric, which provided a grounding in academic literacy. In addition to regular manual work, monks spent several hours each day in sacred reading, which included reading and copying the Scriptures and reading monastic writings and the writings of the Church Fathers. Later in the early medieval period, monastic formation also included the *quadrivium* (the meeting of four roads), which consisted of arithmetic, geometry, music and astronomy. The preparatory work of the *trivium* followed by the *quadrivium* was the prerequisite for the studying of philosophy and theology by clergy in training.[26]

Effects of the English Reformation and the Roman Catholic Counter-Reformation on the training of clergy

It is generally accepted that the Protestant Reformation initiated a radical transformation of the ministry and training of the clergy. David Cornick notes, for example, that English clergy moved from being 'socially separate,' often not living near their churches, to being locally-based parish priests who became known as 'ministers' because of their changed duties, or termed 'presbyters' in contrast to the more catholic term of 'priest'.[27] Bruce Gordon shows that the ministry of the English priest shifted in focus from the administration of the sacraments to an emphasis on preaching, teaching and pastoral discipleship.[28] R. N. Swanson notes that the new functions of reformed clergy required them to be trained as 'professional and self-consciously elite cadres'.[29] Amy Nelson Burnett writes that newly ordained clergy often 'served an apprenticeship through assisting an older priest'.[30]

Over several generations, the training of the English reformed clergy developed and expanded to reflect a change in the understanding of ordained ministry. Two examples offer an insight into these changes. The first comes from John Colet, the Dean of St Paul's Cathedral in London who was also a friend of the reformer Desiderius Erasmus of Rotterdam. In 1512 – five years before Martin Luther came to prominence with the *Ninety-Five Theses*, and a decade before the main developments of the Swiss Reformation – Colet addressed the clergy of the Convocation of Canterbury Province on 'the reformation of the church'. He called for a 'reformation and restoration in ecclesiastical affairs' which would require an exemplary clergy, living simple and non-indulgent lives, who had a focus on personal prayer, private reading of the Scriptures, and a public ministering of the word of God 'for the souls of men'. In attacking abuses and idolatry in the church and calling for a return to the Scriptures – believing that the study of the Bible was the only route to holiness – Colet anticipated the Reformation that would begin around the time of his death.[31]

The second example is from Ordinal of the Church of England, which is usually published alongside the *Book of Common Prayer* (1662). The 1662 Ordinal is a development of Thomas Cranmer's Ordinal of 1550 which reflected the tenets of the European Reformation[32] including some revisions proposed by Martin Bucer, the one-time mentor of John Calvin.[33] The Ordinal affirms that priests are ordained to both the ministry of the sacraments and the ministry of the word, though the greater focus is placed on the ministry of the word; preaching and teaching. In the rite, priests are described as 'messengers' and 'watchmen and stewards of the Lord.' Commenting on this, Paul Avis concludes, 'Thus the tools of their trade are words in the forms of texts and speech.'[34] The Protestant Reformation, in Europe and England, triggered a shift in the ministry of the clergy towards a greater focus on preaching, teaching and pastoral discipleship; the education of the clergy also developed to ensure priests were equipped as ministers of the word.

The Council of Trent – the 19th ecumenical council of the Catholic Church – was held between 1545 and 1563 in northern Italy. It was a turning point in how the church provided education for those training to be clergy. From the early Middle Ages until the beginning of the European Reformation, all theological education took place in monasteries, urban cathedrals and some smaller churches, and later in some of the ancient universities, such as the University of Paris in France, which emerged from the cathedral school of *Notre Dame de Paris*, and also the University of Bologna in Italy. However, it is thought the majority of training taking place in these local episcopal schools was for the *catechumenate* (Greek, those being instructed), who received three years of instruction, usually before being baptized. When considering the role universities played in educating medieval clergy, William J. Courtenay and Jürgen Miethke conclude that 'the vast majority of parish priests throughout the late medieval period had no university education in theology'.[35] The Council of Trent established the first church academic instructions for educating the clergy in training. Commissioned by the Council, the initial colleges were founded in 1563 as *seminaria* (Latin, seedbeds) for ministerial training in the Roman Catholic Church.[36]

When the Council met in 1546 to 'extirpate heresy and reform morals,' it made a provision that every cathedral should teach grammar and Holy Scripture to clerics and poor scholars. A later meeting in 1563 expanded on this so that every diocese should 'train in ecclesiastical discipline a certain number of youths, in a college to be chosen by the bishop for that purpose.' Poor dioceses were encouraged to combine, larger dioceses were permitted to have more than one seminary, and children of the poor were to be prioritized. The colleges were to train boys 12 years of age, or older, who had basic skills of reading and writing, and who were thought to be likely to persevere in the service of the church. In addition to general education, students were taught to preach, to conduct divine worship, and to administer the sacraments.[37]

Ryan P. Bonfiglio suggests there are several changes in how we think about spiritual formation and theological education that result from the Trent. First, in the Tridentine model, theological training becomes professionalized, typically offered as a formal pathway to a professional award. Before 1563, says Bonfiglio, 'it would have been more natural to see theological education as an aspect of discipleship, not an act of professional credentialing'.[38] Second, as the local church began to delegate its work of training to the academy, fewer people received theological training.[39] Last, perhaps a little too romantically, Bonfiglio concludes that local churches that 'were the locus of theological studies and scholarship for nearly a thousand years' began to lose their imagination in how to teach theology, and creativity and the contextualization of training was lost.[40]

Ministerial formation in the Church of England since the end of the Second World War

The training of ordained leaders in the Church of England has seen significant change and development since the end of the Second World War. George Lings concludes that public worship in England has undergone 'nothing short of a revolution since about 1960'.[41] It has evolved from 'a Sunday gathering, conducted in a consecrated building, using the Book of Common Prayer, led by a full-time clergyman for people drawn from one parish.' These landmarks of form and identity have, says Lings, 'virtually disappeared as essential components of being Anglican'[42] giving way to a more mission-focused and diverse pattern of ministry in the Church of England. These changes also affect the training needs of clergy and church planters who need to be selected and equipped to lead mission-focused churches which can engage with a diverse pattern of ministry.[43]

According to the House of Bishops of the Church of England, in their report *Formation Criteria with Mapped Selection Criteria for Ordained Ministry in The Church Of England* (2014), ministerial formation in the Church of England comprises the areas of Christian faith, tradition and life; mission, evangelism and discipleship; spirituality and worship; relationships; personality and character; leadership, collaboration and community; and, vocation and ministry within the Church of England.[44] They later state that each of these areas includes elements of knowledge, skills and Christ-like character.[45]

Conclusion

Our survey of just these limited sources raises several key questions for training. First, we notice the constantly developing nature of formation. This being the case, what does the current context of institutional decline but also entrepreneurial new possibility suggest should be the format and goal of training? Second, having noted the changing approaches, there is nonetheless a long-standing emphasis on character, practice and prayer throughout, from Augustine's residence, where education and training took place in community, or Benedictine communities, where prayer and work formed the foundation for reflective forms of learning, illustrate an integrated approach to ministerial formation. At various points we see clearly how this emphasis takes precedence over institutional requirements or any suggestion of the formation of a clerical class. Last, related to this observation, does the prominence of the requirement for a university award sit at odds with the flexible and practical nature of training earlier in the tradition? Later, in Part 5 and especially Chapter 15, I will make some proposals that pick up these observations, but for now we can note the resources in the history of training for a new approach.

Questions

1 Is it necessary for church planters to be well-educated and suited to study? Might it be sufficient for them to have ministry experience and a sincere faith in Christ?

2 In what ways is living in community with others also in training (perhaps with a shared Rule of Life) beneficial for ministerial formation and training?

3 Thinking of the Tridentine pattern of seminaries (seedbeds), are clergy-in-training being 'planted' as they train? How might this shape our understanding of the process of church planting?

4 Noting the historic and long-standing integrated approach to ministerial formation (e.g. character, practice, study, prayer, etc.) is ministerial training best served by institutional models like those used for other professions?

Notes

1 See Ron Anderson. 'Creative Church Planting Involving Lay People', in *Church Planting in Europe: Connecting to Society, Learning from Experience*, edited by Evert Van de Poll and Joanne Appleton (Eugene, OR: Wipf and Stock, 2015), 216–26.

2 In 1987, Archbishop Robert Runcie outlined his thoughts on the scope of ministerial formation in the Church of England in a speech entitled 'Theological Education Today'. He said that ministerial formation encompasses '[the] intellec-

tual, spiritual, moral, and practical' aspects of theological training. In a more recent example, in 2002, in a report on ordination training, the Archbishops' Council of the Church of England noted that the term 'ministerial formation' can be used variously to describe the entire process of clergy training, or a subset of the process, or as a description of the result. In this chapter, the term 'ministerial formation' is used to refer to the content and method of the initial training and learning of a Christian minister. In this respect, it includes, but is not limited to, biblical theology, systematic theology, Christian history, the practical skills needed for church leadership, and growth in Christian character. See Advisory Board of Ministry. *Theological Education Today: A Speech by the Archbishop of Canterbury*, ACCM Occasional Paper No. 25 (London: Church House Publishing, 1987), 40, and *The Structure and Funding of Ordination Training, the Interim Report of the Working Party Set up by the Archbishops' Council* (London: Church House Publishing, 2002), 2–3.

3 *Didache* 15.1 quoted in Aaron Milavec, *Didache: Text, Translation, Analysis, and Commentary*, 1st edn (Wilmington, DE: Michael Glazier, 2003), 35.

4 *Eusebius* 3.25.4 quoted in Paul L. Maier, *Eusebius: The Church History*, translated by Paul L. Maier (Grand Rapids, MI: Kregel Publications, 2007), 100–01.

5 *Didache* 1.2a quoted in Milavec, *Didache*, 3.

6 John Chapman, 'Didache', *The Catholic Encyclopedia*, Vol. 4 (New York: Robert Appleton Company, 1908), 20–34.

7 Vernon Bartlet, 'The Didache Reconsidered', *The Journal of Theological Studies*, Vol. os-XXII, No. 3, Apr. 1921, 239–49, doi:10.1093/jts/os-XXII.3.239, 242.

8 William Varner, 'The Didache's Use of The Old and New Testaments', *Masters Seminary Journal*, Vol. 16, No. 1, 2005, 127–51, 130–32, 139–40.

9 Claudia Rapp, *Holy Bishops in Late Antiquity: The Nature of Christian Leadership in an Age of Transition* (Oakland, CA: University of California Press, 2013), 26.

10 Quoted in Johannes Quasten, *Patrology: The Beginnings of Patristic Literature* (Notre Dame, IN: Ave Maria Press, Christian Classics, 1983), 80.

11 *Constitutions*, 2.1.1.

12 Rapp, *Holy Bishops*, 30, 179.

13 *Eusebius*, 7.29.2, quoted in Rapp, *Holy Bishops*, 179.

14 Rapp, *Holy Bishops*, 179.

15 John Tracy Ellis, *Essays in Seminary Education*, 1st edn (Anjou, QC: Fides Publishers, 1967), 4.

16 Ellis, *Seminary Education*, 5.

17 Ellis, *Seminary Education*, 5–6.

18 Ellis, *Seminary Education*, 6.

19 Paul Bernier, *Ministry in the Church: An Historical and Pastoral Approach*, 2nd edn (New York: Orbis Books, 2016), 67.

20 *Rule* 60.2 quoted in Timothy Fry, translator, *The Rule of St. Benedict in English* (Collegeville, MI: Liturgical Press, 1980), 273–74; James G. Clark, *The Benedictines in the Middle Ages* (Woodbridge, Suffolk: Boydell Press, 2011), 87.

21 Clark, *Benedictines*, 88.

22 Clark, *Benedictines*, 89.

23 *Rule*, 2, 8, 62.

24 Columba Stewart, *Prayer and Community: Benedictine Tradition* (London: Darton, Longman & Todd Ltd, 1998), 71.

25 Bede, *The Ecclesiastical History of the English People* 5.24 quoted in Venerable Bede, *The Ecclesiastical History of the English People*, edited by Judith McClure and Roger Collins, translated by Bertram Colgrave, new edn (Oxford: Oxford University Press, 2008), 336.

26 Julia Barrow, *The Clergy in the Medieval World: Secular Clerics, Their Families and Careers in North-Western Europe, c. 800–c. 1200* (Cambridge: Cambridge University Press, 2015), 220–21.

27 David Cornick, 'The Reformation Crisis in Pastoral Care', *A History of Pastoral Care*, edited by G. R. Evans (London: Cassell, 2000), 223–51, 223–40.

28 Bruce Gordon, 'Preaching and the Reform of the Clergy in the Swiss Reformation', in *The Reformation of the Parishes: The Ministry and the Reformation in Town and Country*, edited by Andrew Pettegree (Manchester: Manchester University Press, 1993), 63–84, 63–81.

29 R. N. Swanson, 'Before the Protestant Clergy: The Construction and Deconstruction of Medieval Priesthood', in *The Protestant Clergy of Early Modern Europe*, edited by C. Scott Dixon and Luise Schorn-Schütte (London: Palgrave Macmillan, 2003), 1–38, 1.

30 Amy Nelson Burnett, *Teaching the Reformation: Ministers and Their Message in Basel, 1529–1629* (Oxford: Oxford University Press, 2006), 7.

31 John Colet, *A Sermon Preached Before the Convocation at St. Paul's Church London, in the Year 1512* (Detroit, MI: Gale ECCO, 2010).

32 Paul Avis, 'The Revision of the Ordinal in the Church of England 1550–2005', *Ecclesiology*, Vol. 1, No. 2, 2005, 95–110, doi:10.1177/1744136605051929, 95.

33 Avis, 'Revision of the Ordinal', 97.

34 Avis, 'Revision of the Ordinal', 98.

35 William J. Courtenay and Jürgen Miethke, editors, 'Universities and Schooling in Medieval Society', *The Journal of Ecclesiastical History*, Vol. 53, No. 2, Apr. 2002, 245–428, doi:10.1017/S0022046902434240, 254.

36 Ryan P. Bonfiglio, 'Classroom of the Church', *Christian Century*, Vol. 136, No. 4, Feb. 2019, 22.

37 Charles George Herbermann, 'Master of Arts', *The Catholic Encyclopedia: An International Work of Reference on the Constitution, Doctrine, Discipline, and History of the Catholic Church*, edited by Robert C. Broderick (New York: Robert Appleton Company, 1913), 312–13.

38 Bonfiglio, 'Classroom', 22.

39 Bonfiglio, 'Classroom', 23.

40 Bonfiglio, 'Classroom', 23.

41 George Lings, 'The History of Fresh Expressions and Church Planting in The Church of England', *Church Growth in Britain: 1980 to the Present*, edited by David Goodhew (Farnham, Surrey: Ashgate Publications, 2012), 161.

42 Lings, 'History of Fresh Expressions', 161.

43 Robert J. Banks in *Re-envisioning Theological Education: Exploring a Missional Alternative to Current Models* (Grand Rapids, MI: Wm. B. Eerdmans, 1999) explores the paradigms at work in Western theological education, building on earlier work by Edward Farley and David H. Kelsey. Most recently, reviews of theological education in the Church of England published as *ACCM Occasional Paper 22 Education for the Church's Ministry: The Report of the Working Party*

on Assessment (London: Church House Publishing, 1987) and Bishop John Hind's report, *Formation for Ministry in a Learning Church* (London: Church House Publishing, 2003) explore some of the practical and theological questions relating to theological education in ministerial formation.

44 The House of Bishops of the Church of England, *Formation Criteria with Mapped Selection Criteria for Ordained Ministry in the Church of England* (London: Church House Publishing, 2014), 2.

45 *Formation Criteria*, 2.

9

Craft Church Planting

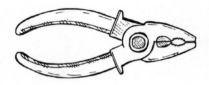

The Church is planted like Paradise in this world.
Irenaeus of Lyons, Against Heresies[1]

The Apostles planted the Church with their blood.
A phrase from medieval liturgy and art

This chapter offers a brief introduction to church planting from the perspective of craft apprenticeship, beginning with an exploration of the origins of 'planting' terminology. For more about church planting in general, please see the bibliography and recommended further reading at the end of this book.

My main focus here is the structures and principles that support a craft perspective of church planting (i.e. apprenticeship, craft-guilds and creativity), rather than a specific technique. In practice, techniques can change very quickly, not least when the planter and their team encounter the contextual realities on the ground. What matters most is the right person having received the right training, in the right role with the right support. Craft apprenticeship is a way that such people can be trained.

In this chapter, and throughout this book, I have followed my preference of using the term 'church planter' to apply interchangeably to those who start new churches and those who revitalize or renew existing churches using church planting methods.[2] Also, I use the term 'church planting' to cover the full range of styles and types of church planting, including fresh expressions of church.

The origins of the term 'church planting'

The term 'church planting' is a curious shorthand for the discipline of creating new churches. Surely many descriptions could be used for this activity – such as birthing, starting, launching, growing, forming, creating, multiplying, etc. – but planting has become a popular and household label for this ministry.[3] The English word 'planting' derives from the Latin word *planta* which refers to a sprout or cutting and the act of planting. This simple, tangible and commonplace metaphor for the process of establishing new churches is helpful because it transcends cultures and ages – everyone, everywhere can easily understand the idea. Also, the practice of church planting encompasses the entire history of the Christian church, since every local church, however long or short its heritage, was once planted. While the popular and contemporary use of the term 'church planting' is modern,[4] the phrase has ancient origins. I suggest there are at least seven historic reasons why the term 'planting' is used to refer to the ministry of starting new churches; considering these usages is one way of understanding the meaning of the term.

Paul: 'I planted the seed'

When writing to the church in Corinthians, Paul uses metaphors of 'planting' ('I planted the seed', 1 Cor. 3.6 NIV) and 'watering' ('Apollos watered it', 3.6 NIV) to describe his ministry as 'one who plants' (3.7, 8),[5] work that he later explains is that of a 'skilled master builder' (3.10). He further clarifies that this labour is reliant on divine activity, since 'only God ... makes things grow' (3.7 NIV). In these verses, Paul associates the various biblical horticultural metaphors and parables with his apostolic calling to proclaim the name of Jesus by sowing and planting seeds in the gospel and kingdom of God.[6]

While most writers cite these verses as a key proof-text for 'church planting', the actual focus of the chapter is to challenge partisan boasting by acknowledging God as the unseen vital agent of kingdom growth. Also, the association of the passage with starting new churches should be as an illustration, not a definition, as later the Corinthian church is also described as a 'field', 'building' (verse 9) and 'temple' (verse 17). So, we might just as well, for example, speak of 'kingdom harvesting', 'church constructing' or 'temple making' as we do church planting. Key then to any terminology derived from these verses is focus on the initial step of 'planting' seeds of the gospel and the kingdom of God; followed by 'watering' of the nurture of embryonic communities of new disciples;

which, with the involvement of God, might result in a new church.[7] If the term 'church planting' is used as shorthand for this, then it is a reasonable one.[8]

Church Fathers

The rapid spread of Christianity in the early centuries indicates that the activity of starting new churches was normative for the Church in that period. So much so that Michael J. Svigel believes the *Didache*, the oldest extant written catechism for leaders, was created as a basic manual for church planters. Svigel suggests this was a way that the Apostolic leaders of the church empowered many of the next generation of emerging leaders.[9]

Although the Church Fathers clearly supported and practised what we call church planting, few used the term 'planting' in their writing. However, a quite beautiful statement on the subject does come from one of the Greek Fathers at the end of the second century. Irenaeus, in his treatise on orthodox Christianity, said '*Plantata est enim Ecclesia Paradisus in hoc mundo*' ('the Church is planted like Paradise in this world'). As far as I am aware, this is the first reference to church planting in Patristic literature.[10] Who wouldn't want this, to bring more of God's Paradise to their neighbourhood?

Plantatio Ecclesiae

The beginning of the twentieth century saw the revival of a medieval Roman Catholic understanding of church planting which is expressed in the term *plantatio Ecclesiae*,[11] which means 'church planting'.[12] The encyclical by John Paul II, *Redemptoris Missio* (1990), on 'the mission of the redeemer' refreshed the modern Catholic understanding of *plantatio Ecclesiae*:

> It is necessary first and foremost to strive to establish Christian communities everywhere, communities which are a 'sign of the presence of God in the world' and which grow until they become churches ... This phase of ecclesial history, called the *plantatio Ecclesiae*, has not reached its end.[13]

Plantatio Ecclesiae suggests an ordered, methodical and systematic approach to evangelization and the fulfilment of the Great Commission, one that is rooted in insights formulated in the first centuries of Christianity. The term refers to the first foundation of the Christian church in a mission field, any further activity after the first planting is merely an extension of that.[14] This certainly includes 'establishing of the visible Church in countries where it had not yet been established',[15] but could be extended to mean the pioneering initiative with an unreached group in society. Interestingly, Gregorius Budi Subanar concludes that the basic theme of the Magisterium teaching documents since 1919 is, '[the] formation of the clergy as the realization of *plantatio Ecclesiae*'.[16] This powerful intrepetation considers all clergy as church planters, or at the very least, a part of the ongoing planting of Christ's Church on earth. While church planting shouldn't stop at the formation of clergy, we can certainly see here reasons for seeing it being central to ordained ministry.

Apostles' sacrifice

An interesting use of the term 'planting' occurs in medieval liturgy and art in the expression '*plantaverunt Ecclesiam sanguine suo*' ([the Apostles] planted the Church with their blood). The phrase is probably a devotional use of *plantatio Ecclesiae*. For example, the phrase has also been used in devotional art: Niccolò Circignani (d. 1597), an Italian late-Renaissance artist also known as Pomarancio, issued an engraving in 1585 titled '*Plantaverunt ecclesiam sanguine suo*' (they planted the church with their blood) showing the martyrdoms of the Apostles Peter and Paul, with the inscription '*Nero persequitur ecclesiam dei. Princeps Apostolorum Petrus affigitur Cruci. Paulus Apostolus securi percutitur*' (Nero persecutes the church of god. Peter the Prince of the Apostles is fastened to the Cross. The Apostle Paul is beheaded). The engraving can be viewed online at the New York Public Library Digital Collections.[17]

The phrase was also adopted by Carmelites in their liturgy and subsequently used in sixteenth-century Jesuit writings.[18] The phrase is similar to a better-known saying attributed to Tertullian (d. 240): 'the blood of the martyrs is the seed of the Church'.[19]

Seedbed

The Council of Trent – the 19th ecumenical council of the Roman Catholic Church which met in northern Italy between 1545 and 1563 – was an important transition point in how the church provided education for those training to be clergy. Before Trent – from the early Middle Ages until the beginning of the European Reformation – all theological education took place either in monasteries, urban cathedrals or selected churches.[20] The Council established a new pattern for the education of clergy through church academic instructions which were called *seminaria* (Latin, 'seed-beds' or more literally 'places for nurturing seeds'). Therefore, just as new churches arise from sowing seeds of the gospel, church planters arise from the planting of seeds: ministerial formation and theological and practical training. These 'seedbeds', whether they be local churches or theological training institutions, are the environment where the seeds of future church planting ministry are best planted and nurtured.

Reformation planting

The European Reformation was a catalyst for radical evangelization through new churches. For example, between 1555 and 1562 John Calvin commissioned at least 88 trained preachers as church planters in France.[21] Their method was first to establish a small group that met in a home to study the Bible. These 'amorphous Bible gatherings' were termed *églises plantées* (planted churches); in time, most developed to became *églises dressées* (churches erected or established churches).[22] This method reproduced and grew quickly through multiplication. In 1555 there was only one *églises dresses* in France, but seven years later there were more than 2,000, the largest of which had 8,000 communicant members; eventually, there were over two million Protestant church members out of a French population of 20 million.[23]

Roland Allen

The modern trigger for the popular take-up of the term church plant-ing comes from the English Anglican priest Roland Allen. At the turn of the twentieth century, Allen noted the challenges of raising indigenous church leaders and contextual church plants through his first-hand experi-ences as a missionary in Northern China and his subsequent research of mission endeavours in India, Canada and East Africa. In his first book, *Missionary Methods, St. Paul's or Ours* (1912), Allen contrasts his study of Paul's missionary methods with the models used by the denominations and mission agencies of his day. He concludes that Paul's method was to establish 'centres of Christian life in ... important places' and, stress-ing the key role of the founding leader, distinguished that Paul 'planted churches' rather than 'gathering congregations', which was the practice of his day.[24] Allen's use of the term planting focused on the vital role of the missioner who first establishes the new church.[25]

Summing up

So, how are churches planted? Without delving into the nitty-gritty of methods, which we have already noted are varied and can change quickly, it might be valuable to summarize our exploration of the origins of the language of 'planting'. The roots of the term offer a useful collection of perspectives on the elements and process of planting a new church, insights that transcend the trends and fashions of church planting techniques. Church planting is when we sow and nurture the seeds of the gospel and the kingdom of God to bring Paradise to earth. Church planting is when strategic churches and their leaders pay the price of following Jesus. Church planting is when we train future leaders who multiply evangelistic groups and apply the Great Commission contextually.

What is craft church planting?

Depending on the example, a church plant is either a nascent or a recently established church. In either case, it follows that all churches were once plants, each with a story of why and how they came to be started. 'Church planters' are the practitioners who establish and develop new Christian communities and 'church planting', the ministry-wisdom and application of this practice. Since few new church contexts (or church planters) are alike, these practices are usually varied and bespoke, but they typically have common overarching characteristics, such as fresh engagement with Christian vision, emphasis on evangelism, and innovation in style and practice.

In what ways might the practice of planting new churches and training church planters be considered a craft? And are there forgotten or neglected craft practices that the contemporary church might benefit from rediscovering, particularly as the Church seeks to be revitalized for mission? Using my three areas of focus in this book – masters and apprentices, guild communities, and creativity – I suggest below some reasons why church planting might be helpfully seen as a craft and how the application of lost craft practices might assist in the renewal of the Church.

Masters and apprentices

At the heart of the craft guild is a master training an apprentice, a relationship that both defines and establishes the craft approach. When applied to Christian ministry, this method of training suggests a model of formation and leadership development that is centred on the context of the local church and the mentoring of proven ministry practitioners who recruit and provide initial formational training for emerging leaders who might plant churches. Master-apprenticeship is a lost model which, in its best expression, goes beyond classic paternalism to something truly empowering, where apprentices go beyond their master because of the humility shown by their master.

Master-apprenticeship training offers an alternative approach to the current pathways for vocational discernment, one more suited to the distinctive requirements of church planting. In this model, the aptitude of novices is tested early through practical engagement with ministry tasks relevant to church planting, under the supervision of those experienced in this craft. I suggest this approach has several advantages. First, it is better suited to nurturing indigenous leaders who can adapt to different contexts. Indigenous leaders are skilled at reading culture and developing contextually relevant approaches to ministry, an ability that is at the heart of starting effective new churches. Second, it produces apprentices that are rooted in foundational practitioner skills. Unlike modern approaches to ministerial formation – where academic theology is usually taught first and ministry skills second – a craft approach begins with basic skills to which learning is added. This method has the advantage of ensuring that learning is focused on understanding ministry, not just learning for learning's sake. Last, it allows for an early assessment of the apprentices' vocation and capacity. In a craft approach, students advance to the next stage of learning when they can produce evidence of the assimilation of knowledge and skills. For example, a church planting apprentice might be trained in methods of mission and discipleship and then tasked with starting a new small group that grew through evangelistic activity and where the leadership of the group was handed on to a member trained by the church planting apprentice.

Guild communities

Within the craft model are several different types of community. The smallest is the workshop, the basic working unit. The workshop is both a place of work (ministry) and learning. In craft planting, each local church has the potential to be a workshop, where the ministry of the church is also a context for training the next generation of ministers;[26] a workshop is a community of practice that is supervised by a master practitioner. Next is the local guild: the community of all those in a locality who share in the practice of the guild, who work together for the common benefit and to ensure the perpetuation of their ministry.

Guild communities support ongoing practice through an approach to training that has the replicability of a viral model – each master trains several apprentices and journeymen, many of whom become masters and train new apprentices. Guilds hold tacit knowledge and ministry-wisdom that might easily be lost, although they were at times guilty of applying a cartel-like grip on power and suppression of innovation. Guilds were also necessary to provide the environment to propagate new workshops (churches).[27]

Creativity

The craft approach fits well with pioneering methods. Just like many types of artist, church planting pioneers bring tried and tested ingredients together in original ways to form a unique piece of work – in this case, a new church. When done well, church planting produces a contextualized expression of the timeless gospel through strong skills and a creative approach. It follows that training in creativity and modelling creativity in training is an important aspect of formation for church planters.

Contextualization, then, is the application of creativity to the culturally sensitive incarnation of new churches: creativity is the trait, contextualization is the application and skill. Whereas a novice church planting apprentice learns tried and tested ministry skills, the same apprentice must eventually augment that emphasis by developing the capacities to self-learn, interrogate new ideas, and bring them together in ways that are relevant to the context. At its heart, this creativity – and the richness of church planting – will flow from intersection of ecclesiology and missiology, where mission forms new church communities and churches are revitalized as they engage in mission. Plants are good not just because they hit growth targets; they are at their heart an expression of creativity. At their best, they bring new cultural, imaginative, communal and generational resources to the church, in an enterprising and expansive way.

Questions

1 What does the medieval expression 'they planted the Church with their blood' say to us today about the sacrifice and cost that might be implicit in effective church planting?
2 How might adopting a master-apprenticeship approach to initial formation reshape the methods of selecting and training women and men as future church planters?
3 How can local churches be helped to become workshops where the ministry context of the church forms a community of practice for immersive on-the-job training for the next generation of church pioneers?
4 In what ways is creativity (bringing tried and tested ingredients together in original ways to form a unique piece of work) important for the process of church planting?
5 If contextualization is the application of the trait of creativity to the incarnation of new churches, how should this affect the design of church plants and the work of church planters?

Notes

1 Irenaeus, *Against Heresies* (c. AD 180), 5.20.2, '*Plantata est enim Ecclesia Paradisus in hoc mundo*'.

2 Making and repairing churches (usually termed planting and revitalizing) are related in craft training thinking. For example, Richard Sennett suggests craftworkers who are proficient in making new products can develop more advanced skills by repairing craft products and tools, he sums up by saying 'it is by fixing things that we often get to understand how they work' see Richard Sennett, *The Craftsman* (London: Penguin, 2009), 194, 199–251.

3 Tom Steffen suggests that church planting is now a household term in global mission and domestic evangelism. See his *The Facilitator Era: Beyond Pioneer Church Multiplication* (Eugene, OR: Wipf & Stock. 2011), 42. However, this is a Western perspective; in the Global South, the term is little used. Churches in parts of South-East Asia, Africa and Latin America are often hesitant to use church planting terminology because of its colonial associations. Instead, they prefer the language of mission or disciple-making movements. In North America, modern church planting has become an industry in itself.

4 Steven Timmis suggests the term church planting only gained popular use in the early 1960s. See his *Multiplying Churches: Reaching Today's Communities Through Church Planting* (Fearn, Scotland: Christian Focus, 2000), 4.

5 Craig Ott and Gene Wilson delineate these roles: 'whereas the ministry of

planting involves primarily evangelism, discipleship, and congregating ... watering involves further teaching and strengthening churches that have already been gathered. Both planters and waterers are essential to the long-term goal of establishing healthy, reproducing churches.' See Craig Ott and Gene Wilson, *Global Church Planting: Biblical Principles and Best Practices for Multiplication* (Grand Rapids, MI: Baker Academic, 2011), 32.

6 There are approximately 30 horticultural metaphors, illustrations or parables in the New Testament – such as Jesus' Parable of the Sower (Matt. 13.3–9) or Paul's analogy of the grafted wild olive branch (Rom. 11.17–24) – used to describe the kingdom of God and the propagation of the Christian gospel. Jesus, Paul and other New Testament writers also use analogies from architecture, agriculture (including animal husbandry, e.g. shepherding) and commerce in similar ways.

7 Roger W. Gehring and Daniel M. McGinnis suggest that Paul's evangelistic strategy is to establish a small nucleus of a church or new Christian households 'cells' of embryonic churches in every city. See Roger W. Gehring, *House Church and Mission: The Importance of Household Structures in Early Christianity* (Peabody, MA: Hendrickson Publishers, 2005), 179–80; Daniel M. McGinnis, *Missional Acts: Rhetorical Narrative in the Acts of the Apostles* (Eugene, OR: Pickwick, 2021), 233–234, 238.

8 Many uses of the word 'planting' in the ante-Nicene period can be traced to this passage. For example, Irenaeus says, 'The Church is planted like the Garden of Eden in this world', see *Against Heresies*, 5.20.2.

9 See Michael J. Svigel, 'Didache as a Practical Enchiridion for Early Church Plants', *Bibliotheca Sacra* 174 (2017), 77–94. However, there are many theories about why the *Didache* was written. Another that is relevant to this book is Aaron Milavec's, who suggests the *Didache* was a manual for master-apprentice relationships, see Aaron Milavec, *The Didache: Text, Translation, Analysis, and Commentary* (Collegeville, MN: Liturgical Press, 2004), 47.

10 *Against Heresies* (c. AD 180), 5.20.2, *Plantata est enim Ecclesia Paradisus in hoc mundo*, author's translation.

11 Stefan Paas reports that he cannot identify any use of the term *plantatio Ecclesiae* before the Middle Ages and that, apart from the Protestant theologian Gisbertus Voetius (d. 1676) and early twentieth-century Catholic documents, the exact origin of the term *plantatio Ecclesiae* is not clear. See Stefan Paas, *Church Planting in the Secular West: Learning from the European Experience* (Grand Rapids, MI: Wm. B. Eerdmans, 2016), 10, 20–21, note 23.

12 First to reuse the term was Benedict XV. Reacting to the impact of the First World War on culture, Benedict wrote the pastoral letter *Maximum Illud* (1919) which, according to the letter's sub-title, was to stimulate 'the propagation of the [Christian] faith throughout the world', particularly in regions outside Europe and North America.

13 *Redemptoris Missio*, 49, quoted in Paas, *Church Planting*, 29.

14 Paas, *Church Planting*, 30.

15 Gregorius Budi Subanar, *The Local Church in the Light of Magisterium Teaching on Mission: A Case in Point: The Archdiocese of Semarang-Indonesia.* (Rome: Gregorian and Biblical Press, 2001), 48.

16 Subanar, *Magisterium Teaching*, 54.

17 Author's translations, see Spencer Collection, The New York Public Library, 'Plantaverunt ecclesiam sanguine suo', *New York Public Library Digital*

Collections, at https://digitalcollections.nypl.org/items/8a2bfac8-460e-241c-e040-e00a18060df5 (accessed 28.1.2022).

18 Subanar, *Magisterium Teaching,* 54; Paas, *Church Planting,* 20–21, note 23.

19 The phrase 'the Apostles planted the Church with their blood' echoes Tertullian (d. 240), who said, 'the blood of the martyrs is the seed of the Church'. See *Apologeticus* 50.13 quoted in Bernie L. Calaway, *History and Mystery: The Complete Eschatological Encyclopedia of Prophecy, Apocalypticism ... Mythos, and Worldwide Dynamic Theology* (self published, www.Lulu.com, 2019), 301.

20 Although, latterly, some of the ancient universities, such as the University of Paris in France and the University of Bologna in Italy, taught theology. The College of Sorbonne, the theological college of the University of Paris, was founded in 1253 by Robert de Sorbon from the Cathedral school of *Notre Dame de Paris.* See Hilde de Ridder-Symoens, *A History of the University in Europe: Volume 1, Universities in the Middle Ages* (Cambridge: Cambridge University Press, 2003), 80, and Ryan P. Bonfiglio, 'Classroom of the Church', *Christian Century,* Vol. 136, No. 4, Feb. 2019, 22.

21 The secrecy of the operation meant few records were kept; however, we do know they experienced persecution because nine of these church planters were martyred.

22 Peter Wilcox, '"Églises Plantées" and "Églises Dressées" in the Historiography of Early French Protestantism', *The Journal of Ecclesiastical History,* Vol. 44, No. 4, 1993, 689–95, doi:10.1017/S0022046900077861, 690–91; Paas, *Church Planting,* 22.

23 For an excellent summary of Calvin's church planting in France, see Jean-Marc Berthoud, 'John Calvin and the Spread of the Gospel in France', in *Fulfilling the Great Commission* (London: The Westminster Conference, 1992), 1–53.

24 Allen's critique applies today, where focus is too much on the infrastructure of the new congregation rather than the role of the founding leaders to 'plant' the church, which he understood to be evangelism and initial discipleship.

25 Allen also suggested that church plants should reflect the local culture and be led by indigenous leaders. He developed this point in his later volume, *The Case for Voluntary Clergy* (London: SPCK, 1923), where he argued for locally trained ministers in new Chinese churches. Allen noted that Chinese missionaries who received ministerial training in English theological colleges returned to China educated but ineffective as pastors. In his next book, *The Spontaneous Expansion of the Church and the Causes that Hinder It* (Cambridge: James Clarke and Co, 1927), he suggested that missional effectiveness was often inversely proportional to educational attainment. Ed Stetzer agrees: '[W]e raise up church planters and pastors by competency, rather than certification' and 'we need a way to raise up church planters and pastors that does not always require formal education'. See Stetzer, 'Why Lay People Can (and Should) Plant Churches', *The Exchange,* at https://www.christianitytoday.com/edstetzer/2018/april/why-lay-people-can-and-should-plant-churches.html (accessed 28.1.2022).

26 An example of this hybrid in the medical world is a teaching hospital.

27 For a longer exploration of this see Ralph D. Winter, 'The Two Structures of God's Redemptive Mission', *Practical Anthropology,* Vol. 2, No. 1, Jan. 1974, 121–39, doi:10.1177/009182967400200109. Winter suggests that 'church' exists in two forms: modal and sodal, the former being typically created by the latter.

PART 4

Wisdom From Experience

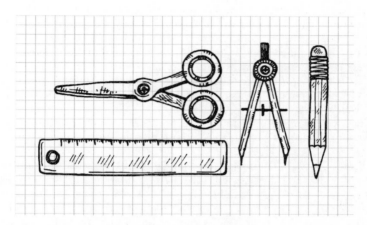

The holder of this travel-book is a companion on a 'traditional walk' ... to increase their understanding of the work practices of people in other countries and thus improve their knowledge about their profession and extend their experience of life. We kindly request everybody – particularly all honourable masters, authorities and other institutions – who meet this companion to assist them in their intention ...

Journeyman Travel-book

Note: Author's translation from the introduction to the *Reisebücher* (German, Journeyman Travel-book), issued by the Conféderation des Compagnons Européens Gesellenzünfte (Strasbourg: Confederation of European Journeymen Associations)

IO

Exploring Master-Apprenticeship

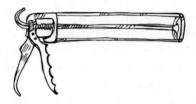

If one is master of one thing and understands one thing well, one has at the same time, insight into and understanding of many things.

Vincent Van Gogh[1]

A pattern of training, mentoring and apprenticeship 'on the job' should be developed, rather than outside or apart from the mission situation where the leader (or potential leader) is exercising their ministry.

Mission-Shaped Church[2]

Introduction to this section

We have now considered the wisdom in biblical and theological sources, and in training and apprenticeship more generally, but how do these insights play out in practice? What is the tacit knowledge held by practitioners? To determine this we need to listen not only to academic sources but to lived experience. Here the wisdom embedded in the practical skills and habits of actual church planters can come alive, speaking for itself in conversation with the more theoretical perspectives we have surveyed up to this point. I have used two sources to develop my thinking: a survey of 560 church planters and interviews with 16 trainers. The first group, who completed an online survey, were church planters from 32 different counties.[3] Of the second group, the trainers, half were church ministers who train church planters and half were artists who train artists. The latter set was drawn from varied roles in different artistic fields – disc jockey, musician, sculptor, actress, painter, conservation artist, model maker and chef – which resulted in a diverse and interesting range of perspectives.

All the church leaders and artists were asked the same set of questions, which were shaped by the content of Part 2 of this book. This revealed interesting areas of common thinking, different shades of thinking and contrasting approaches. The names of the trainers have been changed: the artists have been given names beginning with 'A' and the church leader trainers, names beginning with 'T' (for trainer).[4] Some are well-known figures, certainly in their respective networks, and others are not famous. However, their identities are not important; what is important is that they were selected because they are expert masters – women and men each with 20 years or more experience – who are accomplished in their area of work or ministry, are creative and innovative, and proven as effective trainers of the next generation.

I have distilled the data from the survey responses and interviews – which include more than 93,000 words of transcribed conversation – into 45 lessons about craft apprenticeship that I present in this and the following two chapters. Although the findings are mine, I have tried, as much as possible, to describe these ideas in the words of the church leader trainers, artists and church planters. They reflect the perspectives of those interviewed, and yet there are striking points of similarity which deserve our attention. Strictly speaking, each finding is an unproven observation; the thinking is emergent and needs to be tested, applied and assessed before it can be adopted as best practice. However, by presenting them in this way I hope to enable just this process of further experimentation and verification.

The results have been sorted using the headings that were identified in Chapter 3: master-apprenticeship (this chapter), guild training communities and creativity. Additionally, at the end of this section, in Chapter 13, I briefly describe four examples of craft-type training. These examples highlight some, although certainly not all, of the principles that are set out in this section. First, we begin with understanding master-apprenticeship and the qualities of effective master-trainers.

The qualities of effective master-trainers

There are three essential qualities of an effective master in their training relationships (I use the term 'master-trainer' as a shorthand for a master training in a master-apprenticeship context). The qualities are relevant experience and accomplishments, good communication skills, and being interested in the development of others.

Relevant experience and accomplishments

Relevant experience and past success are key foundational qualities for effective master-trainers; for a master to be qualified to train others they must first have proved their effectiveness as a practitioner. For example, Tom said to me, 'It's the experience I have that gives me credibility, but it also gives me authenticity.' Similarly, Trevor said, 'A church planter needs to accumulate a wealth of on-the-ground experience before they start training others.' Tanner, stressing the importance of a strong performance history, commented that 'significant church planting trainers will have a track-record and recent history of developing young church planters'. April made a comparable observation about artists she has trained: 'A master is someone who has gained mastery of tools and materials and is now teaching the same things to a novice.' Tom best summed up the tone of several comments I heard:

> There is something about having been in that situation: you understand the pressures, the passion, the ups-and-downs, and the challenges you face. I think the way I train someone else is a reflection of my own experience, and that is what gives it credibility to the person learning from me – they can see that I've been in the midst of a situation like that myself.

Of course, there is a need to ensure that respect for the master's past accomplishments does not result in idolization or inappropriate deference. Alan offered this helpful caveat: 'The thought that the master is the best isn't necessarily that helpful, because the master helps people move beyond them.' My own *ad hoc* polling suggests most current senior church leaders were not nurtured in this way – they do not feel that anyone invested in them at an early stage, or that they were inspired to surpass their mentor. When current church leaders feel that they advanced without mentoring, a significant barrier is created to the culture of developing the next generation. In my experience, this produces leaders who are looking for supporters rather than developing successors. For a master to be an effective trainer they need to have done well as a practitioner, but they also need the humility to desire greater things for their pupils.

Good communication skills

The second key trait for masters to be effective trainers is the ability to communicate well. April described the ideal to me: 'An expert who is a good communicator can open up other people's learning and creativity.'

Toby noted the idea that a master needs to be 'consciously competent' – rather than 'unconsciously competent' – to be an effective teacher.[5] By this, he meant that masters need not only to be effective practitioners; they also need to understand why they are effective and be able to communicate their method to others. Again, April summed it up well when she said that a master-trainer is 'someone who has mastery of materials, tools and people'. Her reasons for believing this are based on her experience as a trainer and her understanding of history. She said:

> Historically people who were masters themselves were very quick to acknowledge the importance of their artistic formation, both intellectually and in terms of mastery of the material and the tools that they need to use. That's of course why apprenticeships were so long.

Effective communication, for a master, should include passion. April continued:

> People who are passionate about something love sharing it with other people … Somebody who's a really good mentor and a master has passion and a willingness to share what they have. Their enthusiasm and their love of what they do is such that they want to give the person they're teaching every opportunity to get to the point where they share that enthusiasm, passion and expertise.

It's not enough for a master to be accomplished in their craft, they must also have a contagious passion to impart their knowledge and experience to others. They also need both self-awareness and good communication skills to be effective at stimulating other people's learning.

Interested in the development of other people

The third core trait for an effective master-trainer is to be someone who enjoys being with other people, and who is interested in their development: a people-person. April told me that 'someone who is patient and skilful at explaining is often far more effective than someone who may be creatively brilliant, but not interested in the skill or the expertise and creativity of the other person'. She also described the converse: 'People who are not good teachers are not interested in other people – they're very interested in themselves.' This quality was evident in all of the interviewees. They all demonstrated their interest in developing other people, sometimes giving examples illustrating that they did this out of a genuine desire to develop the next generation.

The relationship between a master and an apprentice

The interview respondents highlighted eight key aspects of the relationship between the master and the apprentice.

Some masters have a parental approach to teaching the apprentice

Masters often take a parental approach to teaching their apprentices, especially when the student is from a younger generation. It was interesting that all the men I interviewed used paternal language to describe their approach to teaching apprentices, however none of the women did. Does this illustrate a weakness in the male perspective on training relationships? In later sections the female interviewees favour qualities such as trust, empowerment and confidence when describing training relationships.

Toby was the most direct when he told me, 'Apprenticeship *is* a paternalistic approach to teaching' (his emphasis). Similarly, when speaking to me about an all-male group he works with, Trevor said, 'Leading groups of emerging leaders has a lot to do with spiritual fatherhood.' He went on to highlight examples drawn from Paul's relationship with his apprentice, Timothy. From Romans 16, he noted four aspects of parental-apprenticeship which he utilizes: the apprentices are 'recognized publicly by their leader', 'with deep affection'; their leader 'knows details about their lives' and 'has a relationship with their whole family'. I spoke to Tom about his experiences as an emerging leader and he commented, 'My training incumbent drew me in almost like a son, I felt I was in a position where I wanted to learn and gain as much as I could from him.' Tom had had a one-hour one-to-one meeting with his training incumbent every week for 15 years. He added that recently someone said to him, 'You are just like [name]', which he received as a 'great compliment'. Tom also used an example from his relationship with his own son to describe a challenge that can emerge in parental-apprenticeship. He explained it like this:

> Imagine a good father with a son with whom he has a good relationship. Sometimes the son wants to break free of their father and the father can sometimes be a bit overpowering. So the father needs to know this moment will come and be ready for it so that they can release their son to break away, to do new things and to be better than them.

The relationship between the master and apprentice is built on trust

Trust is foundational to effective training relationships between masters and apprentices. Half of the people I interviewed highlighted trust as a vital quality in the relationship. Tanya phrased this brilliantly: 'Everything moves at the speed of trust.' When describing her experience of this, she said, 'There needs to have been sufficient relational depth cultivated so that the novice feels able to be unguarded and open about the things that they find most challenging.' Tanya continued by adding that this requires 'trust in the character of the master so that they can be inspired by the master'. Trust then follows relational experience, as Tanya confirms: 'There's a sense that they respect the master, not just for the skills they have, but also for the experience they've acquired.' Trust must also be accompanied by the master's demonstrable love that communicates to the apprentice that they are valued. This was recognized by several respondents. Particularly, echoing 1 Thessalonians 2.8, Trevor said, 'The [master-apprentice] relationship has to be one of love and trust and deep affection', to which Alan added 'mutual appreciation of each other'. Toby expanded that 'a person learns more from those in whom they have trust and confidence – someone in whom they feel a sense of value and who ... cares for them'. Alice described a positive experience that highlighted the result of trust, love and value in a training relationship: 'When I was at drama school, the teacher brought out the best in me by making a space in which I could fail and get it incredibly wrong.' Last, Amanda proposed that the outworking of trust between the master and apprentice should be reciprocal, reflecting: 'We [masters] have to take people's criticism.'

Masters instil confidence in their apprentices

A perhaps unexpected consequence of the master-apprentice relationship is the impartation of confidence to the new apprentice *because* the master chose them. For example, Toby told me: 'Rather than leaving students thinking "my teacher is amazing", a good teacher will leave their students feeling "I am amazing!"' And similarly, Adam told me this had been his experience: 'The master gave me a great deal of confidence.' He went on to say that this formative experience led him to adopt the same approach with his students. Likewise, Amy said of her first mentor, 'He built my self-esteem.' She explained her reasons for this:

> It's going to give the novice self-esteem and self-confidence because the master has considered them worthy to have their time and attention. The novice is going to be in the presence of the master, so they'll be able to witness great art taking place and they can then go and try and emulate it.

Toby described how confidence is imparted: 'this type of learning will teach and reinforce values, beliefs and a deep sense of identity', later adding that this 'centres around faith in self, faith in others, and faith in God'. To impart confidence to their students, an effective master will need to be confident in their role (as someone who is qualified to teach) and humble enough in their approach to allow their students to leave feeling elevated. A humble master might easily underestimate how highly others regard them.

The master aims to empower the apprentice

Empowerment of the apprentice is a distinctive characteristic of master-apprentice relationships – one exemplified in the responses of several of those I interviewed. To be effective in empowering trainees requires close proximity of the student to the master, particularly in the early stages of training. As Alan remarked to me, 'If it's about the master handing on their art form, then the master isn't going to want the apprentice to go too far afield, because they're going to want them to mimic what they do.' However empowerment moves beyond a student merely copying, or even becoming a facsimile themself of, the master. Amy explained that rather than trying to make her like himself, her first mentor was 'trying to bring out the artist in me'. Describing this transition beyond imitation, April observed that 'with all teaching, you see the point at which the person begins to own the quest for themselves'. In her discipline – where she is training students to be researchers and artists – she has noticed:

> You get beyond the point where they're no longer just a student – now they're the researcher; they're the artist. They move across an almost invisible line and they step over it with those tools that you've helped to give them. And then they can begin to develop their [own] art, ideas and intellectual confidence.

Others I interviewed acknowledged that they have personally benefited from empowering students to go beyond themselves. 'It's a win for me as the person who's training somebody', Alan added, 'because I get to learn backwards – individuals I've trained often come back and say, "I've been on this thing", or "I've heard this" or "I read this really good book I thought you might learn from"'. This same phenomenon is observed by Andrew: 'If the master wants the apprentice to go on beyond them then there needs to come a stage when the apprentice is teaching the master.'

Apprentices hold their master in high regard

It is perhaps unsurprising that there are strong benefits to apprentices holding their masters in high regard, since this itself is closely connected to value, prestige, trust and confidence. Several interviewees acknowledged such benefits. April – who is also an academic historian – reflected with me about the way in which medieval people were trained:

> Even into the Renaissance, most of the great artists were the very first people to acknowledge the importance of their master. They were proud to say, 'I was taught by so-and-so' because they valued what they had learned and *whom* they had learned it from. (Interviewee's emphasis.)

Amy, speaking to me about her own positive experiences, remarked that she was inspired that someone so talented could see potential in her that she didn't recognize herself: 'He could see it and – because I looked up to him so much – I knew it must be right. That experience ultimately gave me the confidence to discover a new level of artistry.' Such inspirational relationship is sometimes a forgotten aspect of the master-apprentice dynamic, however, as Andrew highlighted, 'First and foremost it is always about relationship, but not any relationship.'

Furthermore holding a mentor in high regard is not only inspirational but also aspirational, as Amy continued to illustrate: 'When there's a master and you're allowed into their presence you think, "This person *is* everything that I aspire to"' (interviewee's emphasis). However, undoubtedly there also lies a corresponding danger of idolization of a master by an apprentice. In contrast to her positive comments, later in her interview, Amy lamented that her attitude at that time 'almost amounted to a sort of hero-worship'.

The relationship between the master and apprentice is adaptive

Master-apprentice training does not follow a set pattern. Each master-apprentice pairing produces a unique training expression that is defined by the distinctive characteristics of the master, the apprentice, and the training context. I have noticed this characteristic of adaptivity across almost all interviewees. For example, Andrew observed that 'people learn differently', and Tanya remarked to me that she is 'different with different people'. Adaptivity also often manifests in very practical ways, as Toby emphasized: 'My feedback is very tailored to who they are.' Trevor similarly noted that 'some trainees trust their instincts too much. They think they are great, and so are overconfident; whereas others need to be encouraged to trust that God has called them, and [to] believe in themselves.' Ultimately, the adaptive nature of the master-apprenticeship relationship is summarized well by Timothy's approach:

> The master needs to spend time getting to know the apprentice, their dreams, their aspirations, the things they are dreaming to do for the Kingdom and [the master's role is] acknowledging what skills need to be developed, to help that apprentice focus on what they already do very well and the key parts of the craft of church planting that they need to learn before they can become a full master in the craft.

The master's relationship with the apprentice is intimate

The relationship between the master and apprentice is undoubtedly an intimate one due to the confidential closeness and trust necessary when investing in the life of another person. Quite rightly, the modern Church is aware of the potential risks associated with intimate training relationships, especially when one party is in an authority role. Nothing in this section should be read as encouragement to disregard safeguarding practice or support situations that might in any way encourage sexual harassment or bullying. Within the accountable boundaries of a properly safeguarded relationship, this element of trust and sharing can still be a crucial element. Five of those interviewed described this intimacy in various ways. For example, Alex reported sharing his home with those he is training: 'They will need to move into my house and live with my family; they will need to do life with us and eat with us.' Similarly, Toby said, 'Apprenticeship is where somebody is in the house with me.' Living together in the same home might not be essential, however a common strand to the intimacy required in the master-apprentice relationship, as Alan highlighted, is a willingness to go beyond 'sharing information [to] sharing your whole life'. Correspondingly, Timothy commented to me that he tells his church planter trainers that their primary task is not to teach theological content but rather to invest in the lives of their church planting apprentices, and Tina recognized that she is 'discipling [her interns] personally as well as professionally'. Cohering with these perspectives, Alan observed that there is a need for the master to 'share something of [themself] in this process'. He continued, 'Master-apprentice teaching is radically different from the way you are taught in the classroom, which is information-based and less intimate; whereas in the master-apprentice context you are standing with each other.' Alice added that intimacy results from being 'incredibly present and giving [your] entire attention' and Amy said that it involves a 'strong emotional-content component'.

All these elements – holistic sharing of life, personal attentiveness, and being with alongside – are exactly the type of incarnational training practices modelled by Jesus, as Alan recognizes: '[Jesus] is doing life with them and discipleship is happening on the road.[6] There is a balance of teaching, intimate moments and the stuff of life that come together to allow the Holy Spirit to really form people.' Furthermore the intimacy involved is reciprocal, it is not just the master who draws alongside, as Tom's example demonstrates: 'Once when I trained somebody, he called himself my wingman – he just followed me around.' Alan summarizes, 'The master has committed to the apprentice and the apprentice is committed to the master'; they are drawn intimately together in reciprocity.

Masters should choose their apprentices

Finally, the significant relational investment involved means that masters choose their apprentices. Several of those interviewed commented on this process of selection. Alan remarked that 'you can't agree to apprentice just anyone; there are good matches and there are not so good matches – you can't force it', and Timothy similarly highlighted the need for compatibility between master and apprentice: 'I would say the chemistry of the relationship is of far greater importance than what needs to be taught.' Such an important choice of who to train must certainly be made wisely, carefully and with spiritual discernment. As Timothy continued to explain, it is important to 'be in relationship with people that you are really called by God to invest in'. Not only should the decision be made discerningly but also, as Alan emphasized, without undue influence: 'The master needs complete freedom to be able to choose who their apprentice will be.' Later on, Alan said he often asks prospective apprentices, 'Do you want to be invested into?' because he is looking for people who are eager to be trained by him. Essentially then, a master should set high standards for selecting an apprentice, as Tanya practically illustrates: 'I wouldn't just apprentice anyone. I ask myself the questions, "Have they got what it takes to be a team leader?", "Are they able to handle the cost of leadership?", and "Have they proved themselves with a good enough track record and progression of the leadership they've been able to carry?"'

The methodology of master-apprentice training

There are six key methodological aspects to master-apprentice training, which were highlighted by the responses of interviewees. These are: giving time; asking questions and giving feedback; providing on-the-job training experience; delivering basic training; sharing ministry-practice secrets; and releasing when ready.

Giving their time

Training novices to be experts requires a significant investment of time from both apprentice and master. This point was widely recognized by the interview respondents. For example, Amy estimates that it took her approximately 12,000 hours of practice and learning to become an expert musician. 'You can't become a professional artist without tonnes and tonnes of hours of practice and experience,' she remarked. In contrast to classroom-based teaching where a student's personal contact time with a tutor tends to be more limited, an authentic master-apprentice training model requires significant amounts of time from the master. Referencing a typical North American seminary context, Alan told me, 'The dilemma of a classroom seminary setting is that you come to hear a lecture and, if you're lucky, you might be able to chat for a couple of minutes with the professor afterwards. There is little opportunity for mentoring or discipleship.' But in the master-apprentice model, as Alex highlighted, 'there are no shortcuts to proper training, you [the master] have to put in the hours, then more hours, and then more hours'; masters give of their time extensively.

Asking questions and giving feedback

Asking questions and providing feedback are key aspects of master-apprentice training methodology. In fact, half of the interview respondents identified the significance of doing so. Asking questions is a two-way process. Putting a question to an apprentice provides an opportunity for reflective learning, creative problem solving and development of initiative. 'In training someone you're not imposing your view or vision onto someone else,' Alice explained. 'You're saying "What's inside you?"' Likewise, providing space for an apprentice to ask questions of the master is equally important. Tom discussed with me his practice of giving each of his interns an hour a week to do so: 'When we did our one-to-ones, I would encourage them to ask questions about why I made particular decisions.' Tom then asked them how they might approach the same situation when they plant a church, recognizing that he needed to help his apprentices find solutions for themselves without becoming dependent on him. 'What I don't want to do is say "This is the answer",' he remarked. Similarly, Tanya, advocating a reflective methodology, told me that she 'will always encourage [her interns] to put aside some preparation-time before we have our conversation'. Masters cultivate a questioning ethos which then becomes a springboard for trainees to develop these important reflective and problem-solving skills for themselves, as Tom explains:

> What I can do is help the church planter ask the right questions for their context. I do that by helping the apprentice to hear the kind of questions I'm asking of myself and the ways that I've answered those questions. Someone said to me something that stuck, which is, 'A good question is much better than a good answer'. This is because a good question keeps things open and you keep on reflecting on it.

Feedback is a key training companion to question-asking, and can also be bi-directional. The potential impact of a master giving feedback to an apprentice cannot be underestimated, although this often requires a personalized approach. As Trevor highlighted, 'Feedback is very tailored to who they are' – masters need to combine their experience with their understanding of the apprentice when giving feedback. Correspondingly, Tanya mentioned that feedback needs to be 'led by their agenda'. She added that observing how well students receive feedback is a good way of discerning their openness to training and willingness to learn. When training artists, Amanda regularly observed students who were using tools, which provided an opportunity for her to give developmental feedback, such as, 'If you hold the tool like this...', or 'Why not try heating it first?' Similarly, April found that 'it takes expertise to be able to say, "If you try holding the brush in this way", or "The tool will work better if you hold it in this way"', yet she discovered that this type of feedback often 'liberated latent skills and produced rapid development'. Such feedback from a master who has observed the apprentice at work is invaluable, as Amy explained to me, 'My lessons would have enormous amounts of feedback – often quite brutal – but it showed me how to be better.' One way that masters can encourage question asking and feedback is to model the practice themselves by encouraging their students to give them feedback, which might also include suggestions.

Providing on-the-job training experience

Rather than just talking about an activity, masters use their position or resources to enable apprentices to have hands-on training, often from the very beginning of their apprenticeship. As they described their training methodology, all of the interviewees gave examples of contextual practice, placing a strong emphasis on participative learning. Tom remarked that, '80 to 90 per cent of learning is doing it'. Contrasting contextual training with passively viewing a TV cooking show, Trevor explained that you're not 'just watching someone else cook an imaginary meal. You're tasting what they've produced, going through the experience, looking at it together and then you get to do some cooking yourself.' He also described on-the-job training with a dramatic metaphor: 'We like to say that we let our interns play with live ammo', he continued, 'but you give them room to fail and space to try things in the presence of an experienced church planter because an experienced pastor can see things that they don't see.' Timothy has trained several thousand church planters, and he related to me that one of the key values for church planter apprenticeships in his organization is 'residency'. Defining this he went on to say, 'The whole notion of residency is that at an early stage the apprentice spends time with a sending church to be enculturated as a reproducing leader.' Expanding on this theme, later in the interview Timothy lamented that theological training often tends to ignore the practical aspects needed to develop as 'a true relationship builder'. Using the term 'micro-experience', he explained that 'multiplication must be caught not taught', and that 'you have to do it on the micro-level first before you go out and do the macro-level'.

Delivering basic training

In contrast to common contemporary thinking about masters – that they should only work with expert students[7] – one of the master's most important roles is to deliver initial and basic training to new students. When I asked interviewees about this, several of them said they preferred working with apprentices with little prior experience and some said they would only accept apprentices who had not been trained by others. Toby commented to me, 'My job is to put in the basics, and that job is harder if someone else has part-done the same, or if the student has self-taught.' Similarly Alex pointed out that 'it's always better – and easier – to train someone if you can get them from the very beginning before they have bad habits, wrong ideas, half-wisdom or just someone else's methodology in their head'. Comparing a master to a brick layer, basic training can be seen as the structural foundation upon which later skills are built. As Andrew observed, 'The master gives you the foundations and building blocks from which you can launch into your destiny', and Timothy similarly remarked, 'The role of basic training is to set the best foundations from the beginning.' It is essential that these are solid and not poorly laid: masters rebuild them rather than beginning on an unsound base. Expressing this concept another way, Timothy likened the master's role to the basic training soldiers receive in the military: 'Sometimes the instructor will even need to undo your bad habits and prior learning', a point echoed by Amy who noted initial training is about 'stripping things down to the basics'. Importantly basic training does not exhaustively cover every possible eventuality; rather it is lean, responsive and ready to deploy. Toby highlighted this particularly by remarking that this type of training is characterized by a 'just-in-time', rather than a 'just-in-case' strategy. Terry also added that masters should cover topics that are not included in seminary, such as selection of an initial team, fundraising, relationship with superintendents, and evangelism.

Sharing special knowledge

One intriguing aspect of the master's methodology is the idea of 'secrets' as part of training interactions with apprentices. Alex summarized it well when he told me, 'There are some things I only share with people I mentor one-to-one.' Similarly, Alan – who also made the interesting comment that 'information is sacred' – explained he is selective about whom he apprentices because he shares wisdom that has taken him years to gather. He went on to say that 'in sharing their secrets, the master is allowing the apprentice to be as good as them'. Reinforcing this, Alex remarked, 'It's like getting the family recipe from granny – many people have asked her for it, but she'll only pass it on to the person she trusts and loves.' When I asked Toby to share more about secrets, he told me:

> This knowledge is known by the mentor, but they may find it difficult to commit to paper or to explain verbally. The secrets remain hidden in the mind of the mentor and this special 'know-how' gives him or her the winning competitive edge. Hence such learning or wisdom is usually only passed on through the family or to close-knit trusted community members. Such knowledge is context-specific and based upon creative experience and experimentation of the mentor.

Secrets are not just pieces of high-value information, they are also items of tacit or implicit knowledge that are not easily communicated to another person. Some secrets are pieces of information that are only told to select people, and some secrets are information that can only be *shown* to people; so only the few who are personally trained by that person can receive it. What is being shared is hard-won practical knowledge, or wisdom that isn't easily disseminated.

It is important to stress here that, as in all healthy mentoring relationships, appropriate self-disclosure and safeguarding should be remembered; what is being considered here is the sharing of the treasured wisdom of ministry and craft, not salacious information or inappropriate uses of power.

When we were talking more widely about the 'tacit capacity' of institutions, Alan commented that there have been problematic changes in working environments in recent years. He said, 'Many institutions used to have people that worked for them for 40 years; now they work for four months or four years', explaining that the consequence of this is a 'loss of institutional knowledge because institutions are having to reload every few years'.

Releasing when ready

There is not a fixed timeframe for master-apprentice training; masters release their apprentices at the point when they are ready. When asked 'How long does it take to train an apprentice?' the interviewees gave a wide range of responses from one-week intensive church planter courses, to year-long internships to train church interns. Training for some was even longer; for example, Tom was trained by his mentor for 15 years. Hidden within those timeframes are other factors, such as the actual time spent together, the context, other training being undertaken, and the prior training the apprentice has received. Timothy said an apprenticeship should end when there is mutual agreement: 'If you are my apprentice when I say you're ready and when you say you're ready is when you are ready.' Similarly, Alice favoured an evidence-based assessment: 'Your student moves on when they've done what they need to do with you and now they need a bigger context or they need other teachers.' That said, Timothy did later also suggest that 'anywhere between nine and twelve months is an ideal length of time for an apprenticeship', though this is best tailored to the individual.

April observed that 'there is a point at which people can be very talented autodidacts', explaining that an autodidact is a student who has learned enough in one discipline to be able to self-learn other disciplines. She articulated to me that a master can train an apprentice to the point where they become autodidactic, at which stage the apprentice is then able to take ownership of their ongoing learning. She concluded that masters are expert and experienced practitioners who provide the necessary sets of keys to open doors for other people.

If this is the perspective of apprentices and those who train them, what about the kind of communities where this kind of training can happen? We turn to this in the following chapter.

Questions

1 What qualifies someone to be a master-teacher? Is it possible to train church planters if you haven't planted a church yourself?
2 Confident and humble – does that describe your training style?
3 When you develop others, are you training up supporters or successors; do you envisage a stage when the apprentice is teaching the master?
4 How long does it take to develop basic, intermediate and expert ministerial proficiency – is 10,000 or 12,000 hours of practice and learning necessary to achieve mastery?
5 Is a just-in-time model of training preferable to a just-in-case or front-loaded one? Why?

Notes

1 Mark W Roskill, *The Letters of Vincent Van Gogh* (New York: Simon & Schuster, 1999), 110.

2 Recommendation 15 in Cray, *Mission-Shaped*, 147–48.

3 Of the 560 church planters, 86 per cent were male and 14 per cent female. All of the respondents confirmed that they held a leadership role in the church plant and 88 per cent held the senior leader role. Respondents were from 132 countries, of these 49 per cent were from the US and 27 per cent the UK; respondents were drawn from 133 distinct denominations or networks. Just over one-third of the church plants described by the respondents were less than five years old and the majority (88 per cent) were still active and meeting.

4 The artists are Adam (disc jockey), Alan (model maker), Alex (chef), Alice (actress), Amanda (painter), Amy (musician), Andrew (sculptor) and April (conservation artist); the church leader trainers are Tanner, Tanya, Terry, Thomas, Tina, Toby, Tom and Trevor.

5 These terms were first used as part of a model titled 'the four levels of teaching' proposed by Martin M. Broadwell in 1969 and later developed by Paul R. Curtiss and Phillip W. Warren in *The Dynamics of Life Skills Coaching* (London: Training Research and Development Station, Dept. of Manpower and Immigration, 1973).

6 For more on this subject see, for example, Samuel Wells, *A Nazareth Manifesto: Being with God* (Hoboken, NJ: Wiley, 2015).

7 Such as a masterclass, where an expert trains highly experienced students.

Exploring Guild Training Communities

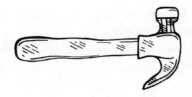

Crafts are teachable; otherwise, good craftsmen would be born, not made.

Aristotle, Nicomachean Ethics[1]

How might modern equivalents to guild communities support training for future church planters? In this chapter we explore the difference between master-apprenticeship training and community training, we consider the different types of training communities, and we unpack the benefits of community training.

The differences between master-apprenticeship training and community training

There is a distinction between master-apprenticeship training – characterized by a one-to-one training environment – and group or community training. However in practice, a mix of master-apprenticeship training *and* group training is often utilized, with one-to-one training typically occurring first. All the interview respondents confirmed that they used a combination of both training methodologies. While important, the initial master-apprentice training experience does have certain limitations. Adam's comments were representative of several other respondents, when he said that 'the trouble with the master-novice relationship is that it tends to be fairly one-dimensional, although the endpoint is very specific'. Likewise, Tom highlighted the constraint of the master's ability to train comprehensively: 'In any training environment or master-apprentice environment, the perspective of the master is limited.' A

similar observation was also made by Andrew: 'The master only special-
izes in one area.' Another drawback of one-to-one training is the relative
social isolation of such a setting, compared to a group environment. Alice
highlighted the social challenge associated with this: 'Groups are necessary because [in a one-to-one setting] the master discusses with them on
their own, so they can feel very isolated and it becomes a challenge for
mental health.'

Because of these limitations, a point invariably arises where there
becomes a need for an apprentice to transition from one-to-one training
with a master, to training communities. Most of the interview respondents
identified the need for such a transition. Alice put it like this: 'One-on-one
stuff is fantastic, but for the individual, it's too safe. Although it feels like
you should stay learning in that safe-space, moving into a group setting is
where you learn much more from other people', and Andrew agreed that
'groups move people beyond the safety of the workshop'. An underlying
impetus for transition, highlighted by April, is that 'you will always have
a different relationship with your master than you will with your peers in
the group. You always look up to your master, but there will always be
things you can't talk to them about.'

There are therefore clear benefits, as I will discuss, to facilitating
apprentices to progress into training communities, and correspondingly,
the importance of a group training environment was recognized by most
of the interview respondents. These perceived benefits include enhanced
learning and peer connectivity. For example, Alice said, 'There is such
huge potential within a group-setting for very deep learning and actually to speed up [that] learning.' Similarly, April remarked that it is very
important 'to try to meet as many people as you can' and noted that
'groups not only help you learn more, they also help you develop social
connections with fellow learners'. The peer group is not only beneficial
for social well-being and mental health then; the enhanced effectiveness
of learning alongside other peers is recognized. 'Because people see things
differently there is an incredible learning power in putting people with
the same interest in a group together' explained Andrew. Summarizing,
Alex agreed that 'peer-power is the best format for learning'.

The types of training communities

There are different types of training communities characterized by
size-dynamics and by purpose, and these distinctions were either directly
described or inferred by our interview respondents. For example, the
relationship between the size and the function of a group was noted by

Alan who commented that 'size-dynamics means groups perform different functions'. He continued by saying that, 'like Methodist societies, there is a role for groups of 50 to 75 people, there is a role for a small class meeting size of under 20 people, and there is also a role for a group of between three and five'. When discussing church planting with Black-majority churches in North America, Terry explained that the variety of needs for different church plants is illustrated by his observation that there are at least 16 different types of support-community for Black-majority church planters. A more pragmatic reflection about group-size was made by Thomas, who commented that 'the size of groups is determined by the bandwidth of relationships'.

Some communities are led by a master; in others, a master may be present; and some groups are peer-led. This variation was identified by Alice and other interviewees, who also suggested to me that groups ideally comprise learners who are at a similar stage of development. In contrast, Trevor proposed that 'you must get people who are less experienced together in the same room as more experienced people' – there are certainly pros and cons to both approaches.

In the section below we will explore six different types of training community. All six were described by the respondents, though this is not intended to be an exhaustive list. These have been classified as follows: intimate groups, tutorial groups, groups of 12, learning communities, micro-networks and church planting networks.

Intimate groups

The benefits of an intimate group of, for example, three people, include openness, efficiency and flexibility. Very small groups enable the deepest level of personal sharing – a phenomenon that Adam observed. Groups of this size, as Toby commented to me, are also the easiest to establish and organize, and – because they are small – they are able to address many aims simultaneously, such as personal encouragement, mutual support and accountability, and quick adaptation to contextual needs, as Tanner explained. Recalling his own experience of being in a group with two other people at different life-stages, Alan summarized that 'everyone needs a Paul and everyone needs a Timothy – older leaders we're learning from and younger leaders we're investing in'.

Workshops or tutorial groups

The tutorial group can be defined as a master-led small group of typically less than six. While tutorial groups are commonplace in UK theological colleges, two of the interviewees – both theological educators – bemoaned the absence of small master-led groups in the North American seminary experience. Referring to these communities by the term 'master-workshops', Alan commented to me that '[North American] seminaries are missing the dynamic of three to five people meeting with the professor, which is the master-apprentice workshop relationship.'

Groups of 12

Groups of 12 are popular, and this is unsurprising given the exemplar of Jesus' engagement with the Twelve disciples, where the apprentice remains connected with the master and does not become lost or overlooked in a larger crowd. Six of the interviewees said that groups of approximately 12 people are an ideal size, and some associated this group with Jesus' training model. There are sound, practical reasons for preferring this size, as Tanya highlighted. If there are 'more than 12, ... you find the quiet people are not contributing. The ideal size is probably between eight and twelve, so there's space for everybody to communicate but it's not too big that you end up with too many lines of communication.'

Learning communities

A commonly found type of community, termed a 'learning community', is a particularly popular model across America, but is also practised in Europe. A learning community consists of a group meeting regularly, with shared objectives, learning together through collaborative and supportive interaction. 'Most church planting networks in America use a learning community model', Alan acknowledged, where 'people meet monthly, weekly or quarterly, with between 5 and 20 people having structured and supportive conversations about the key issues about church planting'. Learning communities are essentially egalitarian groups where ideas and experiences can be shared interactively to influence praxis, as Tom reflected to me: 'When we created a group for church planters, we made it into a learning community. It was a flat learning experience where people can cross-pollinate.'

Micro-networks

A micro-network is a less institutionally structured form of church planting support that operates, often locally, either within or across denominational boundaries. These effectively fulfil the function of church planting affinity groups. Both Trevor and Tanner highlighted the role of such support networks, which Tanner terms 'micro-networks'. Sometimes, as Trevor has observed, these communities span denominations and, in other examples, they connect church planters working within a single denomination. Explaining the concept further, Tanner remarked that 'we all need to be part of a denomination and part of networks. The first is a tribe and a tradition, but [church planters] also need an affinity network. Oftentimes these micro-networks are small and regional.' Despite clear benefits to this type of training community, Tanner conceded that most denominations, even those involved in church planting, do not yet provide these kinds of church planting affinity groups.

Church planting networks

The last type of learning community highlighted by the interviews is the church planting network. These are organizational, operational networks which are run by churches involved in church planting. They are similar to the micro-networks described above, however they are often larger, and arise as a strategic community from groups of churches working together who want to create a church planting pipeline. Of those I interviewed, Thomas spoke most clearly about these communities. Having worked with many hundreds of examples of this type of community, he observed that 'a network of churches working together to do this reduces the overall risk' of a church plant failing. He also suggested that, ideally, these communities should be socially and economically diverse. Arguably, this type of community is observed in the earliest churches, as Thomas explained: 'The New Testament suggests a relational model of church planting, which means networks of churches should be involved in both the raising up and the sending out of the planter, in order to make sure that that planter has relational connections [which they] can rely on.' From his own practical experience, Thomas proposed a taxonomy: a group of four to six churches is a network, and a group of six networks is a movement.

The benefits of community training

In this section, we will consider the benefits of community training in greater depth. In the context of church planting, a significant proportion of subjects who participated in the survey of church planter trainers found community training to be effective. Specifically, when asked about their experiences of church planting communities, approximately half agreed 'planting communities' are effective in increasing the effectiveness of church planter training.[2]

Following analysis of the comments of interview subjects, I have been able to further identify six key perceived benefits of training communities which contribute to their effectiveness. These are personal support, feedback and review, opportunity for participation, teamwork, increased productivity, and deep learning.

Personal support

One key benefit of training in community is the opportunity to give and receive personal support. Smaller groups are more naturally relationship focused and easier to join than larger groups; furthermore, groups with a relational focus often spontaneously facilitate mutual support. Contrastingly, when speaking about seminary training, Tanya observed that 'classrooms tend to isolate people' – she found that recent seminary graduates needed to be trained to avoid isolating themselves. Groups, on the other hand, provide emotional support and encouragement, a fact Amy highlighted.

However, connecting with a group is not always straightforward. For example, Alice pointed out that 'people are very exhausted by modern life and often find it hard to commit time to a group'. Consequently – and perhaps counterintuitively – people in need of support might not connect with a group that is able to support them. Similarly, Terry also felt this paradox was an insight into modern life: 'Groups are around today for the fragmentation in our society.' In this respect, supportive groups model a positive message to a society in need of support; and creating a supportive community requires overcoming these obstacles of isolation and social fragmentation. Yet, as Trevor discussed with me, a significant challenge exists: many new church planters wrongly believe that a unified vision alone is sufficient to create such community. As he wisely remarked, 'If we don't love each other *and* want to work together, then being committed to a clear vision won't be enough ... Most churches and even denominational churches are functionally independent' (interviewee's emphasis).

Feedback and review

Groups are particularly beneficial environments for feedback and review, due to their shared, interactive format which facilitates honest, reflective discussion. For example, Trevor recounted to me how he works to create an atmosphere of feedback in the small groups that he forms for new church planters. Using a sporting analogy, he said 'We game tape problems', which he explained to mean that he encourages groups to review and critique ministry performance, such as reviewing a sermon. This type of feedback often touches upon issues of identity, as Trevor observed: 'If our righteousness is our deepest identity – who we are in Jesus – we can take critique.' That said, it takes wisdom to get the level of challenge right, as Toby noted: feedback must provide 'enough to challenge but not too much to discourage. Nevertheless, the master must be a truthful critic.'

Opportunity for participation

Training communities provide novices with the opportunity to participate at an early stage in their training experience. When speaking about developing young musicians in a church band, Amy commented to me that she has 'given absolute beginners the chance to be in the band right from the word go'. She felt this practice was vital to encouraging musicians who were at the beginning of their learning: 'Even as a beginner you *need* to start playing with others – you can't be learning your musical instrument for three years before having a go in public' (interviewee's emphasis). Early participation builds confidence and encourages development of contextual skills.

Teamwork

Training communities create environments for effective engagement in teamwork and there are a number of advantages to this, highlighted by six of the interview respondents. First, teamwork facilitates access to a wider breadth of knowledge and ability. For example, Alan commented that 'if you've only got one person [the master], you've only got one thread to pull on and then you're only going to get one solution; when you've got several people that you're learning from, you have different options to play around with'. Teamwork encourages specialisms to develop which can serve the whole. As Terry put it, 'Groups mean that we don't have to be a generalist.' Explaining the effect of this to me, he added that 'we can focus on the things we are gifted in because we are in a team with other people with complementary gifts'.

There is also a mutual benefit of collaborative teamwork, as Alice noted: 'You're on an individual journey, but there's this communal journey that you're all in. You're investing in each other and they're all in something bigger than just yourself and you're creating something that's beyond just you.' However, Amanda pointed out that 'people need to be taught to collaborate', and this recognition that teamwork *itself* is a learnable skill was highlighted by others. In some disciplines, teamwork is not just optional, it's vital – as Amy expressed, giving the example that 'it's impossible to become a team player musician without being put in a team to do it'. Similarly, April made the observation that 'although some artists work in a very solitary way, for others working together is intrinsic to the craft. For example, so much music-making involves teamwork.' Therefore learning teamwork skills can often be a significant training objective – one facilitated by training communities. In this respect, Amy reinforced that 'if your craft is all about other people, then you're already learning that aspect of it [when you train in a team]', and April, speaking about her training work, said, 'Our work is done in studios, so it's inherently part of our work *and* training that we operate in community and as a network' (interviewee's emphasis).

Teamwork also enables multidisciplinary learning. 'The nice thing about the group', Amanda remarked, 'is that you're in a room with a wider range of talents.' April added, 'There's a degree of creativity that comes out of working with people who have different perspectives and different skills' and, summarizing these advantages, Trevor concluded that 'we are able, by God's grace, to lead more wisely with input from multiple layers of leaders than from just one leader'.

Increased productivity

Learning communities stimulate greater productivity from their members than learning in isolation, and this was reflected in the responses of the interviewees. Providing a sporting analogy, Thomas noted that in football, 'the team wins together', because the team is helping each player improve his or her individual performance by working together. Similarly, Terry remarked to me that 'coaching networks immeasurably help people to perform better', and Amy highlighted one reason why this might be the case: 'Groups bring an edge of competitiveness.' Team working certainly stimulates competitive performance gains, but there is a further effect –

when a group works well together, it can achieve more than it can apart. As Trevor observed, 'Being part of a network or a group means that there are times when the group can accomplish something that no one person could pull off.'

Observations that I received regarding collective productivity are brought together well by April who said, 'If creativity is about looking outwards, then being part of the network that enabled you to do that will help you discover that there's always something more to be learned, so you get better.'

Collective memory and learning

Lastly, communities enable collective and ongoing learning. One of the greatest benefits of training in community, which Terry discussed, is the capacity of a group to facilitate multigenerational learning. Likewise, Alan also affirmed to me the value of groups in promoting intergenerational learning. Recognizing that there is a collective memory or wisdom that can be passed on, Terry expressed to me that groups can hold the lore of the discipline or craft and thereby facilitate deeper learning. Collective learning is deep in the sense that it transcends any one individual's knowledge base or experience. In this way, communities enable existing leaders to continue to learn – one reason why this can happen, Andrew suggested to me, is because 'there's always going to be somebody better than you in the room'. The collective memory of groups provides a mimetic environment for information to pass from generation to generation as a cultural phenomenon that transcends any one individual's knowledge base. In summary, Alice reflected that

> there is such huge potential within a group-setting for very deep learning and actually to speed up the learning. One-on-one stuff is fantastic but, for the individual, it's safe … Moving into a group setting is where you dig deep and learn from other people.

We return in Part 5 to the role groups play in training, but we should be clear at this point that a range of appropriate groups, networks and communities of practice are crucial in developing the craft of church planting.

Questions

1 How do we create peer groups that stretch, support, deepen and accelerate the development of church planters in training?
2 What types of training communities have you participated in – small groups, workshops, learning communities, micro-networks, church planting networks, etc. – and what benefit did you receive from them?
3 What role can church planting networks play in supporting church planting within denominations?
4 How do we facilitate groups that preserve the lore of church planting – collective memory, tacit knowledge and secret wisdom – so it can be passed from one generation of practitioners to the next?

Notes

1 Aristotle, *Nicomachean Ethics* 2.1.
2 Forty-five per cent either agreed or strongly agreed with the statement that 'the planting community I was in before I planted my first church plant was effective in increasing my training as a church planter'; 50 per cent either agreed or strongly agreed that 'the planting community I was in while I planted my current church plant was or is effective in increasing my training as a church planter'.

12

Exploring and Applying Creativity

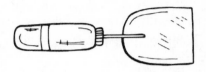

all men and women are entrusted with the task of crafting their own life ... they are to make of it a work of art, a masterpiece.

Pope John Paul II[1]

Inside the artist there are two men: the poet and the craftsman. One is born a poet; one becomes a craftsman.

Émile Zola[2]

Christian spirituality is like jazz music.

Donald Miller[3]

This chapter considers the ways in which creativity is significant for training church planters. The findings are categorized below under three main headings: observations about the aspects of creativity that are significant for church planting, observations about the aspects of creativity that are significant for training church planters, and observations about how creativity is developed and released.

Aspects of creativity that are significant for church planting

Creativity plays a significant role in the activity of church planting, and this was confirmed by the responses of all three groups of participants in this study. For example, Alan commented to me that 'church planting is fundamentally a creative process'. Echoing this observation, Thomas 'wished we use the terminology "the art of church planting" more, because planting is about creativity'. The activity and process of creativity often begins with listening to God in prayer, as Tanya has highlighted:

We place quite a bit of weight on the prophetic when training planters. We are very much encouraging people to hear from God and let him [God] speak into the identity of the emerging church communities as they're being established.

This link between creative people and prophetic people was also affirmed by Alan who noted that 'a lot of prophets are artists'. The same idea – of the importance of creativity as a revelation of God – was also noted by Amanda, who compared church planting with the illumination that can result from artistic creation: 'When an artist paints a painting, a miracle happens – the blind see.'

When asked about the importance of creativity in church planting, almost all of the subjects who participated in my interviews agreed that creativity is an important part of the process of church and that church planting is more effective with leaders who are creative.[4] The same subjects were asked to list the words or phrases that came to mind when they thought of creativity in the context of church planting and training church planters. The most common keywords were 'innovative', 'flexible' and 'out of the box', such as in the statements 'innovation releases new creativity', 'flexibility allows for new things from old' and 'you need "out of the box" thinking in a new context'.[5] Figure 12.1 shows a word-cloud representation of all the keywords that occurred more than once.

Figure 12.1: Word-cloud of keywords describing creativity

Creativity in the revitalization of the wider church

Creativity can also play an important role in the revitalization of the wider church through church planting, and this was emphasized by some of the interview respondents. For this to occur, creative people must be both valued and effectively enabled. Acknowledging the inflexibility of some historic church denominations, Tom said, 'The challenge to the church today is to make space for people who don't fit. If they're able to hold creative people in some way, that becomes a blessing to the whole and it begins to give permission for other creative stuff to happen.' The process for this, as Tom argues, begins by 'enabling creativity to happen on the edge' with the result that, in time, 'the centre of gravity of the whole movement or denomination moves towards that creativity'.

Creativity in the contextualization of church planting

Contextualization – the tailoring of the Christian message, and faith expression, in order to communicate with relevance to a specific socio-logical context – is vital for effective church planting. Highlighting the importance of this, Tanya said, 'The whole thing about church plants is that they are contextual.' Furthermore, the application of creativity in the activity of church planting results in, and promotes, contextualization. This association between creativity and contextualization was recognized by several of the interview respondents. For example, Thomas noted that 'the concept of artistry and creativity in each plant is uniquely gifted by God and the call to a specific context of people in a place and a time'. Similarly Alan observed that cultural awareness – 'that is, understanding your context through culture and understanding how to engage' – is a vital precursor to contextualization. Both require, and are enriched by, creativity: 'the artistic spirit is dynamic, adaptable, and pliable'.

If, as Thomas expressed earlier, we can speak about the 'art of church planting', then the church planter should be considered as a type of artist. Tina made this very association when she remarked that 'by thinking like an artist in the church planting world, I have the capacity to create something unique and important inside the body of Christ'. For Thomas, there is a stark contrast between the prevailing culture of church planter training and new ideas for training that are highlighted when talking about creativity:

Let me just speak to the West. We have tried the pipeline model of church planting, ... but we've missed the artistry model ... I've written down in my journal a few times that it would be better if we treated church planters like artists and trained them as artists, create studios for them to create, and places where they can learn the craft and experiment.

Later in his interview, Thomas reinforced that this way of thinking has not always been encouraged: 'I believe that we've done a disservice to not allow a church planter to identify themselves as an artist.' Correspondingly, others that I interviewed lamented the lack of creativity in some church planter training models, likening the result to cloning. Tanya said:

The church plant needs to fit the context and can't just be a clone or a copy of the church that they are being sent from. I'm encouraging people to listen deeply to the context ... and [listen] to God. Something's being created that is bespoke and unique to fit that context ... You know, anything is possible. Also, [I believe in] the value of experimentation and that mistakes are okay.

And reflecting on her own experience as a church planter, Tina realized that the biggest difference between herself and her colleagues is that they approached church planting as technicians whereas she approached it as an artist. She went on to say that in her experience, 'church planting is about creating a piece of art, not a big-box factory for saved people'.

As a caution, Thomas observed a negative trait in artists: '[Later in their life] the artist tends to look over his or her shoulder and sees their whole body of work as the culmination of the journey that got them to that place.' He said that this type of reflection, which occurs in older practitioners, can result in church planters who are too focused on themselves and no longer open to new creativity.

Aspects of creativity that are significant for training church planters

Creativity and human identity

Creativity is an essential part of being human – one that enriches individuals and groups of people. When commenting on the aspects of creativity that are significant to the training experiences of church planters, a number of those interviewed highlighted the association between creativity and human identity. 'To be creative is to be human', Alice explained, 'we are naturally creative beings.' She continued to say, 'If we don't have creativity in our lives, we are just living some kind of mechanized life.' Recognizing the power of the arts to draw people and communities together in shared appreciation, Amy extended this idea: 'When you share your life, the creative thing that you share creates common humanity with those people.' She later explained that this is because 'artists enhance, empower and enrich the lives of other[s]'.

Creativity and God

God created humans to be creative – we are anthropic artisans, made in God's image, reflecting and expressing divine intention through our own creativity. Although self-identifying in the interview as a person who does not believe in God, Alice nevertheless recognized the association between creativity and something lying beyond ourselves: 'My creativity is something that is so much vaster and not of me', she remarked, continuing by adding that 'creativity is lifeblood, that is, essential to being human. I think creativity is something that connects us to something deeper inside us and something bigger than us all, ... so, to me, it does something quite spiritual.' Expressing a similar idea, Andrew told me: 'Creativity is one of the deepest expressions of the character and nature of God in [our] reflecting him as an image-bearer. When we create we are mirroring who God is. For me, creativity is birthing something from nothing.'

Everyone is creative

Perceptions of what typically constitutes creativity can be stereotypical, for example fine art, music, dance, etc. Yet several of the interview respondents spoke about the idea of creativity applying to activities that might not commonly be thought of as artistic, such as asking open questions, being willing to do something in a different way, or working with different people. Reflecting this, Alice remarked that 'what we define as creativity can be a bit limited. It is not just about creating a work of art on a wall or a performance on a stage. Because creativity is fundamental to living a fully human life, it applies to anything and everything that we make.' Foundationally then, every single person is creative – and this belief was expressed by nearly all of those that I interviewed. For example, Tom suggested that while there are degrees of creativity, 'everyone is creative; some people are just off the scale creative', and Amanda added that when some 'people say "I'm not creative", I fundamentally disagree with that. I believe that we are all infinitely creative.' However, creativity is not always automatically released; sometimes it needs unlocking in people who are being trained, as several respondents noted. Paraphrasing the theatre director, Declan Donnellan, Alice said, 'We're all infinitely creative, but some of us are less blocked than others.' As Donnellan continues, 'the talent is already pumping away, like the circulation of the blood. We just have to dissolve the clot'.[6] For some church planters, training is necessary – like an anticoagulant – to release and restore the flow of creativity. April put it like this: 'Creativity is something that is ever-present to all of us, Some are lucky enough [to] access it automatically; others need help with skills or processes to tap into it.'

Creativity as empowerment

An interconnection exists between creativity, a culture of empowerment and the development of people – which several respondents identified. When asked why creativity was important to church planters, Trevor told me, 'It is important to believe in the gifts of young leaders and to bless their gifts so that they will have ideas. We need to help them to know that there is space for them to play.' Similarly, Alan expressed this empowerment as 'permission to solve a problem', and Alex defined the creative person as 'someone who thinks around a problem'. When I asked Alan, 'How does problem-solving link with creativity?' he replied, 'In my experience, scarcity produces creativity.' Problems themselves often call for creative solutions, and these will emerge when training church planters are effectively empowered to step out creatively.

Creativity and risk-taking

Risk-taking is an important quality relevant to church planting training. The idea that a challenge can create an environment that cultivates creativity was described by some of the respondents interviewed, when they emphasized the connection between creativity and risk-taking. 'You can never truly release creativity without being willing to take risks', Amanda acknowledged, 'sometimes big risks'. Enabling a culture of risk-taking involves allowing each other the freedom to fail, and recognizing the ability to alter course. As Alice noted, 'if you're approaching things from a creative perspective, then you are committing yourself to making mistakes ... or to being able to change your mind and be flexible'. Risk-taking is also necessary for innovation – something Alan identified: 'You need to be able to make mistakes, and see any way that you will learn to be an innovative and risk-taking exercise.'

The development and release of creativity

As discussed, when asked 'How can people be trained to be creative?', all of the interview respondents affirmed the idea that everybody is creative. April summarized that, rather than 'a gift that you either have or don't have', creativity is 'a skill that anyone can develop through hard work'. Correspondingly, a number of respondents suggested practical approaches which accord with the understanding that creativity can be effectively developed and released in others. We will consider these in eight categories.

Creativity is nurtured and released in two distinct stages

A synthesis of the comments of the respondents suggests that creativity is nurtured and released in a two-stage process. The first stage is characterized by investment in basic skills and abilities, typically through stimulation experiences and repetitive skill-tasks. Commenting on this stage, Amanda said: 'Without skills, you can't liberate your potential and you'll become stifled'; furthermore, 'if you try to be creative without the skills behind you it becomes frustrating and it dampens down creativity'. The second stage is characterized by imaginative engagement with challenges, accompanied by a playful and youthful approach. Considering this stage, Amanda continued, 'There's a point in your training where it can stifle your creativity if you're just repeating and repeating … You need to encourage ideas and start experimenting.' We can therefore identify different components in each of these two stages. Alex used an organic metaphor which summarizes the overall process: 'First you plant the seeds, add good nutrients, and some water. Then you wait, and nothing seems to happen. But eventually, with sunlight and time, something amazing grows.'

The master as a coach

A factor in navigating the transition between these two stages is the role of the master. Several interviewees recognized that the master can function in a coaching capacity to unlock creative expression: 'If the master can become a coach, then they can be a guide to draw out creativity from people', Terry explained, adding that 'a good coach can help people to be more creative than they would be if left on their own'. Similarly, the catalytic task of the master was identified by April: 'the role of [the teacher or trainer] is to be a facilitator to give people the tools, the confidence and the encouragement'. Highlighting a greater significance of this transition, Amy noted that 'as soon as you introduce creativity you're introducing autonomy'. This means being given permission to imaginatively experiment (stage two), rather than becoming a clone of existing practitioners, or feeling constrained by 'a set of rules'. The benefits of coaching a student into an autonomous creative stage – as Amy confirmed from her experience – include better mental-health and an improved sense of self-worth and personhood. In her words, 'the person comes alive because they've got in touch with something inside that they didn't know was there'.

Creativity takes significant work

The development of creativity takes a significant amount of work, and this is something that was recognized by all of the respondents who commented on this aspect. 'You've got to practise the art', remarked Amanda, and Alex told me that 'all true creatives have to work very hard on what they do'. Likewise, April frankly admitted that 'to develop creativity there's a lot of [expletive] hard work involved'.

In summarizing the first stage of the development of creativity (skill-building), April reflected that from the 'field of art [comes both] the understanding of working with materials, and how the learning of basic skills by instruction will release latent creative potential'. She brings insight here by highlighting that development of creativity is contextual – it depends on the 'materials' being worked with – and contextual creativity is nurtured by developing familiarity with those materials and basic skills. For church planters, materials are the various people they engage with (those outside of the church, newcomers, new disciples, emerging leaders, etc.) and basic skills include spiritual disciplines; preaching, teaching and mentoring; and leadership and ministry roles, such as shepherding. In April's words, 'All creativity needs to flow from an understanding of the potentials of those materials.'

Affirmed identity and creativity

A further foundation for the first, skill-building stage of developing creativity is secure identity. A lack of understanding of our personal identity in Christ and a lack of individual confidence can result in a reluctance to try new things, as Tina reflected: 'If you know who you are in Jesus, then you walk in authority that unleashes those creative juices.'

Two factors were observed by Amy: 'We were created in God's image by a creative God to be creative', and later she said, 'As we are being creative, we are the most deeply rooted in our God-given humanity.' She summarized her understanding of the process: 'Creativity is allowing someone to connect with something they feel inside and find a way to just let it come out.' She described one aspect of the result when she said, 'It's almost like creativity is how you present yourself.'

The more confident a church planter is in their identity in God, including the connection between God's identity as a creator and their own creative work, the more effective they will be in expressing and applying their creativity.

Other comments about developing creativity

The first, skill-building stage of developing creativity can involve a variety of other approaches. Perhaps counterintuitively, it is often better for the master to ask questions rather than offer advice. As Tom explained to me, this 'leads to much more creativity because you are helping them to apply thinking to their context'. Meeting the right people is also equally important, April pointed out, because 'people who can be facilitators, encouragers, and guides can help you by giving you the tools you need to express creativity to its fullest degree'. She went on to remark that 'there's a degree of creativity that comes out of working with people who have different perspectives and different skills'. Others I interviewed went a step further, taking new trainees to visit art galleries, in order to stimulate imaginative and innovative thinking. Thomas 'took a bunch of prospective church planters to the National Gallery to look at ways that people express themselves'. 'One of the things I do with my new ordinands', Alan explained, is 'take them to the Tate Modern – even if they're techy non-artists – and we ask ourselves, "What [are] the artists trying to communicate?", "What are they communicating?", and "How are they using their art form to communicate?"' Ultimately, as Tom put it to me, 'all creativity is grown through doing it'. Thomas extended the image further: 'The cycle of creativity is like a flywheel, once you begin to embrace it in small doses then you're more willing to get out there.'

Time to release creativity

Moving on to consider the second stage of developing creativity (imaginative engagement with challenges), it is important in this phase to allow sufficient time to release creativity. Speaking about this, Alan remarked: 'To function as a creative person you need to have space to contemplate, space to create and space to dream.' Tina regretted that when she was younger she 'neglected the incredible value of thinking time', and further reflected that 'all the great innovators in the world were people who had big chunks of time to think, big chunks of time to walk and big chunks of time to pray. Your creativity needs that room: it needs the mental space and the spiritual space to blossom.' Applying this practically, Tanya therefore tells prospective church planters, 'Have white-space in your diary for your head to ponder, imagine, think, dream and create. Whether it's retreat days, or [getting] away for a couple of days walking in the mountains or on the beach'; similarly, Tom recommends that apprentice church planters 'put time in [the] diary to "kick leaves"', echoing Rob Parsons's advice that leaders allow sufficient time in their week to ponder ideas.[7]

Confidence to take risks

We earlier considered the general importance of risk-taking, however this becomes particularly significant in the second stage of developing and nurturing creativity. Interview respondents highlighted the importance of having the confidence to take risks, in order to release creativity. Andrew observed that 'creativity comes when we set ourselves free from the fear of failure'. Creativity can only be expressed when there exists a willingness to try new things combined with willingness to accept that ideas may not work, as Alex noted:

> You have to be able to experiment, to try new things and to have the cover and support of a mentor or a master. Inventing something comes after you've tried a hundred times: it doesn't come the first time. So a new model, or a new technique, or a new art form, or whatever, will come through experimentation and getting it wrong many times.

Youthful and playful

Finally, the adoption of a youthful or a playful approach is most significant in the second stage of developing creativity, where play stimulates imaginative and fluid approaches to meeting challenges. 'Creativity comes from a sense of trust and a sense of play', affirmed Alice. She continued by sharing with me that her preferred way of working with others involves 'a combination of challenging people with a sense of playfulness, and permission to fail', concluding, 'I find that gives us an ability to reach beyond what we think we're capable of.' Andrew added that when releasing and enabling creativity, 'there is a need and opportunity for play and fun – not taking yourself too seriously – and enjoying the process'. And, from her study of history and experience training other artists, April observed that:

> the most open people are generally the people who are the youngest and least experienced because they have nothing to lose. I think the danger [occurs] when people get older and more established – in some instances they find it harder to admit there are things they don't know or things they might be able to learn.

She also reflected that 'it's fascinating that some of the greatest artists have always seemed very young, whatever their literal age. They always seem young because they keep that freshness and their desire to know and to interact with the world around them.' This can occur, Andrew suggested, through encouraging a perspective-shift in the mind of students by imagining themselves as children again. He remarked that 'children are a great example – they're not worried about getting marked out of ten or being graded: it's just not in their thinking. They're developing the thing they love doing and don't care what anyone thinks.' In summary, creativity will be catalysed when church planting training facilitates fluid, youthful and playful approaches; and it will flourish when imaginative, innovative ideas are allowed to find full expression.

As these accounts show, creativity is more than attractive window-dressing of the Christian faith; it is the outflow of deeply-held convictions about the life and purpose of God. It is a Christian vision of creativity that keeps apprenticeship from being programmatic or paint-by numbers. It holds relationships open to the freedom of God and the surprises of the Spirit. Ultimately, it distinguishes true disciples of Christ from slavish religious reproduction. Only by holding apprenticeship and guild-like learning communities together with this liberative impulse can we hope to foster the kind of church planting ethos which does justice to the gospel.

Questions

1 What might be gained and released by considering church planting as an art, not just a science?
2 If everyone is creative, how might we design training programmes for church planters that nurture and release the flow of creativity?
3 What is the relationship between challenges, risk-taking, and permission to fail and the activation of creativity?
4 How might church planters (and all ministers) create white-space in their schedule to ponder, imagine, think and dream to release the freedom of God and creativity?
5 How can we give permission for the youthful and playful approach (not taking yourself too seriously, enjoying the process, imitating children) that is vital to releasing creativity and the surprises of the Spirit?

Notes

1 Pope John Paul II, *Letter of His Holiness Pope John Paul II to Artists* (Pauline Books and Media, 1999), 2.1.

2 Letter to Paul Cézanne on 16 April 1860, published in Alex Danchev, *The Letters of Paul Cézanne* (Los Angeles: The J. Paul Getty Museum, 2013).

3 Donald Miller, *Blue Like Jazz: Nonreligious Thoughts on Christian Spirituality* (Nashville, TN: Thomas Nelson Publishers, 2003), 239.

4 Eighty-seven per cent either agreed or strongly agreed with the statement that 'in churches I have planted, creativity was an important part of the process of church planting'; 77 per cent either agreed or strongly agreed that 'church planting is more effective with leaders who are creative'.

5 This question was answered by 97 per cent of the respondents, who supplied 1,475 answers which were then classified according to researcher-assigned keywords which grouped closely related themes or repeated phrases. In total there were 1,026 keyword assignments for keywords which occurred more than once, drawing on 106 distinct keywords.

6 Declan Donnellan, *The Actor and the Target*, revised edn (London: Nick Hern Books, 2005), 5.

7 Rob Parsons, *Almost Everything I Need to Know about God: I Learned in Sunday School* (Nashville, TN: Thomas Nelson Publishers, 1999), 133.

13

From Principle to Practice:
Some Examples of Craft Apprenticeship

When the dogs stop barking and the postman knows your name, it's time for the journeyman to leave.

Advice to a modern Journeyman[1]

How do these principles of craft apprenticeship play out in practice? This last chapter before the conclusions seeks to illustrate this by way of some brief examples.

Such a process is not entirely straightforward. Historic examples of craft guild apprenticeship are hard to come by. In fact, the precise details of what training looked like in medieval guilds is a mystery. It may be that once-written accounts have been lost over time or, in a less literate age, never written at all. Their scarcity might be due in part to the secrecy of guilds: masters were keen to protect knowledge that was vital to their economic competitiveness. Or it may simply be that the guild method of training meant that books were not a priority because masters personally trained apprentices in the basics and in how to learn for themselves. Whatever the reasons, beyond small snippets, we have no full accounts of training encounters in the historic medieval guilds.[2]

Relevant contemporary accounts are also limited. Few modern institutions operate according to craft principles, and any that do typically utilize a hybrid model of ancient and modern approaches. Also, for the most part, modern artisans often work alone, rather than in training-workshops as their medieval forebears did. That said, we can find expressions of craft apprenticeship in some modern examples of historic industries, in new forms of formal apprenticeship, in small indigenous manufacturing, and in modern contexts that are rediscovering old ways, sometimes by accident.

Below are four contemporary examples which should help in illustrating some of the principles identified in the previous three chapters. These samples may also remind you of your own examples – something you have seen or done yourself that embodied a craft approach. The first is from a personal visit to The House of Waterford Crystal in the Republic of Ireland, which includes an explanation of the methods of training apprentices and the 'Apprentice Bowl'. The second is from an interview with David Switalla, a modern-day German journeyman stonemason and sculptor who describes his *Wanderjahre* (German, Wandering-years). The third is taken from an ethnographic study of handicraft pottery in China. The last is a report on training preachers at G2, an innovative church in York.

The 'Apprentice Bowl' at Waterford Crystal

Glass-cutting apprentices have been trained at Waterford since 1783.[3] Typically, prospective apprentices must perform a proficiency test to establish their initial suitability for training. For example, as evidence of their basic agility, current applicants must cut an eight-point star on a circular piece of crystal using a sandstone wheel. If accepted, new apprentices join a six-person team, known as a Bench, so named because of a bench-mounted motor that turns the wheels of the six-man shop. Each Bench is led by a 'first man' who is a master. The first man works with a second, known as the first helper, who is assisted by a second helper and three apprentices. As Benches are run on a piece-rate system, the productivity and financial rewards of the working group are dependent on the competence of every member of the team. The job of the master and first helper is to hand-cut the first rough cut of each pattern or design with a carborundum wheel in such a way as to make it easy for the apprentice to join all the points in a diamond-shaped pattern with a smooth sandstone wheel. In past times, every cutting element was done in two stages: rough and smooth. For example, the master would rough-cut sixteen-point stars and it would be the job of the newly appointed apprentice to smooth out the rough cut and bring the star design to a perfect centre. Over five years apprentices learn numerous cuts such as, cross-hatch cutting (also known as caro); rosettes; different point stars; swerve cutting; upright cutting; horizontal cutting; and the skills to smooth out the rough cuts made by the master or first helper. This also requires the ability to profile glass in a two-stage grinding process using a carborundum wheel followed by a finer sandstone wheel. Last, apprentices have to learn how to do 'scollops', which refers to the process of shaping the tops of crystal pieces.

After five years of training, apprentices can graduate as cutters by producing evidence of their knowledge and skill by making an 'Apprentice Bowl'.[4] To make this, an apprentice is given a plain glass bowl approximately eight inches in diameter and four inches high. They are required to produce a finished bowl that demonstrates approximately 600 hand-made two-stage cuts which incorporate all of the types of cut used in the workshop. During the test, apprentices can request the advice of other cutters, including the master craftsmen, provided that the other craftworkers do not touch the bowl. Apprentices are only permitted three attempts at an Apprentice Bowl: if they fail three times, they must restart their apprenticeship training. Typically, a bowl takes one week to complete. When all the smooth cutting is completed, the bowl is graded by the cutting shop manager who assesses it according to the intricacies of the cuts, the free-flowing movement, hand-depth perception, and mitre-cutting qualities. If the bowl passes it is inscribed by the Bench master, polished in acid, and the apprentice graduates as a glass cutter.

David Switalla – 'my wandering years'

David Switalla is a modern-day German *steinmetz und steinbildhauermeister* (stonemason and sculptor) whose journeyman travels followed the methods of the stonemason guilds of his country.[5] Switalla worked as an apprentice stonemason in the city of Neu-Ulm in Germany from 2005 to 2009. In September 2009 he embarked on his travels as a journeyman to receive new training that would help him qualify as a master.

On the day that he began his journeyman-walk, Switalla was accompanied to the city boundary of Neu-Ulm by his training master, family members, younger apprentices from his workshop, and past and present journeymen. His master drew a line on the ground in chalk to remind him that, for the next three years and a day, he should not return within 30 kilometres of the workshop where he had trained as an apprentice. Switalla's friends then helped him to climb over the city sign (this was a local and recent tradition) and he walked away with his fellow journeymen without looking back. He was expected to carry everything he needed with him as he travelled. He also agreed not to carry a mobile phone, and his first job was to make a personalized walking stick. At his leaving party, his master pierced his ear – using Switalla's hammer and a nail Switalla had made – as a sign that Switalla would return to his master's workshop after his educational travels.

In his years as a journeyman, Switalla learned many life skills, new masonry skills, and skills in other complementary crafts that he discovered as he travelled. He was told that during his journey he should seek out stonemason masters and from them receive short-term paid work that would provide opportunities to learn new skills and ideas. These mini employments should not last longer than three months. To remember this, Switalla was told, 'When the dogs stop barking [at you]', and 'when the postman knows your name' it is time to leave. On his travels, he carried a small notebook that served as an education log for his journey. For each visit, Switalla asked the local master to write a short report on the work that had been done and what he had learned.

Geoffrey Gowlland – pottery-making skills in China[6]

This report is quoted from Geoffrey Gowlland, research associate at the Department of Anthropology and Sociology at the School of Oriental and African Studies, University of London. It is based on a modern ethnographic study of ceramics workshops in Dingshu in Jiangsu province, China. It highlights some of the stages and techniques used in teaching and learning pottery-making skills.

[T]he apprentice will learn the different techniques of the craft in the order of the normal sequence of production, starting with the basic building blocks of the craft, that is, clay sheets and disks beaten into shape with a mallet. Learning these basic techniques until the components are made absolutely flat can take months of tedious, repetitive practice. In the early stages of learning, and when a new technique is learned or an error is corrected, a customary practice is for the teacher to stand behind the apprentice who is sitting at the work table, grab his or her hands, and move them into place, demonstrating the 'correct' movements. Gradually, the teacher will rely less on this method of teaching and more on verbalizing instructions ... The learning process thus evolves from more direct interaction to control at a distance through words. These two methods, direct control of the hands and control through the voice, are modes of teaching through scaffolding, meaning that the tasks to be learned by the apprentice are made more accessible through the intervention of the expert who will direct the student's efforts. Another substantial part of learning does not take place by recourse to scaffolding; rather, techniques are made visually available to observation, making it possible for learners to pick up techniques without explicit instruction nor direct intervention ... The physical proximity of apprentice and master in the workshop was often pointed out by my informants as essential in the learning process. Usually the worktable of the apprentice is placed in close proximity to that of the master, which enables mutual visual access to the work of master and apprentice. The teacher will quickly spot a mistake being made, by regularly glancing up from his or her own work, while the apprentice can easily raise the gaze to observe her teacher at work and strive to better understand a certain technique.

Training apprentice preachers at G2 York

'Ignition' was a programme to develop new preachers and teachers at a church called G2. It was inspired in part by 2 Timothy 1.6 ('ignite the gift of God that is within you', author's translation) and delivered through 'Ignition Sunday' – a termly service where four novice speakers delivered a five-minute talk. Participation was open to any member, provided they had not previously done a talk in the church. Most participants were in their twenties, the oldest was aged 72 and the youngest, 11.

Candidates were encouraged to choose the subject of the talk themselves – the suggestion was to select a single verse of Scripture, although some chose a theme or a personal story. All the Ignition speakers received individual mentoring from a more experienced speaker, although in some cases this person had only done a handful of talks themselves. All the speakers participated in a group preaching rehearsal where peer feedback was valued as highly as comments from experienced leaders. The aim of the rehearsal was to create a forum for positive feedback in a coaching format, rather than to vet the talks. Many commented that the rehearsal instilled confidence and helped them to be more creative. After the event, all the speakers received feedback with a bias towards positive comments and encouragement. Some went on to become regular speakers, conference speakers and church leaders.[7]

Notes

1 David Switalla, 'My Journeyman Years: A Living Tradition from a German Perspective', *York Festival of Ideas* (York: University of York, 10 June 2019 at All Saints Pavement in York and a short private interview on the same day).

2 Sheilagh Ogilvie, a key researcher of medieval guilds, has compiled a qualitative database of 12,051 observations about European guilds between 1095 and 1862, but is not able to offer any examples of training narratives between masters and apprentices in medieval guilds. See Sheilagh Ogilvie, *Qualitative Guilds Database*

(Cambridge: Faculty of Economics, Cambridge University), at http://www.econ.cam.ac.uk/people-files/faculty/sco2/Ogilvie-Guilds-Qualitative-Database-1-Nov-2018.xlsx (accessed 28.1.2022).

3 This report draws on my recollections of a visit to the factory of The House of Waterford Crystal in Kilbarry in the Republic of Ireland in 1997. It is supplemented from a blog maintained by James Connolly, who is a retired Waterford Crystal Master Craftsman. See 'Waterford Crystal Apprentice Bowl', *Waterford Crystal Collection*, at http://waterfordcrystalcollection.com/waterford-crystal-apprentice-bowl (accessed 28.1.2022).

4 Actually, a Waterford Crystal apprentice can graduate at any time provided they successfully produce an Apprentice Bowl; however, it typically takes five years before they are proficient enough to do this.

5 This report draws from a public lecture delivered as part of the *York Festival of Ideas* on 10 June 2019 at All Saints Pavement in York and a short private interview on the same day. See David Switalla, 'My Journeyman Years: A Living Tradition from a German Perspective', in *York Festival of Ideas* (York: University of York, 10 June 2019).

6 See Gowlland, 'Learning Craft Skills in China: Apprenticeship and Social Capital in an Artisan Community of Practice', *Anthropology & Education Quarterly*, Vol. 43, No. 4, Nov. 2012, 358–71, doi:10.1111/j.1548-1492.2012.01190.x, 363–64.

7 G2 was a church plant I led between 2007 and 2021, at http://g2york.org (accessed 28.1.2022). My last in-person service as the leader of G2, the Sunday before the first UK Coronavirus lockdown, was 'Ignition 100' where our 100th speaker preached.

PART 5

Conclusions

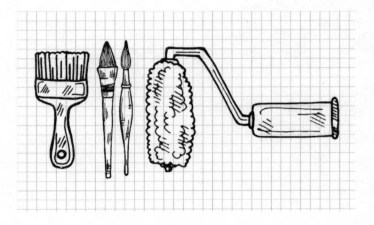

The conclusion does not belong to the artist.
Émile Zola

Note: Letter to Paul Cézanne on 16 April 1860, published in Alex Danchev, *The Letters of Paul Cézanne* (Los Angeles: J. Paul Getty Museum, 2013).

14

Applying a Craft Approach to Training Church Planters

So it is with every artisan and master artisan who labours by night as well as by day ... All these rely on their hands, and all are skilful in their own work ... they maintain the fabric of the world, and their concern is for the exercise of their trade.

Ecclesiasticus 38.27, 31, 34

The craft of church planting

The provision of resources for training in Christian ministry has never been greater. There are more theological books available today than at any other point in history; the Internet has made it possible for digital material to be accessible by anyone, anywhere in the world; and seminaries and theological colleges offer students a 'high-quality education' provided by 'professional academic instructors' delivering 'university-backed awards.'[1] High-quality didactic training resources are certainly available in abundance; however, truly effective training for future church planters in the Church of England – training that brings together theory and practice – is limited and still in infancy. Most church planters to date have had to learn as they planted for the first time or have taught themselves from books or conference resources, few have been directly apprenticed by a seasoned practitioner. This is the type of challenge Paul has in mind when writing to the Corinthians: 'you might have ten thousand basic instructors available to you, but you do not have many spiritual parents' (1 Corinthians 4.15, my paraphrase).

Arguably, modern models for training leaders have been significantly shaped by industrial and post-industrial organizational worldviews.[2] In the industrial perspective, most organizations function like machines – workers are trained to operate like cogs in an organizational mechanism, and success is measured by the efficiency of assembly-line production of identically constructed products. By contrast, the craft model is in closer harmony with the organic metaphors of the New Testament, because craft workers are trained and empowered as artisans, every context is seen as distinctive and unique, and churches are planted, not manufactured. The craft guild approach to apprenticeship, when it makes space for contextual creativity, offers a flexible model that is particularly suited to training pioneer ministers, especially for the development of ministerial character, practitioner skills, and innovation in models and approaches to mission and ministry. Central to this model is the mentoring role of a training practitioner we might call a church planting master: an expert practitioner of church planting who personally tutors the next generation of church planters, having been trained the same way themselves. Does the Church again need to consider the mode of training best suited to developing the future ministers and pioneers of the Church? One where local churches and theological colleges work in concert to create a new 'seedbed' for nurturing future church planters.

In this book, I have explored the craft of church planting from historical, biblical and theological perspectives and through management theory, the history of ministerial formation and church planting theory. I have used my own research to bring these perspectives together to form a craft perspective of training in the context of church planting. My conclusions are in three parts: below, I suggest one way that craft training might be delivered; in the next chapter, I propose five practical recommendations; and in the closing chapter, I offer some final thoughts on restoring the craft of church planting to the Church. In addition, many other suggestions, ideas and reflections (too many to summarize here), and the detail of how the craft approach works, can be found in the earlier sections of this book, especially in Part 4 which reported findings from original research with experts.

A craft approach to training church planters

What might a craft approach to training church planters – one inspired by the apprenticeship model of the medieval guilds – look like? What follows is one suggestion of what it could look like, although there are many possible variations, depending on circumstances such as training for ordination or lay ministry; full-time or part-time training; leading to full-time, part-time, bi-vocational, or co-vocational forms of ministry; variations due to experience and age; local ministry or nationally deployable; and finally, adjustments based on the requirements of the intended church plant.

Nevertheless, I suggest three key phases that apply in all scenarios: first, recruitment, initial training and testing; next, self-directed further learning in new contexts; and finally, mastery and supervising the training of the next generation. Those familiar with the existing training methods of the Church of England and other Christian denominations in the West will notice a few similarities with some of the elements of this outline. This should not be a surprise, since the guilds have had a significant effect on historic patterns of training in England, and the Church of England has formed its practices of training within this culture. Even though the guilds have gone, some echoes of their wisdom, culture and practice remain in the methods of the English Church. However, the approach outlined below is distinctive in several respects: the intent, the process of selection, the ordering of training elements, the priority of experience-based learning, the training context, the selection of trainers, and how students progress.

Phase one – recruitment, initial training and testing

Recruitment by an established church planter

As the saying goes: 'It takes one to know one.'[3] The initial selection of a potential future church planter should begin with (or at least be confirmed by) an experienced church planting master. The master's key skill is to discern who might make a future church planter.[4] Moreover, the recruitment will usually be personal, because the master is likely to be selecting someone to be *their* apprentice, not simply nominating a candidate for the wider Church to train. I recognize this approach has significant potential for bias; nevertheless, all the examples referenced in this book have been of masters who selected their apprentices. Potential apprentices that are not recruited might move to other contexts for a chance to find a master who is willing to take them.

Immediate deployment and participation in a church planting context

Apprenticeship training happens on-the-job and is a 'ministry-first' approach: the student begins in the workshop with practice. Inevitably this will include praxis learning from reflection on the theory embedded in practice and questioning why methods are used. More than that, there might be basic instruction in some areas or elementary theological discussion and education as the apprentice learns through observation and elementary participation. The context for training a church planter (the workshop) is a church involved in church planting, either a recent church plant or a church involved in resourcing church planting. This should also mean the minister of the church will be an accomplished church planting practitioner – thus providing the training workshop and training-master.

Direct supervision by a master

The initial formation comes from a master, who models and directs how ministry is done and observes and nurtures the student in their first steps. In several ways, this initial stage is a period of testing: the apprentice is exploring, or testing out, their vocation; they are also strengthening and developing their character and skills;[5] and the master is assessing and testing their potential. In time a person might engage with several masters, but at this initial stage an experienced practitioner needs to lay basic foundations.

Learning with others

Ideally, the student isn't learning on their own, they are part of a group of other learners either at the same or different stages of development. Perhaps the church has interns and other new trainees or is part of a network of other training churches. This provides the apprentice with one or more communities of practice that complement and support instruction from the master.

Phase two – self-directed further learning in new contexts

Graduation from apprenticeship

In time, evidence of initial learning and future potential is assessed by the successful completion of one or more suitable ministry projects.[6] Some novices may not reach this stage, or some may not wish to progress further – in a church committed to training new leaders this first phase might simply be part of their common pipeline of training leaders. Some do progress to the next phase: self-directed learning.

Internship

This second phase of training – self-directed further learning in new contexts – is equivalent to the journeyman or wandering years. The aim is for the intern to continue to learn, by experiencing contexts beyond their initial training church. They learn by continuing to do ministry and by learning from other interns and masters. In the tradition of the guilds, this phase of ministry requires the intern to leave their home church, although, a similar outcome could be achieved through a new role in the same church.

Phase three – mastery and supervising the training of the next generation

Evidence of mastery

Evidence of an effective internship is demonstrated by three master skills: first, evidence of self-directed learning which builds on the core skills learned in initial instruction; second, demonstration of creativity and innovation beyond things learned by instruction from others; and last, a desire and aptitude to train others. In the classic model, the first two of these are shown by a 'masterpiece' that provides evidence of skills learned in basic training and of the creative incorporation of learning from their travels.[7] By this stage, the intern will have worked alongside many interns and apprentices, which should provide evidence to assess their aptitude and desire to train others.

Training others

In the guild model, mastery and supervising the training of others are inseparable parts of a master's role.[8] Arguably the greatest test of the master is their ability to recruit new people to train: do people want to learn from them? In this final stage, a master continues as a practitioner who is also training others.[9] Some may not progress to this next stage, either because of aptitude, or because they prefer to remain focused as a practitioner.

Leading networks

Although all masters were senior members of their guild, some had a role leading the guild. They were called 'guild masters', who were network leaders who invested in the vision, strategic leadership and culture of their guild; they also played a key role in appointing new masters. For church planting, the equivalent of this role are leaders of networks of church plants which, in some cases, might be networks of churches and leaders they have personally trained and sent out.

Stages of training

I suggest then, from a guild perspective, there are four stages or categories of training for church planters: apprentice, new practitioner, sending church leader and strategic director.[10] *Apprentices* are novices training for church planting in the future, either as lay or ordained leaders, as the primary leader or as part of a wider team. This early stage of training and formation is often explorative. *New practitioners* are developing-leaders who are involved in church planting for the first time, perhaps at early stages. This is a vulnerable stage where support and additional practical training, often categorized as just-in-time training, is needed. *Sending church leaders* are established practitioners who are training and commissioning others. They are 'apostolic' in the sense that they are sending others. Last, *strategic directors* are senior leaders overseeing church planting and networks at a strategic level, beyond a single local church.

Theological study and ordination

How do theological study and ordination fit in the craft model of training? In the past, both were considered essential requirements for leading the ministry of a church. I have said little about theological study in this book because it is a well-established and longstanding component of the process of ministerial formation; nor have I intended to diminish the importance of theological study in the process of training future church planters – theological study has been a key part of my initial ministerial formation and ongoing refreshment.[11] Instead, in this book I have focused on elements of a craft approach to training, most of which are less familiar. In the last few centuries, ministers-in-training have received their theological training through residential university or college-based programmes; more recently, theological training has been offered in different ways, such as mixed-mode training where theological training is concurrent with training through ministry experience. The guild approach takes this one step further, by focusing on the ministry context (a church plant) as the primary place of learning, rather than the college or academy. Nevertheless, it is important to note that although guild training and university training models are historically distinct, they have significantly influenced each other. For example, the modern three-stage pattern of university further education (i.e. BA, MA, PhD) derives from the phases of training in guilds: an apprentice learning to be a bachelor of their art (i.e. bachelor of arts), a journeyman learning to be a master of their art,[12] and some senior masters learning to be a doctors (Latin, teachers) that teach others.

Here's one possibility of how theological training might fit alongside guild training for a leader training for ordination: In the early stages, the emphasis could fall on biblical studies, preaching, mission and initial theological reflection. During their intern years, this could be extended with reference to church history, doctrine and elementary pastoral studies. It may be at this point they are ordained as they start, or begin to revitalize, a church (which will be their masterpiece). As they prepare to become a master the circle of learning could be broadened further to include biblical languages, leadership studies, church administration and training skills. A lay leader might follow a similar pattern, or a reduced version, through study on a part-time course running on regular weekday evenings or monthly Saturdays.

The publication of *Mission-Shaped Church* and the development of legislation for fresh expressions of church, and other recent initiatives, have made it increasingly common for lay people to lead churches in the Church of England, though not parish churches.[13] And guidelines for Ordained Pioneer Ministry have also highlighted the necessity of evidence of effective pioneering ministry *before* selection for ordained ministry.[14] In a craft model, a lay person might plant churches, or start one or more churches or ministry projects as part of their journey towards ordination.[15] Again, there is no single pattern for the process of ordination in a craft guild model of training church planters. For those with a charism of planting, ordination to the diaconate might accompany graduation from apprenticeship and priesthood could be related to the role of being a master. Bishops, too, could become so as their role as a senior master is recognized. Of course, the church may also want to recognize those with other gifts among these orders (pastors, educators, chaplains and those who 'water' the planted church).

As the Church continues to rediscover the ancient practice of starting and revitalizing Christian communities, the ministry of the church planter will become a more common and normal form of ministry. Applying the lost wisdom of apprenticeship training is one way that this transition might be achieved: using experienced church planters as trainers, delivering training in the context of a church plant, recognizing creativity as an important component of church planting and training, using training models that are accessible to a wide range of candidates, and recognizing the value of church planting networks for ongoing development.

Notes

1 Quotations from 'Common Awards in Theology, Ministry and Mission' (Durham: Durham University, Cambridge Theological Federation in partnership with Durham University and the Church of England), at https://www.durham.ac.uk/departments/academic/common-awards (accessed 28.1.2022).

2 Lance Ford, Rob Wegner and Alan Hirsch say, 'the unconscious guiding metaphor for ecclesiology in the West is that of the "industrial complex"', see *The Starfish and the Spirit: Unleashing the Leadership Potential of Churches and Organizations* (Grand Rapids, MI: Zondervan, 2021), 110; see also 8, 105 and 174 for further comparison between industrial and pre-industrial views of work and how they have affected views of training and leadership in the church.

3 Although this late-nineteenth-century saying is typically a slur response to a negative trait highlighted by a critic, I use it to mean that practitioners are best suited to identify those with the potential to be trained. See Gregory Y. Titelman, *Random House Dictionary of Popular Proverbs and Sayings* (New York: Random House, 1996).

4 I once asked a *vigneron* (French, winemaker) how he knows which grapes will make good wine. He told me it is an intuitive process that novice winemakers often get wrong because it takes up to 30 years to become a *maître* (master) who can tell which grapes will make the best wine. Experienced winemakers learn to assess the potential of unprocessed grapes (even though the taste is different from the wine they produce) through the accumulation of experience from past results, evidence from multiple sources (taste, touch, smell sight, soil conditions, weather and modern chemical tests) and what he referred to as 'clues', micro-evidence that only expert winemakers understand.

5 For example, James 1.3 ('the testing of your faith produces endurance').

6 Examples might include pioneering a small group, leading and developing a ministry area, running an effective mission project, etc.

7 Whereas the evidence (pieces) produced by an apprentice demonstrate competence in what they have been taught, the masterpiece must show that an intern has learned beyond that which their master(s) taught them, including the ability to innovate and think creatively.

8 In the medieval guilds some did remain as perpetual journeymen: expert craftworkers not directly training others. For some this was a free choice, however, some guilds limited the numbers of masters, and some journeymen lacked the financial resources to establish a workshop or buy into the guild.

9 Perhaps like the role of an experienced physician in a teaching hospital.

10 These are the categories of training that I use in the St Hild Centre for Church Planting. Gareth Robinson has a similar categorization: dreamers, doers, doners and directors. See his *Stones and Ripples: 10 Principles for Pioneers and Church Planters* (London: 100 Movements Publishing, 2021), 3.

11 To explore some of the recent thinking on reimagining theological education,

see Robert Banks, *Reenvisioning Theological Education: Exploring a Missional Alternative to Current Models* (Grand Rapids, MI: Wm. B. Eerdmans, 1999) and David Heywood, *Reimagining Ministerial Formation* (London: SCM, 2021).

12 Before the rise of the university system, the term bachelor had the meaning of apprentice worker. By 1215, in the University of Paris, a graduating apprentice was granted a bachelor's licence and permitted to train for mastership (the degree of master). See Harry Beck Green, 'The Origin of the A. B. Degree', *The Journal of Higher Education*, Vol. 17, No. 4, Apr. 1946, 205–10, 206–7.

13 But note, clergy are part of 'the people of God' (*laos*), not separate from it.

14 The selection criteria for Pioneer Ministers says they should 'have a track record of innovation', at https://www.churchofengland.org/life-events/vocations/vocations-pioneer-ministry (accessed 28.1.2022).

15 For example, Dr John Gollapalli, who is Bishop of the Free Methodist Church of South India and a theological educator, once told me he will not have a vocational conversation with a lay person unless they have planted at least three village churches. In the West, this is perhaps equivalent to starting large house groups by evangelism.

15

Five Summary Recommendations

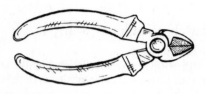

But where shall wisdom be found? And where is the place of understanding? ... God understands the way to it and he alone knows
where it dwells.

Job 28.12, 23 NRSV

Late have I loved you, O Beauty ever ancient, ever new.

Augustine of Hippo, Confessions[1]

When faced with a significant challenge, we might be tempted to focus
only on big issues or on incremental changes; in fact, in complex situations, both approaches are needed. So, before I list a few (big) key
recommendations, it is worth remembering the value of small changes.
Occasionally a small change is a revolution in disguise or a key that
unlocks a new pathway of action and thinking; similarly, sometimes
a big result can be derived from the accumulated effect of many small
changes.[2] Small suggestions like these are peppered through this book,
but, although I repeat a few below, there are too many to catalogue comprehensively here. Instead, I encourage readers to 'pan for gold' by sifting
through what has gone before for nuggets of wisdom from God.

This book seeks to revive lost wisdom about training church planters
and church planting. As neither of these activities are new, I am not so
much proposing brand-new patterns of ministry as the rediscovery of
ancient ways made relevant for today. My conviction is that much of what
we need to learn and discover in ministry today is a rediscovery of the
insights of the saints of old. In this, I agree with T.S. Eliot who said: 'the
end of all our exploring will be to arrive where we started.'[3]

So, what are the key recommendations to take the ideas in this book forward? I propose there are five, although you may have others. Let me acknowledge that implementing any such set of suggestions may come with challenges; however, rather than diluting or qualifying my proposals, I offer them as the beginning of a conversation, rather than the final word.

1 Experienced church planters as trainers

I propose that accomplished church planters should play a leading role in the selection, training and ministerial formation of future church planters, especially in the early stages of training.[4] For the sake of terminology, I refer to these people as 'church planting masters' or 'master-trainers'; they are expert planters who have proved their learning and experience by founding new churches and are now also involved in training the next generation of practitioners. The key qualities for effective master-trainers are: relevant experience and accomplishments, a passion and enthusiasm for their ministry, and the desire and ability to develop emerging leaders.

Additionally, church planting masters should have the freedom to select or recruit their apprentices, partly because selecting apprentices is part of their gift, and partly to facilitate a more direct training relationship. In some cases, it is likely that church planting apprentices will remain in their existing churches, having arisen through a process of discipleship and leadership development in a church involved in church planting.[5]

As apprentices become interns, they will seek out other master-trainers in different churches for new learning experiences. So, the network of church planting masters or master-trainers is also important to the training process. Church planting masters can have a significant and defining impact on the initial teaching experiences of apprentices, and the ongoing learning of interns, because of their insights as practitioners. In these training relationships, experienced practitioners can shape the formative learning experiences of the apprentice. The training contributions from other theological educators remain important but should be concurrent with or following the contribution from the master church planter.

Finally, because of their experience and role in training, church planting masters should be invited to play an advisory role in contexts that are wider than their local settings, such as their deanery, archdeaconry, diocese or province. This might include advising on church planting strategy, training options and deployment; involvement in the vocational discernment of prospective church planters at various stages of their journey; and mentoring prospective church planting masters.

2 Apprenticeship training in the context of a church plant

A significant part of the training of any future church planter, certainly in the initial stages, should be rooted in the context of a recent church plant or a church that is actively involved in church planting. This training should be characterized by an on-the-job format where the apprentice is personally involved in relevant ministry activities under the direct supervision of a master-trainer who – in addition to delivering other training – provides developmental feedback on ministry performance. This approach provides apprentice church planters with an immersive experience where they can have legitimate participation in the ministry of church planting. It will allow them to observe ministry and – more importantly – be observed by more experienced practitioners as they engage in ministry. In part, this is the approach used by colleges that offer mixed-mode training;[6] however, I am suggesting we go further so that the church context becomes the beginning and the centre of the whole learning experience.

Currently, ministers-in-training in the Church of England learn in two phases: the first rooted in a theological college and the second in a local church. I suggest that church planters might be better trained if the order of these is changed so that college-based training is subservient to initial and long-term practical ministry training.[7] In the craft model, emerging church planters can be tested at an early stage through the normal ministry of the local church. This testing can identify and develop not just skills but also character, which is arguably a vital foundation for any set of ministry skills. A person's character – which can only be assessed holistically, in proximity, and over time – illustrates how they are likely to behave in the future, especially in real-life ministry situations. If we are to raise up leaders who will be effective at starting and renewing churches – bearing the distinctive challenges that are often experienced in pioneering work – we need training models that can facilitate deep character formation alongside the acquisition of ministry skills and theological and practical knowledge. In this respect, a local church will always be a preferable formational environment to a theological college, which can play an important, but secondary or supportive, role in the overall training process.

3 Creativity is an important component of church planting

To be fully effective at planting churches in a post-Christendom era, church planters need to be nurtured in the ability to think and act creatively, to maximize their ability to start churches that are relevant to their context. Creativity was a key aspect of the pre-industrial view of work and, in the present age of rapid change, it has become a vital component of contemporary church planting. All new churches should be contextual, that is, an authentic expression of the Christian church in that place and with those people. Creativity is a key skill to achieve this. Accordingly, all church planting apprentices should be helped to develop and release creativity as part of their ministerial formation.

Creativity is developed and released in two stages. First through investment in basic skills and abilities, typically through stimulation experiences and repetitive skill-tasks; most churches have many opportunities for this type of basic ministry experience, such as roles in evangelistic courses or teams that support Sunday church services. The second stage is released by imaginative engagement with challenges accompanied by a playful, youthful and risk-taking approach. These two components should be incorporated into the stages of training. Trevor Hart's illustration of human creativity being like jazz improvisation was particularly helpful in describing the application of creativity. In jazz, something new is made from things that already exist. The jazz-artist learns to be creative by learning basic skills and practising the music of others, before creating their own music. In this respect, creativity is a skill that brings together existing elements in a distinctive way to fit a context and need.

Creativity is important because it enables church planters to work contextually. This application of creativity stands on the more basic skill of listening; that is, being able to read, learn and understand culture and context. The combination of creativity and listening produces contextualization that is incarnational and relevant. My own research showed that most church planters believe that creativity is important in church planting (87 per cent) and that church planting is more effective with leaders who are creative (77 per cent). The same respondents offered key ideas that they associated with the concept of creativity. The most popular keywords used were innovative, flexible, 'out of the box', contextual, entrepreneurial, visionary, adaptability, bold, imaginative and risk-taking.

Finally, the Church of England should adopt a more positive approach to risk-taking in the context of church planting, by involving and affirming creative innovators.[8] Taking greater risks ensures that church plants are not 'playing it safe' and thereby potentially missing opportunities, and will encourage a greater variety of styles of church plant that will reach a broader range of people. A stronger culture of risk-taking will attract a greater number of creative practitioners and innovators as church planters. Such people will have a revitalizing effect on the Church of England, as creativity-on-the-edge, in time, results in the whole Church moving towards more creative and imaginative models of ministry.

4 Apprenticeship models of training are more accessible to some

Apprenticeship and context-based models of training are accessible to a wider range of people than those located in theological colleges that are centred on academic study. Self-supporting students and students who are less academically inclined are less able to access training if it is centred on theological colleges and academic assessment. Bishop Jill Duff makes this point when she contrasts Paul with Peter, saying 'I'm not convinced that Peter – the rock on who Jesus built his church – would easily navigate his way through selection and ordination training in the Church of England.'[9] A craft approach will make training accessible to a wider range of candidates, including younger emerging leaders who can begin to explore their calling as self-supporting volunteers in the church, or people who learn like Peter, a working man training on-the-job, rather than Paul, a high-flyer who might thrive in the environment of the academy.[10]

Of course, the Christian church needs some expert theologians, and the literacy and complexity of society probably makes formal theological education a more necessary component of general ministerial training today than in the ancient world. However, effectiveness in ministry and church planting is not determined by academic education alone, especially in pioneering contexts. In his book *The Spontaneous Expansion of the Church and the Causes that Hinder It* (1927), Roland Allen goes so far as to suggest that, in his day, missional effectiveness was often inversely proportional to educational attainment.[11] In the present time, Ed Stetzer agrees with Allen's point and adds: 'we [should] raise up church planters and pastors by competency, rather than certification' and 'we need a way to raise up church planters and pastors that does not always require formal education.'[12] The best and most effective training is a blend of on-the-job learning, mentoring and instruction – a combination which is offered by a craft apprenticeship approach.

One thought-provoking point that emerged from the historical study of ministerial formation is that not all priests and bishops in the past were well-educated. For example, in the Patristic period, although most clergy did receive the equivalent of a 'good education'[13] of their day, some were not suited to study and academic learning. It seems when faced with this dilemma – what should be done with a candidate not suited to academic learning? – the answer was sometimes to appoint them anyway. The guiding questions in these situations seem to have been: 'Do they have a vibrant personal faith?', 'Do they know the Scriptures?', and, 'Is there evidence of spiritual fruit from their preaching and personal ministry?'[14] Illiterate bishops and priests in the early church were sometimes appointed without formal study provided they were judged to have a vibrant and effective faith.

The story of John Wesley and the early Methodists is a more recent example of a movement where many uneducated and self-supporting leaders led the ministry of a rapidly growing movement of new churches.[15] Alan Hirsh notes that American Methodism grew for nearly a hundred years with 'uneducated leaders' until 1850, at which point local ministers and circuit riders were required to complete four years of theological studies to hold their appointment. Within a few years, the movement stopped growing.[16]

5 Denominational churches need church planting networks

Denominational churches need to both create and work with church planting networks that function like guilds of church planting. Communities and networks that provide church planting practitioners with opportunities for peer support, feedback and review, and deep learning should be encouraged as best practice for the ongoing support and development of existing church planters. Some communities may function in a similar way to existing forums (e.g. deaneries), either replacing or complementing them.

Various types of church planting communities are necessary for the ongoing learning of church planters and the development of future church planters. These might include small groups, workshop or tutorial groups, learning communities and micro-networks. Some of these groups might be peer-led, others might be led by or resourced by a church planting master or started by an apprentice church planting master as part of their development.

Church planting networks are also a key component of resourcing church planting at scale. Networks can play a strategic role in releasing church planting capacity in a region by identifying planting opportunities, formulating comprehensive planting plans, establishing leadership pipelines, increasing the capacity of churches and teams to deliver, allocating resources strategically, and creating and aligning systems and support.

The emerging church planting movement within the Church of England has the potential to play a significant role in the revitalization of historic churches and the wider structures of the church. Indeed, arguably we need more church planting networks, including those expressive of Anglo-Catholic and mainstream Anglican traditions, and networks better reflecting the concerns of under-resourced groups such as low income estates and minority ethnic groups. But the structural legacy and emerging network elements within the Church are in mutual need of each other. For this reason, church planting strategy and networks and the revitalization of inherited church structures should be considered together and work together for common good.

Notes

1 Augustine of Hippo, *Confessions*, 10.27.

2 One theory is 'the aggregation of marginal gains' which was utilized by Dave Brailsford for the British cycling team at the 2008 Beijing Olympics. Brailsford sought to improve cyclist's performance a small amount in many areas to produce a large result. See Eben Harrell, 'How 1% Performance Improvements Led to Olympic Gold', *Harvard Business Review*, 30 October 2015, at https://hbr.org/2015/10/how-1-performance-improvements-led-to-olympic-gold (accessed 28.1.2022).

3 T. S. Eliot, *Collected Poems 1909–1962* (London: Faber & Faber, 2002), 200–9.

4 As an aside, the recommendations in *Mission-Shaped Church* for training pioneers offer no comment on *who* should train future church planters. While it might be inferred from the report that suitably qualified people should be the ones training and mentoring future church planters – perhaps presuming that structure, teaching content and methodology will result in an effective training experience – it is not defined. See Graham Cray et al., editors, *Mission-Shaped Church: Church Planting and Fresh Expressions of Church in a Changing Context* (London: Church House Publishing, 2004), 147–48.

5 My friend Dave Ferguson calls the action of a church leader regularly calling out the ministry potential in church members 'ICNU' (an acronym wordplay of 'I see in you'). He suggests established leaders should verbalize specific examples of the potential they see in emerging leaders, such as, 'I see in you someone who could be a great preacher'. See Dave Ferguson and Warren Bird, *Hero Maker: Five Essential Practices for Leaders to Multiply Leaders* (Grand Rapids, MI: Zondervan, 2018), 95–112.

6 Mixed-mode training, which is sometimes called context-based training, began to appear after the publication of *Mission-Shaped Church*. In this model students spend a significant proportion of their training time in the same church context throughout their entire course. For example, St Hild College was formed in 2017 to 'combine rigorous academic theology and mission-focused Christian practice in a community of shared learning', see St Hild College, 'Our Vision', http://www.sthild.org/vision (accessed 30.1.2022) par. 1; St Mellitus College was established in

2007 to deliver theological education 'at the heart of the local church', see Jonathan Aitken, The St Mellitus Story (Private Publication, 2017), 3–4.

7 I teach at St Hild College, where Anglican, Baptist and independent students learn together. I have observed that, unlike Anglicans, Baptist ministers-in-training and independent students of church planting have often served the equivalent of a curacy before they come to theological college.

8 Examples might include postulants (pre-ordinands), ordinands and training curates being allowed or encouraged to plant churches under supervision and including the goal of raising up local leaders to succeed them. Other areas of risk-taking might include using experimental and as-yet unproven models or taking a subsidiarity approach to choosing what to do (that is, allowing novice practitioners rather than those in seniority to choose the planting project).

9 See 'Estates and the Gospel', a paper delivered at the Urban Estates Evangelism Conference in 2017.

10 For an example from history the Wesley brothers and the early British Methodists made leaders of uneducated people. See Howard A. Snyder, The Radical Wesley and Patterns for Church Renewal (Westmont, IL: InterVarsity Press, 1982), 53. For a recent example, see the 'Peter Stream' in the Diocese of London, at https://www.london.anglican.org/support/ministry-and-vocations/christian-vocation/the-peter-stream (accessed 28.1.2022).

11 Roland Allen, The Spontaneous Expansion of the Church and the Causes that Hinder It (Eugene, OR: Wipf & Stock Publishers, 1927). The titles of many of Allen's books give away his convictions about mission and church planting: Missionary Methods, St. Paul's or Ours?; The Case for Voluntary Clergy; Pentecost and the World, Educational principles and missionary methods; The Place of Medical Mission.

12 Ed Stetzer, 'Why Lay People Can (and Should) Plant Churches', The Exchange, at https://www.christianitytoday.com/edstetzer/2018/april/why-lay-people-can-and-should-plant-churches.html (accessed 28.1.2022).

13 Claudia Rapp, Holy Bishops in Late Antiquity: The Nature of Christian Leadership in an Age of Transition (Oakland, CA: University of California Press, 2013), 29–31.

14 Rapp, Holy Bishops, 29–31.

15 The Wesley brothers and the early British Methodists made leaders of uneducated people who were nearly all self-supporting. John Wesley also broke the taboo of women as ministers and leaders in the Church. See Howard A. Snyder, The Radical Wesley and Patterns for Church Renewal (Westmont, IL: InterVarsity Press, 1982), 53.

16 The reasons for this result may be more complex; nevertheless, the shift to an academic model of ministerial training clearly had a key effect. Winfield Bevins, Marks of a Movement: What the Church Today Can Learn from the Wesleyan Revival (Grand Rapids, MI: Zondervan, 2019), 148.

16

Restoring the Craft of Church Planting

In the land of the blind, the one-eyed man is King
Erasmus of Rotterdam, Collectanea Adagiorum[1]

Craftwork is as ancient as society. From the most ancient of times craft-workers have produced practical art for the benefit of others – some, for example, showing creativity by carving stone for buildings that last many generations, others by baking bread for daily life. Originally through family units, and in time through organizations like the medieval guilds, craftworkers have transmitted their skills by apprenticing the next generation and encouraging creativity through a pilgrim approach to learning. This pattern is as evident in the historic Christian church in Britain and Europe as it is in the work of stonemasons and artisan bakers. But like many trades, the Church has lost much of her craft wisdom.

In every age, the mission of the Church needs to be refreshed and revitalized. Like any living organism, each local church, all networks of churches, and every Christian denomination pass through stages of life, such as birth, innovation, growth, stagnation, decline, and sometimes demise.[2] Although no two organizations follow the same path, whatever the timescale, history suggests that – without intervention – decline is the inevitable outcome of most, if not all, Christian organizations.[3]

Of course, movements and churches can be renewed. This is exactly the hope offered in Christianity: what is destined to die can be resurrected to new life by Jesus Christ.[4] So, no person, local church or denomination is beyond the transforming power of God to bring new or renewed life. But, just as mission is a co-labour with God,[5] God's renewal of the church requires the church to offer itself.

So, who will renew the mission of the Church? Certainly, it is Jesus who builds his church (Matt. 16.18) and we are the apprentices who co-labour with him. Councils, synods and committees will all have their role to play, but an indispensable element – at times, the most vital – will be the front-line practitioners who understand the craft of church planting. These are the pioneers who will safeguard the future of the church by re-seeding the gospel to the different contexts of society through creativity in orthodoxy and innovation in mission.[6] Of course, this is not a new idea, it is one affirmed in the words heard by every Church of England minister at their ordination and licencing:

> The Church of England ... professes the faith uniquely revealed in the Holy Scriptures and set forth in the catholic creeds, *which faith the Church is called upon to proclaim afresh in each generation.* (emphasis added)[7]

And since, for the most part, mission and evangelism are practically and theologically inseparable from the local church, one implication of the commission above is that each generation must also refresh and renew the church. As Jesus said, 'do not pour fresh wine into old wineskins ... but instead pour fresh wine into renewed wineskins' (Matthew 9.17, my translation).[8] So, in each generation, the Church must be strengthened and refreshed so that it can receive and grow from the results of fresh mission; Lesslie Newbigin makes this relationship between mission and the renewal of the Church clear when he says: 'mission changes not only the world but also the church.'[9]

Today we are at such a moment – the Church needs a great renewal. Parts of the Church in England are stagnant, and many churches are in long-standing decline – a picture that is also seen in varying degrees in all the historic denominations. It is sad to observe that, in England, many local churches and some denominations are nearing closure. This book proposes that the Church needs to renew the craft of church planting to release a fresh phase of mission innovation and growth that will renew the Church and birth new churches. The leading agents of this ministry will be church planters – specialist pioneer ministers who are selected and trained to renew the Church through revitalization and church planting. Moreover, it is reasonable to suggest that in the future *all* ordained leaders should expect to be involved in church planting in some way: either personally involved in planting, or training a church planter, or otherwise working with one.[10] Furthermore, the importance of this ministry and the growing number of church plants will inevitably adjust the ministry focus of the Church. As in any season of innovation, leading practitioners are usually best informed about the methods and approaches that are most effective in their area of ministry – certainly, they have a key contribution to make as practitioner theologians and architects of change.[11] In this season, we need to be guided by these pioneer church planters, who may themselves be still learning and perfecting their craft but have much to offer a continually learning church.

Nurturing, training and releasing a myriad of emerging church planters requires a fresh pedagogy of ministerial formation, one where the superiority of the classroom approach gives way to rediscovering the best of the old ways of craft apprenticeship training in context. In this model, ministry is a craft learned from established masters through participation in the vocational context alongside other fellow learners. The next few decades will require thousands of these ministers, who are equipped to start new worshipping communities, revitalize existing churches, and minister in mutable circumstances. The guild method offers an approach that develops people like artists through the acquisition of craft skills and the nurturing of personal creativity and distinct style. An approach that accents master-apprentice initial formation, evidenced-based progression, group learning, self-learning, contextual training in churches involved in church planting, and participation in church planting networks.

I hope this book will contribute to the important conversations about church planting and training church planters in the Church of England and other denominations. This book has focused on the Church of England; however, most of the ideas are directly transferable to other Christian denominations and networks. I find that church planters are naturally ecumenical and pioneers from different traditions seem to be particularly able to work together and learn from each other. Although this text is far from definitive on this topic, it is perhaps a first word. The next step is for each reader to explore and experiment with these principles and be part of this rediscovery of ancient methods. Perhaps one small thing all of us can do is to find an apprentice.[12]

As the church learns again this craft of church planting, may we be schooled by the greatest Master of them all, Jesus Christ, the one who said, 'I will build my church.' Jesus, the master church planter, is still calling women and men today to apprentice alongside him as fellow craftworkers in the mission of the Church. Few sum this up better than the scholar, poet and church planter Eugene Peterson:

It is [a] 'long obedience in the same direction' which the mode of the world does so much to discourage ... we are people who spend our lives apprenticed to our master, Jesus Christ. We are in a growing-learning relationship, always. A disciple is a learner, but not in the academic setting of a school-room, rather at the worksite of the craftsman. We do not acquire information about God but skills in faith ... we are people who spend our lives going someplace, going to God, and whose path for getting there is the way, Jesus Christ.[13]

Notes

1 Author's translation of '*In regione caecorum rex est luscus*'. This Latin proverb is from Erasmus of Rotterdam, *Collectanea Adagiorum* 3.4.96 first published in 1500. A later edition, published under the title *Adagiorum Chiliades* in 1509, contained a similar passage: '*Inter caecos regnat strabus*' (Among the blind, the squinter rules), at https://archive.org/details/proverbschieflytooblaniala/mode/2up (accessed 28.1.2022).

2 Several authors (including, for example, Aristotle and Plato) have proposed a 'cyclical theory' for the rise and fall of political or non-governmental organizations. Ibn Khaldûn suggests that each stage lasts one generation (approximately 30 years) and a typical cycle unfolds in four stages over approximately 120 years. See Murat Önder and Fatih UlaÐan, 'Ibn Khaldûn's Cyclical Theory on the Rise and Fall of Sovereign Powers: The Case of Ottoman Empire', *Adam Akademi Sosyal Bilimler Dergisi*, 8.2, 201), 231–66, at https://doi.org/10.31679/adamakademi.453944 (accessed 28.1.2022).

3 Jim Collins suggests that, although no organization can grow indefinitely, there is an opportunity to start a fresh growth cycle, provided the intervention occurs before decline sets in. See his *How the Mighty Fall: And Why Some Companies Never Give In* (London: Random House Business, 2009).

4 For example, after referencing a plot to kill Lazarus, who Jesus raised from the dead (John 12.9–11), and explaining the meaning of Jesus' forthcoming death, John reports Jesus telling his disciples: 'unless a grain of wheat falls into the earth and dies, it remains just a single grain; but if it dies, it bears much fruit' (12.24).

5 For example, 1 Corinthians 3.9: 'we are co-workers in God's service', NIV.

6 I use the word 'orthodoxy' here not to suggest a particular theological position but to mean the Christian faith as received by the Church.

7 From the preface to the Declaration of Assent. See *Common Worship: Services and Prayers for the Church of England* (London: Church House Publishing, 2000), xi.

8 However, note the previous verse: 'No one sews a patch of unshrunk cloth on an old garment, for the patch will pull away from the garment' (Matthew 9.16), where *new* cloth is unsuitable for an *old* garment. From 9.16 and 17, we might conclude: old (but not broken) churches are spoiled by importing unsuitable/unseasoned new methods and new mission is wasted if added to damaged (old) churches.

9 Lesslie Newbigin, *The Open Secret: An Introduction to the Theology of Mission* (Grand Rapids, MI: Wm. B. Eerdmans, 1995), 59.

10 A comment made by the principal of a theological college. Another told me that he predicts at least one-third of current ordinands who do not currently expect to be involved in church planting will be in the next decade.

11 When I teach about church planting, I use the term 'practitioner theologian' to highlight the distinctive role planters can have in developing a theological

understanding of church planting. I define a practitioner theologian as 'a ministry practitioner who is engaged in dynamic theological research whereby the theory and practice of the public understanding of their ministry area is being informed and developed through their privileged research, informed study, and reflection on their ministry experiences, often with others.'

12 This is how I started, I offered to help someone learn how to lead a Bible study in a small group.

13 Eugene H. Peterson, *A Long Obedience in the Same Direction: Discipleship in an Instant Society* (Westmont, IL: InterVarsity Press, 2019), 17.

17

Apprenticeship Acknowledgements

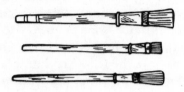

For we are God's masterpiece. He has created us anew in Christ Jesus,
so we can do the good things he planned for us long ago.

Ephesians 2.10 (NLT)

When I began this research project, I never imagined how rewarding and
fulfilling the process would be. It has also proved to be important, as I
can see now that I started my studies at a time when I was in danger of
becoming bored with the sacred work I am called to as a minister in God's
church. This project has been a gift that has brought personal renewal and
enlargement of my vision for what God is doing to revive the church in my
nation and around the world. Writing this book has also been intellectu-
ally cathartic for me: as an introvert, I've written for the audience of one,
but I hope my thoughts will be useful to many others. Part of me wishes
that I had done this a decade ago, but I don't think I would have gained
nearly as much as I have from doing it now. God's timing is perfect: I
suspect ten years ago I was not ready to become a master.

So, I hope it doesn't sound too bold to say that I consider this book
my *chef-d'oeuvre élevé*, my masterpiece. What I have written here – I
hope – is evidence of my basic training in Christian ministry, ongoing
self-directed learning, and mastery of the craft of church planting. In the
tradition of the guilds, this stands as confirmation of my qualification to
train others, just as I was nurtured by my masters and fellow journeymen.

Like all apprentices, I have been trained in the basics by the masters who
believed in me when I was just beginning. They gave me my first opportunities to step out, they modelled by example the methods I needed to
follow, they provided advice and feedback, challenged me when I needed
it, and they encouraged me to do the next things. Most of them took a

small (or sometimes big) risk in offering me an opportunity to learn. For example, Mike invited me to try church, Steve asked me to host a Bible study, Graham gave me my first chance to preach, Peter let me help him lead a church, Ray said I was ready for more, Andy called me to plant my first church, Roger gave me a second chance, Rebecca made me a director, Graham said I was needed, Gavin told me to not give up, Matthew has been a constant encourager, and Mark believed in my vision. To these and my other training-masters, I owe a great debt of thanks.

As this book has demonstrated, sometimes you can learn as much from your fellow novices in the workshop as you can from established experts. So, alongside the masters are the fellow co-learners in my various communities of practice along the way, they also deserve credit for how they have helped me learn. And here, perhaps, the tidiness of the role labels begins to loosen a little, because on occasion another apprentice can teach you like a master and a good master is often also your companion in learning.

I began my apprenticeship of following Jesus when I was at university in 1988. Along the way there have been many encouragers and fellow learners; when I started writing names in my notebook I got to 50, too many to list here – to all of you, thank you. I have also served my wandering-years, although I think mine lasted for about 15 years. I didn't travel the world, but I did learn from many masters, again too many to list. Some of these learning experiences were over a coffee or during ministry trips, others were through watching or asking questions, and many of these ministry experiences were in the form of jobs. In particular, four pioneering groups have helped me to master the craft of church planting.

G2 York

The first is 'G2' – an innovative church plant in the City of York.[1] Started in 2005, G2 York is a church plant with a vision to help people discover hope through Jesus Christ. It was my privilege to co-found this church and for 14 years to be the Ordained Leader. Our adventure of church planting, mission and raising-up leaders was the groundwork and part inspiration for this book. At G2 I was able to be a training-master as I continued to learn new skills – I trained G2, but G2 also trained me. I've forgotten many of the things we discovered together, but here are a few: we learned how to connect with people who had never been to a church through café-church, we raised more leaders by going multi-site and planting new churches, we discovered how to empower local mission through Hub groups, we realized that students are amazing, we developed innovative apprenticeship-methods of training leaders, we developed Big Ideas, we empowered women to lead, we didn't look down on younger leaders,[2] we pressed on in, prayed through the night, and we trained 100 preachers through 'Ignition'. However, I can't take credit for all that we did or learned at G2 because there have been so many partners in our shared journey of re-imagining a church for the next generation. They all deserve to be honoured but – again – the list is long (more than 100 names), to all of you: thank you.

Alpha International

Working for Alpha International and Holy Trinity Brompton (HTB) for 15 years gave me an incredible grounding in global mission, church unity and later church planting.[3] I can still remember an experience in the first week of my new job when attending an Alpha International Conference at HTB. With me on my row was a Southern Baptist minister, a New-frontiers elder, a Vineyard pastor, a Russian Orthodox bishop (wearing his kamilavkas hat), a Church of England bishop (in plain clothes) and a French Roman Catholic priest. As a group we were as varied in our church-styles as we were in visual appearance, but, when we were asked to pray as a group for our friends and family to come to faith in Jesus, we discovered that we did indeed share a common faith and mission. The unity reflected in this example is one small illustration of the diversity and breadth of the global impact of the Alpha course that was developed by Nicky Gumbel.[4]

The vision of Alpha is bold: 'to play our part in the evangelization of the nations, the revitalization of the church and the transformation of society.'[5] From small steps of expansion, beginning in the early 1990s, Alpha has run in churches in 169 nations; at one point my team were working with half of the prisons and 10,500 churches in the UK – from every denomination – all running Alpha at least once a year. While it is hard to measure the full impact of large-scale initiatives like this, one Church of England bishop told me that half of the people he confirmed cited Alpha as part of their journey to faith.[6] It is equally hard to measure the impact Alpha has had on the culture of the Church in England and beyond, but, certainly, Alpha has played a key part in encouraging and enabling churches to be outward-looking and mission-focused. It is not surprising that an organization so committed to local mission would end up multiplying churches through evangelism and become a leading voice in church planting: to date and since 1985, HTB and its network have planted 99 churches across the country, with a further three international plants.[7]

St Hild College

My personal involvement with St Hild began several years before the College started in a conversation with Mark Powley, who would later become the founding Principal of this pioneering theological college based in Yorkshire. One afternoon, at the end of a workshop on mission, we found ourselves musing about the potential for a theological college to seed church planting across a region. At that point our ideas were just a theory, perhaps for someone else? Little did we know that a few years later we would work together to turn our thesis into a bold project as part of St Hild College.

In 2019, this resulted in me joining the staff team to develop training resources for church planting. Much to my surprise, I discovered there was virtually no provision for church planting training in the Common Awards syllabus of modules.[8] Because of this, one of our first priorities was to pioneer new teaching modules that take a distinctive approach to teaching church planting as an integrated discipline.[9] These modules have enabled the formation of a 'Church Planting Track' for cohorts of students wanting to receive comprehensive theological and practitioner training which is focused on starting new churches. Moreover, because every church leader now needs to know how to plant a church, train a church planter, or work with a church planter, we now see church planting as core learning for any minister-in-training.

In 2020, anticipating a rapid growth of interest in church planting, we launched a Centre for Church Planting, as part of the College. This Centre is now a national resource for church planting offering direct support to churches in the North of England. The vision is to resource the Church in the North of England in its mission to reach people through planting and revitalizing churches.

Asbury Theological Seminary

It is not well known in the United Kingdom, but Asbury Theological Seminary is the fourth largest seminary in the United States and the world's largest in the Wesleyan tradition. The focus on being evangelical, charismatic and sacramental made the seminary campus in Wilmore, Kentucky something of a home-from-home for my annual visits for residential study. I am grateful beyond words to the Beeson Scholar Program, whose generosity made it possible for me to study in the Doctor of Ministry programme; this kindness has been matched by the support and encouragement of the Doctor of Ministry team, who have provided generous amounts of wisdom, support and Southern hospitality along the way.

The study that has given birth to this book would not have happened without the encouragement of my doctoral supervisor and friend, Winfield Bevins, who always manages to bring the theory and practice of church planting together in inspirational ways. Your short article 'What is the Biggest Change Evangelical Seminaries Need to Make Right Now? Think Like St Patrick' provided a key initial thought for my research and this book.[10] Thank you also to the Asbury class of 2020: my cohort of fellow students. What a privilege it has been to get to know each one of you. Through you, I have learned so much about the global church and the diversity of God's work. Sharing accommodation and meals, late-night chats, many video calls, and an unforgettable pilgrimage week in England concluding on The Holy Island of Lindisfarne where we remembered some of the great British saints who pioneered as church planters, has been a life-changing experience. Doctors (and prospective doctors) Bryan Collier, C. J. Tillinghast, Ellen Marmon, Graham Singh, Gregg Okesson, Jay Moon, Jeff Horsman, John Ryberg, John Valentine, Patrick Dommati, Ric Thorpe, Theo Burakeye RIP, Tom Tanner, William Chaney Jr. and Winfield Bevins – I thank you for being such wonderful companion journeymen.

As I close, let me also recognize the people who have been kind enough to review draft chapters of this book and offer feedback and suggestions. Each of you has helped me make this book better. Thank you Ben Walker, David Watkis, Gavin Wakefield, Graham Cray, Jenny Lander, John McGinley, John Valentine, Jonathan Crabtree, Josh Cockayne, Mark Powley, Matt Morgan, Matthew Porter, Miriam Swanson, Ric Thorpe, Will Foulger and Winfield Bevins for your help. Of course, any shortcomings that remain are mine.

Traditionally, the last position in the acknowledgements is saved for the person who receives the greatest honour. Here this place is reserved for Amanda, my wonderful wife of 25 years, who has endured a few too many late nights and weekends, Christmases and holidays inconvenienced by my reading lists, assignments and, most recently, this book manuscript. Amanda, I love you.

Notes

1 I've lost count of how many times I've been asked why the church is called 'G2' (and how many incorrect explanations I've heard). Here is the correct story: The initial idea was to explore the dynamics of a church meeting in a third-space –

a venue that is neither a private home nor a workplace (nor a church building). As we were planning the church plant, and before we named the church, we selected a health-club/gym, that at the time was called 'Next Generation Gym', as the venue. Because of this, we considered 'Next Generation Church' as the provisional name for the church. At some point, we concluded that, although we liked the sentiment of the name, it wasn't a good public label. Our dilemma was resolved by Jim Roberts, who proposed the name 'G2'. As I recall, he said his inspiration came when reading the weekend supplement of the *Guardian* newspaper, which is called G2. So, G2 is shorthand for 'next generation'.

2 We had in mind 1 Timothy 4.12 (NIV), which says: 'Don't let anyone look down on you because you are young.'

3 HTB Group comprises five entities that share a common vision and some shared elements of governance, staffing and resourcing. The constituent organizations are Holy Trinity Brompton (HTB), which is the founding organization, Alpha International, St Paul's Theological Centre, the Church Revitalisation Trust, and Caring for Prison Leavers (formally Caring for Ex-Offenders).

4 The Alpha course was founded at HTB in 1977 by Charles Marnham. It was adapted and developed by Nicky Gumbel during the late 1980s when he was an assistant curate at HTB. The first Alpha course outside of HTB was in 1991/2. The origins of some of the material used by Marnham may have come from David Watson and Donald Werner at St Michael le Belfrey, York in the late 1960s and early 1970s.

5 The use of the Roman Catholic term 'evangelization' is deliberate – it emphasizes that evangelism is a journey, not a single event. This philosophy of mission is reflected in the relational focus and multi-week approach of the Alpha course.

6 This bishop told me that, for approximately half of the people he confirmed, Alpha was either the beginning, the middle or the end of their evangelistic journey to faith.

7 The 'HTB Network' consists of churches planted from HTB and daughter and grand-daughter churches of these plants. Some of these churches are listed at https://www.htb.org/network (accessed 28.1.2022).

8 Common Awards is a framework administered by Durham University that is used by the Church of England and some other denominations for training ministers. Other than modules specifically focused on fresh expressions of church, I could only identify one half-credit introductory module associated with church planting.

9 Typically, church planting is taught as either a sub-discipline of ecclesiology or mission. An effect of this is that church planting training becomes the application of another discipline which in turn can easily reduce the teaching programme to a 'how to' experience. In these modules, I sought to teach church planting as a discipline in its own right; to locate church planting as an integrating concept whereby other theological disciplines can be seen, examined and applied from and to church planting; and to illustrate the wide variety of possible models and approaches to the task. Each of these three ideas is summed up with the word 'perspective'. The modules are TMM3861 *Church Planting in Perspective* and TMM46120 *Advanced Church Planting in Perspective*, further details are at https://www.durham.ac.uk/departments/academic/common-awards/policies-processes/curriculum/modules (accessed 28.1.2022).

10 Winfield Bevins, 'What is the Biggest Change Evangelical Seminaries Need to Make Right Now? Think Like St Patrick', *Christianity Today*, Vol. 56, No. 10, 2012, 34–36.

Select Bibliography and Recommended Further Reading

Below are several lists of suggested key reading drawn from a selected bibliography of the material referenced in this book and some additional recommendations for further study. The full list of all books and articles referenced in this book can be found in the notes at the end of each chapter.

Church planting, mission and church growth

Addison, Steve, *Pioneering Movements: Leadership That Multiplies Disciples and Churches* (Westmont, IL: InterVarsity Press, 2015).

Addison, Steve, *The Rise and Fall of Movements: A Roadmap for Leaders* (London: 100 Movement Publishing, 2019).

Allen, Roland, *The Case for Voluntary Clergy* (London: SPCK, 1923).

Allen, Roland, *The Spontaneous Expansion of the Church and the Causes that Hinder It* (Cambridge: James Clarke and Co, 1927).

Allen, Roland, *Missionary Methods; St. Paul's or Ours: A Study of the Church in the Four Provinces* (Eastford, CT: Martino Publishing, 2011).

Alvarez, Iosmar, *Viral Multiplication in Hispanic Churches: How to Plant and Multiply Disciple-Making Hispanic Churches in Twenty-First Century America* (Nashville, TN: Discipleship Resources, 2019).

Anderson, Ron, 'Creative Church Planting Involving Lay People', in *Church Planting in Europe: Connecting to Society, Learning from Experience*, edited by Evert Van de Poll and Joanne Appleton (Eugene, OR: Wipf and Stock, 2015), 216–26.

Barna Group, *Talking Jesus: Perceptions of Jesus, Christians and Evangelism in England* (London: Church of England, Evangelical Alliance and HOPE).

Bevins, Winfield ed., *Global Voices: Stories of Church Planting from Around the World* (Wilmore, KY: Asbury Church Planting Initiative, 2019).

Bevins, Winfield, *Church Planting Revolution: A Handbook for Explorers, Planters, and Their Teams* (Franklin, TN: Seedbed Publishing, 2017).

Bevins, Winfield, *Marks of a Movement: What the Church Today can Learn from the Wesleyan Revival* (Grand Rapids, MI: Zondervan, 2019).

Bevins, Winfield, *Marks of a Multiplying Movement: Lessons from the Wesleyan Revival for Church Multiplication* (Chicago, IL: Exponential Publishing, 2017), at https://exponential.org/resource-ebooks/marks-of-a-movement (accessed 28.1.2022).

Bevins, Winfield, *Plant: A Sower's Guide to Church Planting* (Franklin, TN: Seedbed Publishing, 2016).

Beynon, Graham, *Planting for the Gospel: A Hands-on Guide to Church Planting* (Fearn, Scotland: Christian Focus, 2011).

Brisco, Brad, *Covocational Church Planting: Aligning Your Marketplace Calling & The Mission of God* (Nashville, TN: Missional Press 2021), at https://www.namb.net/send-network/resource/ebook-covocational-church-planting (accessed 28.1.2022).

Bullivant, Stephen, *Catholic Research Forum Reports 3: The 'No Religion' Population of Britain: Recent Data from the British Social Attitudes Survey (2015) and the European Social Survey (2014)* (Twickenham: Benedict XVI Centre for Religion and Society, St Mary's University, 2017), at https://www.stmarys.ac.uk/research/centres/benedict-xvi/docs/2017-may-no-religion-report.pdf (accessed 28.1.2022).

Bullivant, Stephen, *Europe's Young Adults and Religion: Findings from the European Social Survey (2014–16) to Inform the 2018 Synod of Bishops* (Twickenham: Benedict XVI Centre for Religion and Society, St Mary's University, 2018), at https://www.stmarys.ac.uk/research/centres/benedict-xvi/docs/2018-mar-europe-young-people-report-eng.pdf (accessed 28.1.2022).

Church Growth Research Programme, *From Anecdote to Evidence: Findings from the Church Growth Research Programme 2011–2013* (London: Archbishops' Council of the Church of England, 2014).

Church of England Working Party on Church Planting, *Breaking New Ground: Church Planting in the Church of England; a Report Commissioned by the House of Bishops of the General Synod of the Church of England* (London: Church House Publishing, 1994).

Cottrell, Stephen, *GS 2223: Simpler, Humbler, Bolder – A Church for the Whole Nation which is Christ Centred and Shaped by the Five Marks of Mission* (London: General Synod of the Church of England, 2021), at https://www.churchofengland.org/media/24449 (accessed 28.1.2022).

Cray, Graham et al., editors, *Mission-Shaped Church: Church Planting and Fresh Expressions of Church in a Changing Context* (London: Church House Publishing, 2004).

Crider, Caleb, Larry McCrary, Rodney Calfee and Wade Stephens, *Tradecraft: For the Church on Mission* (Portland, OR: Urban Loft Publishers, 2013).

Croft, Steven. ed., *Mission-shaped Questions: Defining Issues for Today's Church* (London: Church House Publishing, 2009).

Croft, Steven, ed., *The Future of the Parish System: Shaping the Church of England for the 21st Century* (London: Church House Publishing, 2006).

Croft, Steven J. L. and Ian Mobsby, *Ancient Faith, Future Mission: Fresh Expressions in the Sacramental Tradition* (Norwich: Canterbury Press, 2009).

Dadswell, David and Cathy Ross, *Church Growth Research Project: Church Planting* (Cuddesdon: Oxford Centre for Ecclesiology and Practical Theology, Ripon College, 2013), at https://www.churchofengland.org/sites/default/files/2019-06/cgrp_church_planting_from_cgrd_website.pdf (accessed 28.1.2022).

Davison, Andrew and Alison Milbank, *For the Parish: A Critique of Fresh Expressions* (London: SCM Press, 2010).

Devenish, David, *Fathering Leaders, Motivating Mission: Restoring the Role of the Apostle in Today's Church* (Milton Keynes: Authentic Media, 2011).

Dever, Mark, *Nine Marks of a Healthy Church*, 3rd edn (Wheaton, IL: Crossway, 2013).

DeYmaz, Mark, *Building a Healthy Multi-Ethnic Church: Mandate, Commitments, and Practices of a Diverse Congregation* (Hoboken, NJ: Jossey-Bass/John Wiley, 2007).

Donovan, Vincent J., *Christianity Rediscovered: An Epistle from the Masai* (London: SCM, 1978).

Drane, John W., *The McDonaldization of the Church: Spirituality, Creativity and the Future of the Church* (London: Darton, Longman & Todd Ltd, 2000).

Emery White, James, *The Rise of the Nones: Understanding And Reaching The Religiously Unaffiliated* (Ada, MI: BakerBooks, 2014).

Ferguson, Dave and Jon Ferguson, *Exponential: How You and Your Friends Can Start a Missional Church Movement, Exponential Series* (Grand Rapids, MI: Zondervan, 2010).

Finney, John, *Recovering the Past: Celtic and Roman Mission* (London: Darton, Longman & Todd, 1996).

Foppen, A., S. Paas and J. V. Saane, 'Personality Traits of Church Planters and Other Church Leaders in Europe (II)', *Journal of Empirical Theology*, Vol. 31, No. 2, 2018, 288–308, https://doi.org/10.1163/15709256-12341377

Garrison, David, *Church Planting Movements: How God Is Redeeming a Lost World* (Larkspur, CO: Wigtake Resources, 2003).

Garrison, David, '10 Church Planting Movement FAQs', *Mission Frontiers: The Bulletin of the US Center for World Mission*, Vol. 22, No. 2, Apr. 2011, 9–11 at https://www.missionfrontiers.org/issue/article/10-church-planting-movement-faqs (accessed 28.1.2022).

Gehring, Roger W., *House Church and Mission: The Importance of Household Structures in Early Christianity* (Peabody, MA: Hendrickson Publishers, 2005).

General Synod of the Church of England, *GS 2142: A Mission-Shaped Church and Fresh Expressions 15 Years On* (London: Archbishops' Council of the Church of England, 2019).

Gill, Robin, *The Myth of the Empty Church* (London: SPCK, 1993).

Goodhew, David and Rob Barward-Symmons, *New Churches in the North East* (Durham: Centre for Church Growth Research, St John's College, 2015), at https://churchgrowthresearch.webspace.durham.ac.uk/wp-content/uploads/sites/144/2021/04/NCNEreportFINAL.pdf (accessed 28.1.2022).

Goodhew, David, ed., *Growth and Decline in the Anglican Communion: 1980 to the Present*, 1st edn (London: Routledge, 2016).

Goodhew, David, ed., *Church Growth in Britain: 1980 to the Present* (Farnham, Surrey: Ashgate, 2012).

Goodhew, David, ed., *Towards a Theology of Church Growth* (Farnham, Surrey: Ashgate, 2015).

Harvey, Michael, *Creating a Culture of Invitation in Your Church* (Oxford: Monarch Books, 2015).

Hirsch, Alan, *The Forgotten Ways: Reactivating the Missional Church* (Grand Rapids, MI: Brazos Press, 2006).

Hull, John M., *Mission-Shaped Church: A Theological Response* (London: SCM Press, 2006).

Hunter III, George G., *The Celtic Way of Evangelism: How Christianity Can Reach the West ... Again*, 10th Anniversary edn (Nashville, TN: Abingdon Press, 2010).

Hunter III, George G., *The Recovery of a Contagious Methodist Movement* (Nashville, TN: Abingdon Press, 2011).

Hunter, Todd, *Autopsy Reports of Failed Churches: Church Pathology Report* (London: Association of Vineyard Churches, 1986).

Jackson, Bob, *Hope for the Church: Contemporary Strategies for Growth* (London: Church House Publishing, 2002).

Jackson, Bob, *Leading One Church at a Time: From Multi-Church Ministers to Focal Ministers* (Cambridge: Grove Books: 2018).

Jackson, Bob, *What Is Making Churches Grow?: Vision and Practice in Effective Mission* (London: Church House Publishing, 2015).

Jones, Peyton, *Church Plantology: The Art and Science of Planting Churches* (Grand Rapids, MI: Zondervan, 2021).

Keller, Timothy, 'Process Managing Church Growth: How Strategy Changes Over Time', *Cutting Edge*, Spring 2008, 4–9, 26–27.

Keller, Timothy, 'The Missional Church', *Theology Matters*, 10.4 (2004), 1–16.

Keller, Timothy, 'Why Plant Churches?' (New York: Redeemer City to City, 2002), 1–6, at https://download.redeemer.com/pdf/learn/resources/Why_Plant_Churches-Keller.pdf (accessed 28.1.2022).

Keller, Timothy and Stefan Paas, *Center Church Europe: Doing Balanced, Gospel-Centered Ministry in Your City* (New York: Redeemer City to City, 2014).

Keller, Timothy, *Center Church: Doing Balanced, Gospel-Centered Ministry in Your City* (Grand Rapids, MI: Zondervan, 2012).

Kinnaman, David and George Barna, *Churchless: Understanding Today's Unchurched and How to Connect with Them* (Carol Stream, IL: Tyndale House Publishers, 2014).

Kinnaman, David and Mark Matlock, *Faith for Exiles: 5 Proven Ways to Help a New Generation Follow Jesus and Thrive in Digital Babylon* (Grand Rapids, MI: Baker Books, 2018).

Lings, George and Stuart Murray, *Church Planting in the UK Since 2000: Reviewing the First Decade* (Cambridge: Grove Books, 2012).

Lings, George and Stuart Murray, *Church Planting: Past, Present and Future* (Cambridge: Grove Books, 2003).

Lings, George, *The Day of Small Things: An Analysis of Fresh Expressions of Church in 21 Dioceses of the Church of England* (Sheffield, Yorkshire: Church Army Research Unit, 2016), at https://churcharmy.org/wp-content/uploads/2021/04/the-day-of-small-things.pdf (accessed 28.1.2022).

Lings, George, *Encountering the Day of Small Things – An Analysis of Fresh Expressions of Church in 21 Dioceses of the Church of England* (Church Army Research Unit, 2016), at https://churcharmy.org/wp-content/uploads/2021/04/encounteringthedayofsmallthings-web.pdf (accessed 18.1.2022).

MacMillan, Neil, 'Building a Church-Planting Movement in a Traditional Denomination', *Foundations International Journal of Evangelical Theology*, 72, Spring 2017 (2017), 41–60.

Male, David, *How to Pioneer (Even If You Haven't a Clue)* (Church House Publishing, 2016).

Mallon, Fr. James, *Divine Renovation: Bringing Your Parish from Maintenance to Mission* (Twenty-Third Publications, 2014).

McGinnis, Daniel M., *Missional Acts: Rhetorical Narrative in the Acts of the Apostles* (Eugene, OR: Pickwick, 2021).

Moon, W. Jay and Fredrick J. Long, *Entrepreneurial Church Planting: Engaging Business and Mission for Marketplace Transformation* (Wilmore, KY: GlossaHouse, 2018).

Moore, Ralph, *Starting a New Church* (Grand Rapids, MI: BakerBooks, 2014).

Moore, Ralph, *Starting a New Church: The Church Planter's Guide to Success* (Grand Rapids, MI: BakerBooks, 2014).

Moynagh, Michael, *Being Church, Doing Life: Creating Gospel Communities Where Life Happens*, 1st edn (Oxford: Monarch Books, 2014).

Moynagh, Michael, *Church for Every Context: An Introduction to Theology and Practice* (London: SCM, 2012).

Moynagh, Michael, *Church in Life: Innovation, Mission and Ecclesiology* (London: SCM Press, 2017).

Murray, Stuart, *Church Planting: Laying Foundations* (Paternoster Press, 1998).

Murray, Stuart, *Planting Churches in the 21st Century: A Guide for Those who Want Fresh Perspectives and New Ideas for Creating Congregations* (Herald Press, 2010).

Newbigin, Lesslie, *The Open Secret: An Introduction to the Theology of Mission* (Grand Rapids: MI, Wm. B. Eerdmans Publishing Company, 1995).

Newbigin, Lesslie, *Foolishness to the Greeks: The Gospel and Western Culture* (London: SPCK, 1986).

Newbigin, Lesslie, *The Gospel in a Pluralist Society* (London: SPCK, 2014).

Newbigin, Lesslie, *The Household of God: Lectures on the Nature of the Church* (London: SCM Press, 1953).

Newbigin, Lesslie, *The Open Secret: An Introduction to the Theology of Mission* (London: SPCK, 1995).

Newbigin, Lesslie, *Truth to Tell: The Gospel as Public Truth* (London: SPCK, 1991).

Nicholson, Steve and Jeff Bailey, *Coaching Church Planters: A Manual for Church Planters and Those Who Coach Them* (Chicago: Association of Vineyard Churches USA, 1999).

Okesson, Gregg A., *A Public Missiology: How Local Churches Witness to a Complex World* (Baker Academic, a division of Baker Publishing Group, 2020).

Orr-Ewing, Francis (Frog), *Victorian Church Planter, Thomas Gaster and Church Missionary Society, India 1857–1904*, PhD thesis (University of Oxford, 2017), at https://www.academia.edu/36999447/Rev_Thomas_Joseph_Gaster_An_Urban_Missionary_in_Historical_and_Theological_Context (accessed 28.1.2022).

Ott, Craig and Gene Wilson, *Global Church Planting: Biblical Principles and Best Practices for Multiplication* (Grand Rapids, MI: Baker Academic, 2011).

Paas, Stefan, 'Church Renewal by Church Planting: The Significance of Church Planting for the Future of Christianity in Europe', *Theology Today*, 68.4 (2012), 467–77, https://doi.org/10.1177/0040573611424326

Paas, Stefan, *Church Planting in the Secular West: Learning from the European Experience* (Grand Rapids, MI: Wm. B. Eerdmans Publishing Company, 2016).

Paas, Stefan, *Pilgrims and Priests: Christian Mission in a Post-Christian Society* (London: SCM Press, 2019).

Payne, J. D., *Discovering Church Planting: An Introduction to the Whats, Whys, and Hows of Global Church Planting* (Westmont, IL: InterVarsity Press, 2009).

Payne, J. D., *Apostolic Church Planting: Birthing New Churches from New Believers* (Westmont, IL: InterVarsity Press, 2015).

Petersen, Jim, *Church Without Walls* (Global Commerce Network, 2018).

Pope Francis, *Evangelii Gaudium: The Joy of the Gospel: Apostolic Exhortation on the Proclamation of the Gospel in Today's World* (London: Catholic Truth Society, 2013), [also available at https://www.vatican.va/content/francesco/en/apost_exhortations/documents/papa-francesco_esortazione-ap_20131124_evangelii-gaudium.html].

Pope John Paul II, *Redemptoris Missio: Encyclical Letter of Pope John Paul II on the Permanent Validity of the Church's Missionary Mandate* (London: Catholic Truth Society, 2003), [also available at https://www.vatican.va/content/john-paul-ii/en/encyclicals/documents/hf_jp-ii_enc_07121990_redemptoris-missio.html].

Pope Paul IV, *Evangelii Nuntiandi: Evangelization in the Modern World* (London: Catholic Truth Society, 1975) [also available at https://www.vatican.va/content/paul-vi/en/apost_exhortations/documents/hf_p-vi_exh_19751208_evangelii-nuntiandi.html].

Powell, Neil and John James, *Together for the City: How Collaborative Church Planting Leads to Citywide Movements* (Westmont, IL: InterVarsity Press, 2019).

Robinson, Gareth, *Stones and Ripples: 10 Principles for Pioneers and Church Planters* (100 Movements Publishing, 2021).

Sanders, Brian, *Microchurches: A Smaller Way* (Independently published, 2019).

Schwarz, Christian A. and British Church Growth Association, *Natural Church Development Handbook: A Practical Guide to a New Approach* (Moggerhanger, Beds.: British Church Growth Association, 1996).

Searcy, Nelson and Kerrick Thomas, *Launch: Starting a New Church from Scratch* (Grand Rapids, MI: BakerBooks, 2017).

Selvaratnam, Christian, *Alpha as a Church Planting Tool* (London: Alpha International, 2017), at https://www.academia.edu/72797878/Alpha_as_Church_Planting_Tool (accessed 28.1.2022).

Snyder, Howard A., *The Radical Wesley and Patterns for Church Renewal* (Westmont, IL: InterVarsity Press, 1982).

Steffen, Tom, *The Facilitator Era: Beyond Pioneer Church Multiplication* (Eugene, OR: Wipf and Stock, 2011).

Stetzer, Ed, 'Why Lay People Can (and Should) Plant Churches', *The Exchange*, at https://www.christianitytoday.com/edstetzer/2018/april/why-lay-people-can-and-should-plant-churches.html (accessed 28.1.2022).

Stetzer, Ed and Daniel Im, *Planting Missional Churches: Your Guide to Starting Churches That Multiply*, 2nd edn (Nashville, TN: B&H Academic, 2016).

Stetzer, Ed and Warren Bird, *Viral Churches: Helping Church Planters Become Movement Makers*, 1st edn (San Francisco, CA: Jossey-Bass, 2010).

Surratt, Geoff, et al., *The Multi-Site Church Revolution: Being One Church in Many Locations* (Grand Rapids, MI: Zondervan, 2009).

Taylor, Steve, *First Expressions: Innovation and the Mission of God* (London: SCM Press, 2019).

Tennent, Timothy C., *Invitation to World Missions: A Trinitarian Missiology for the Twenty-First Century* (Grand Rapids, MI: Kregel Publications, 2010).

The House of Bishops of the Church of England, *Church Planting and the Mission of the Church: A Statement by the House of Bishops*, HB(18)05, House of Bishops of the Church of England, May 2018 at https://www.churchofengland.org/media/10519 (accessed 28.1.2022).

Thorlby, Tim, *Love, Sweat and Tears: Church Planting in East London. The Centre for Theology and Community* (2016), at http://www.theology-centre.org.uk/wp-content/uploads/2013/04/ChurchPlanting_Final_online.pdf (accessed 28.1.2022).

Thorpe, Ric, *Resource Churches: A Story of Church Planting and Revitalisation Across the Nation* (London: CCX, 2021).

Timmis, Steve, ed., *Multiplying Churches: Reaching Today's Communities Through Church Planting* (Fearn, Scotland: Christian Focus, 2000).

Valentine, John, *Jesus, the Church, and the Mission of God: a Biblical Theology of Church Planting* (Nottingham: Apollos, 2023).

Wakefield, Gavin and Nigel Rooms, eds., *Northern Gospel, Northern Church: Reflections on Identity and Mission* (Durham: Sacristy Press, 2016).

Wigger, John H., *American Saint: Francis Asbury and the Methodists* (Oxford: Oxford University Press Inc., 2009).

Winter, Ralph D., 'The Two Structures of God's Redemptive Mission', *Practical Anthropology*, Vol. 2, No. 1, Jan. 1974, 121–39, https://doi.org/10.1177/00918 2967400200109

Woodward, J. R. and Dan White Jr., *The Church as Movement: Starting and Sustaining Missional-Incarnational Communities* (Westmont, IL: InterVarsity Press, 2016).

Guilds, apprenticeship and training

Aitken, Jonathan, *The St Mellitus Story* (Private publication, 2017).

Archbishops' Council, *Formation for Ministry within a Learning Church: The Hind Report* (London: Church House Publishing, 2012).

Banks, Robert, *Reenvisioning Theological Education: Exploring a Missional Alternative to Current Models* (Grand Rapids, MI: Wm. B. Eerdmans Publishing Company, 1999).

Bevins, Winfield, 'What is the Biggest Change Evangelical Seminaries Need to Make Right Now? Think Like St Patrick', *Christianity Today*, vol. 56, no. 10, 2012, 34–36, at https://www.christianitytoday.com/ct/2012/november/what-is-biggest-change-evangelical-seminaries-need-to-make.html (accessed 28.1.2022).

Billett, Stephen, 'Apprenticeship as a Mode of Learning and Model of Education', *Education + Training*, 58.6 (2016), 613–28, at https://doi.org/10.1108/ET-01-2016-0001

Billett, Stephen, 'Mimesis: Learning Through Everyday Activities and Interactions at Work', *Human Resource Development Review*, 13.4 (2014), 462–82, at https://doi.org/10/gfs7r7

Billett, Stephen, 'Situating Learning in the Workplace – Having Another Look at Apprenticeships', *Industrial and Commercial Training*, 26.11 (1994), 9–16, at https://doi.org/10.1108/00197859410073745

Black, Antony, *Guilds and Civil Society in European Political Thought from the Twelfth Century to the Present*, 1st edn (London: Methuen Young Books, 1983).

Bolsinger, Tod E., *Canoeing the Mountains: Christian Leadership in Uncharted Territory*, Expanded Edition (Westmont, IL: InterVarsity Press, 2018).

Bolton, Bill, *The Entrepreneur and the Church* (Cambridge: Grove Books, 2006).

Breen, Mike and Walt Kallestad, *The Passionate Life* (Kingsway Publications, 2005).

Claudia Rapp, *Holy Bishops in Late Antiquity: The Nature of Christian Leadership in an Age of Transition*, Reprint edn (Oakland, CA: University of California Press, 2013).

Clinton, J. Robert, *The Making of a Leader: Recognizing the Lessons and Stages of Leadership Development*, Rev. edn (Colorado Springs, CO: NavPress, 2012).

Collins, James C., *Good to Great: Why Some Companies Make the Leap – and Others Don't* (HarperBusiness, 2001).

Collins, James C., *How the Mighty Fall: And Why Some Companies Never Give In* (London: Random House Business, 2009).

Croft, Steven J. L., *Ministry in Three Dimensions: Ordination and Leadership in the Local Church* (London: Darton Longman & Todd Ltd, 2008).

Davis, Ken L., 'Mentoring Church Planters', *Journal of Ministry and Theology*, 14.2 (2010).

Donald Miller, *Blue Like Jazz: Nonreligious Thoughts on Christian Spirituality* (Thomas Nelson Publishers 2003).

Drucker, P. F., 'The Discipline of Innovation', *Harvard Business Review*, 76.6 (1998), 149–57

Duffy, Eamon, *The Stripping of the Altars: Traditional Religion in England 1400–1580*, 2nd edn (New Haven, CT: Yale Univ. Press, 2005).

Epstein, Stephan R., 'Craft Guilds in the Pre-Modern Economy: A Discussion', *The Economic History Review*, 61.1 (2008), 155–74, https://doi.org/10.1111/j.1468-0289.2007.00411.x

Epstein, Stephan R., 'Craft Guilds, Apprenticeship and Technological Change in Preindustrial Europe', *The Journal of Economic History*, 58.03 (1998), 684–713, https://doi.org/10.1017/S0022050700021124

Epstein, Stephan R., 'Transferring Technical Knowledge and Innovating in Europe, c.1200–1800', ed. Jonathan Adams, *The Nature of Evidence: How Well Do 'Facts' Travel?*, 1 (2005), 1–40.

Epstein, Stephan R. and Maarten Roy Prak, eds., *Guilds, Innovation, and the European Economy, 1400–1800* (Cambridge: Cambridge University Press, 2008).

Etienne Wenger-Trayner and Beverly Wenger-Trayner, *Communities of Practice: A Brief Introduction* (2015), at http://wenger-trayner.com/introduction-to-communities-of-practice (accessed 28.1.2022).

Etienne Wenger, *Communities of Practice: Learning, Meaning, and Identity* (Cambridge: Cambridge University Press, 1998).

Eugene H. Peterson, *A Long Obedience in the Same Direction: Discipleship in an Instant Society* (London: IVP Books, 2019).

Ferguson, Dave and Warren Bird, *Hero Maker: Five Essential Practices for Leaders to Multiply Leaders* (Grand Rapids, MI: Zondervan, 2018).

Ford, Lance, Rob Wegner and Alan Hirsch, *The Starfish and the Spirit: Unleashing the Leadership Potential of Churches and Organizations* (Grand Rapids, MI: Zondervan 2021).

Fuller, Alison, and Lorna Unwin, 'Learning as Apprentices in the Contemporary UK Workplace: Creating and Managing Expansive and Restrictive Participation', *Journal of Education and Work*, 16 (2003), 407–26, https://doi.org/10.1080/1363908032000093012

Gamble, Jeanne, 'Modelling the Invisible: The Pedagogy of Craft Apprenticeship', *Studies in Continuing Education*, 23.2 (2001), 185–200, https://doi.org/10.1080/01580370120101957

Gardner, Sally May, 'From Training to Artisanal Practice: Rethinking Choreographic Relationships in Modern Dance', *Theatre, Dance and Performance Training*, 2.2 (2011), 151–65, https://doi.org/10.1080/19443927.2011.603593

Gladwell, Malcolm, *Blink: The Power of Thinking Without Thinking* (London: Penguin Books, 2006).

Gladwell, Malcolm, *Outliers: The Story of Success* (London: Penguin Books, 2009).

Gladwell, Malcolm, *The Tipping Point: How Little Things Can Make a Big Difference* Reprint edn (London: Abacus, 2009).

Gowlland, Geoffrey, 'Apprenticeship as a Model for Learning in and Through Professional Practice', in Stephen Billett, Christian Harteis and Hans Gruber, eds., *International Handbook of Research in Professional and Practice-Based Learning* (New York: Springer, 2014), 759–79.

Gowlland, Geoffrey, 'Learning Craft Skills in China: Apprenticeship and Social Capital in an Artisan Community of Practice', *Anthropology & Education Quarterly*, 43.4 (2012), 358–71, at https://doi.org/10.1111/j.1548-1492.2012.01190.x

Hart, Trevor A., *Making Good: Creation, Creativity, and Artistry* (Waco, TX: Baylor University Press, 2014).

Hasaki, Eleni, 'Craft Apprenticeship in Ancient Greece: Reaching Beyond the Masters', in Willeke Wendrich, *Archaeology and Apprenticeship: Acquiring Body Knowledge, Identity and Communities of* Practice, Reprint edn (Tucson, AZ: University of Arizona Press, 2013), 171–202.

Heitzenrater, Richard P., *Wesley and the People Called Methodists* (Abingdon Press, 1995).

Hersey, Paul, and Kenneth H. Blanchard, 'Life Cycle Theory of Leadership', Training & Development Journal, *Life Cycle Theory of Leadership*, 23.5 (1969), 26–34.

Heywood, David, *Reimagining Ministerial Formation* (London: SCM, 2021).

Jolley, Andy, and Ian Jones, 'Formation for Mission in Urban Britain: The Birmingham Mission Apprentice Scheme', *Journal of Adult Theological Education*, 13.1 (2016), 33–47.

Kelsey, David H., *Between Athens and Berlin: The Theological Education Debate* (Eugene, OR: Wipf & Stock, 1993).

Lave, Jean and Etienne Wenger, *Situated Learning: Legitimate Peripheral Participation* (Cambridge: Cambridge University Press, 1991).

Maxwell, John C., *The 360 Degree Leader with Workbook: Developing Your Influence from Anywhere in the Organization* (Thomas Nelson: 2011).

Milavec, Aaron, *The Didache: Text, Translation, Analysis, and Commentary* (Collegeville, MN: Liturgical Press, 2004).

Ogilvie, Sheilagh, *The European Guilds: An Economic Analysis* (Princeton, NJ: Princeton University Press, 2018).

Oxbrow, Mark and John Kafwanka, eds., *Intentional Discipleship and Disciple-Making: An Anglican Guide for Christian Life and Formation* (Anglican Consultative Council, 2016), at https://www.anglicancommunion.org/media/220191/intentional-discipleship-and-disciple-making.pdf (accessed 28.1.2022).

Polanyi, Michael, *Personal Knowledge: Towards a Post-Critical Philosophy* (Chicago, IL: University of Chicago Press, 1958).

Polanyi, Michael, *The Tacit Dimension* (Garden City, NY: Doubleday, 1966).

Rogoff, Barbara, *Apprenticeship in Thinking: Cognitive Development in Social Context* (New York: Oxford University Press, 1990).

Ryan, P., 'The Institutional Requirements of Apprenticeship Training in the Context of the British Isles', in L. O'Connor and T. Mullins, *Apprenticeship as a Paradigm of Learning: Proceedings of the 3rd Annual Conference* (Cork Institute of Technology, 2005), 15–35.

Sennet, Richard, *The Craftsman* (London: Penguin Books, 2009).

Simpson, Rick, *Supervising a Curate: A Short Guide to a Complex Task* (Cambridge: Grove Books, 2011).

Swanson, Heather, 'The Illusion of Economic Structure: Craft Guilds in Late Medieval English Towns', *Past & Present*, 121, 1988, 29–48, at https://doi.org/10.2307/650910

The House of Bishops of the Church of England, *Formation Criteria with Mapped Selection Criteria for Ordained Ministry in the Church of England* (The Church of England, 2014), [available at https://www.churchofengland.org/sites/default/files/2017-10/formation_criteria_for_ordained_ministry.pdf].

Thrupp, Sylvia L., 'Medieval Gilds Reconsidered', *The Journal of Economic History*, 2.2 (1942), 164–73, https://doi.org/10.1017/S0022050700052554

Tillott, P. M., ed., 'The Later Middle Ages: Craft Organization and the Guilds', in *A History of the County of York: The City of York* (London: Victoria County History, 1961), 91–97.

Unwin, George, *The Gilds and Companies of London* (Barnes & Noble, 1964).

Wolek, Francis W., 'The Managerial Principles Behind Guild Craftsmanship', *Journal of Management History*, 5.7 (1999), 401–13, https://doi.org/10.1108/13552529910297460

Other

Pope John Paul II, *Letter of His Holiness Pope John Paul II to Artists* (Pauline Books and Media, 1999).

Preface to the Declaration of Assent in *Common Worship: Services and Prayers for the Church of England* (Church House Publishing, 2000), [also available at https://www.churchofengland.org/prayer-and-worship/worship-texts-and-resources/common-worship/ministry/declaration-assent].

Smith, Adam, *The Wealth of Nations: Books I–III* (Kiribati: Penguin Publishing Group, 1982).

Venerable Bede, *The Ecclesiastical History of the English People*, edited by Judith McClure and Roger Collins, translated by Bertram Colgrave, new edn (Oxford University Press, 2008).

Ancient and medieval primary sources

Aristotle, *Nicomachean Ethics*
Augustine of Hippo, *The Confessions of St Augustine*
Bede, *The Ecclesiastical History of the English People*
Benedict, *The Rule of St Benedict*
Erasmus, *Collectanea Adagiorum*
Eusebius, *Historia Ecclesiastica*
Irenaeus, *Against Heresies*
Khaldûn, Ibn, *The Muqaddimah*
Kohelet Rabbah
Pirke Avot
Plato, *Symposium*
Tertullian, *Apologeticus*
The Apostolic Constitutions
The Didache

Index of Biblical and Apocryphal References

Old Testament

Apocryphal books

New Testament

Index of Subjects and Names